The Optimistic Child

The Optimistic Child

**A PROVEN PROGRAM TO
SAFEGUARD CHILDREN
AGAINST DEPRESSION AND
BUILD LIFELONG RESILIENCE**

Martin E. P. Seligman, Ph.D.

with Karen Reivich, M.A., Lisa Jaycox, Ph.D.,
and Jane Gillham, Ph.D.

HOUGHTON MIFFLIN COMPANY
Boston • New York

Library of Congress Cataloging-in-Publication Data
Seligman, Martin E. P.
  The optimistic child : a proven program to safeguard children against depression and build lifelong resilience / Martin E. P. Seligman, with Karen Reivich, Lisa Jaycox, and Jane Gillham.— 1st Houghton Mifflin pbk. ed.
      p. cm.
  Originally published: 1995. With new afterword.
  Includes bibliographical references and index.
  ISBN-13: 978-0-618-91809-6
  ISBN-10: 0-618-91809-4
  1. Optimism in children. 2. Resilience (Personality trait) in children.
3. Child rearing. 4. Positive psychology. I. Reivich, Karen. II. Jaycox, Lisa.
III. Gillham, Jane. IV. Title.
  BF723.O67S45 2007
  155.4'124—dc22   2007025480

Printed in the United States of America

DOC 20 19 18 17 16 15 14 13 12 11

To the Five Seligman Children

First to Darryl Zachary Seligman, born 1993
To Nicole Dana Seligman, born 1991
To Lara Catrina Seligman, born 1989
To David Alexander Lavie Seligman, born 1973
To Amanda Irene Seligman, born 1969

Contents

The man bent over his guitar,
A shearsman of sorts. The day was green.

They said "You have a blue guitar,
You do not play things as they are."

The man replied, "Things as they are
Are changed upon the blue guitar."

—Wallace Stevens
The Man with the Blue Guitar (1937)

PART ONE

Why Children
Need Optimism

1

The Promissory Note

I WAS THE CATCHER for the Lake Luzerne Dodgers, a catcher with meager talent, a catcher in awe of Danny and Teddy. Danny was the first baseman and Teddy, the coach's son, was the left fielder. They were natural athletes: they could hit fastballs (a small miracle of hand-eye coordination that I never mastered), and they glided around the base paths with the grace of gazelles. They were, to a ten-year-old who was batting .111, the embodiment of beauty and summer and health. As I drifted to sleep at night, it was often with the image of Danny, horizontal and three feet off the ground, spearing a line drive, or of Teddy stretching a single into a double by slipping under the tag.

In the early hours of a chilly, August, upstate New York morning, my father woke me. "Danny's got polio," he said. A week later Teddy got it too. My parents kept me indoors, away from other kids. Little League was suspended, the season unfinished. The next time I saw Danny, his throwing arm was withered and he couldn't move his right leg. I never saw Teddy again. He died in the early fall.

But the next summer, the summer of 1954, there was the Salk vaccine. All the kids got shots. Little League resumed. The Lake Luzerne Dodgers lost the opening game to the Hadley Giants. The fear that kept us housebound melted away and the community resumed its social life. The epidemic was over. No one else I knew ever got polio.

Jonas Salk was my childhood hero, and long into my own professional life as a psychologist, his way of doing science was my model:

not knowledge for its own sake, but knowledge in the service of healing. By exposing children's bodies to tiny, manageable doses of polio, Salk had made their immune systems more capable of fighting off the real thing. He had taken the new, pure science of immunology and applied it successfully to the worst epidemic of our time.

I met Jonas Salk thirty years later, in 1984, in an encounter that changed my life. The occasion was a heated face-off between prominent psychologists and immunologists, and the issue was what to do about another fledgling discipline, this one with the graceless name of psychoneuroimmunology — PNI. A representative of the *P* wing, I was invited because I had helped found a field called "learned helplessness" in the 1960s.

When I began my doctoral studies in experimental psychology at the University of Pennsylvania in 1964, I was burning with an ambition kindled during my Lake Luzerne years, an ambition that has since become unfashionable and is widely regarded as naive. I wanted to understand the psychological mysteries that hold people in chains and make human miseries legion. I had chosen experimental psychology as my life's work because I was convinced that the experiment is the best way to find the root causes of psychological suffering, by dissecting it in the laboratory, and then discovering how to cure and prevent it. I had chosen to work in the animal laboratory of Richard L. Solomon, one of the world's leading learning theorists. I chose to work with animals because I believed that experimentation on the causes of psychological suffering could not be carried out ethically with human beings.

When I arrived, the animals wouldn't behave and the laboratory was in an uproar. Solomon's graduate students were trying to find out how fear energized adaptive behavior. They gave dogs experience with Pavlovian conditioning (a signal paired with electric shock) and later put them in a chamber in which running to the other side would turn off shock. To the annoyance of the graduate students, the dogs didn't escape the shocks. They just sat there passively without moving. The experiment, too, had come to a standstill because the animals didn't do what everyone predicted they would do — run away from the shock.

To me, the animals' passivity was not an annoyance, but the phenomenon I had come to study. Here was the essence of the human reaction to so many of the uncontrollable events that befall us: giving up without even trying. If psychology could understand this, the cure and even prevention of human helplessness might be possible.

My coworkers, Steve Maier and Bruce Overmier, and I spent the next five years working on the cause, cure, and prevention of helplessness. We found that it was not shock, but being able to do nothing about it, that caused the dogs' symptoms. We found that we could cure helplessness by teaching animals that their actions had effects, and we could prevent helplessness by providing early experience with mastery.

The discovery of learned helplessness created a stir. Learning psychologists were upset. As behaviorists they maintained that animals and people were stimulus-response machines and could not learn abstractions — whereas learned helplessness required learning that "nothing I do matters," an abstraction too cognitive for stimulus-response learning theory. Clinical psychologists were intrigued because learned helplessness looked so much like depression. In the lab helpless animals and people — passive, slow, sad, without appetite, drained of anger — looked exactly like depressed patients.* So I proposed

---

*Because our society's attitudes toward animal experimentation have changed since the 1960s, as have my own, I want to say a few words here about the ethics of such work. My views differ from those of many of my fellow scientists. Because producing suffering in animals is wrong, it can be justified only if the experiments promise to help alleviate much more suffering in humans (or animals), and only if there is no other feasible method. My belief three decades ago was that research into learned helplessness showed such promise, and I turned out to be right. New therapies and new ways of preventing depression were developed as a result of this work. Indeed, this book is about one of the prevention programs. An understanding of the brain chemistry of helplessness and of posttraumatic stress, as well as new psychological therapies that show lifesaving promise in cancer and heart disease, have also followed.

But I also maintained that as soon as we had documented the basic facts in dogs and had found out how to cure and prevent helplessness, we should stop our experiments on dogs. This we did in the late 1960s, as we began to apply our findings to help human beings.

that learned helplessness was a model of depression and that whatever we discovered that relieved helplessness in the laboratory would
also be a cure for real depression.[1]

When we tested the learned helplessness model of depression in
the late 1970s, we discovered that certain people, pessimists, were
more likely to give in to helplessness. Such people were also at greater
risk for depression. Optimists, on the other hand, resisted helplessness and did not give up when faced with unsolvable problems and
inescapable noise. It was this project — identifying people at special
risk for giving up and becoming depressed and strengthening these
people so they could resist helplessness — that consumed me day and
night. It did, that is, until my encounter with Jonas Salk.

Conferences of American academics are usually cordial, logroll-
ing affairs. Because there is no bottom line, the coin of the realm is
mutual congratulation. The heartier it is, the more successful everyone feels. This conference, in contrast, was barely civil. It was punctu-
ated by fierce turf squabbles. The issue was who would get research
money, a great deal of it. On the table was a proposal that the Mac-
Arthur Foundation, the Croesus of foundations, underwrite PNI in
order to get the field up and running. The psychologists supported the
idea, pointing to two new findings: People under stress were more
vulnerable to cancer, and helpless animals with sluggish immune systems failed to reject implanted tumors. So rigorous evidence seemed
to show that emotional problems worsened physical disease. This had
long been claimed by preachers, grateful patients, and M.D.s out of
the mainstream, but it had never been demonstrated in the laboratory, where it could be dissected and understood, and where new
therapies could be developed.

"Surely," the psychologists contended, "we should explore how
emotional states weaken the immune system and bring on disease. We
can then work out psychological therapies to bolster the immune
system."

"We can't even trace the path from one immune event to another,
or from the immune system to cancer," carped the immunologists.
"Trying to trace the path from stress to emotion all the way through
the immune system and finally to cancer would be a colossal waste of

money. MacArthur should spend its wealth elsewhere." It wasn't hard to guess where.

Dr. Salk was a trim, quiet figure, standing above the fray, and when things got too heated, he would gently encourage both sides to find some patch of common ground. The common ground repeatedly became battlefields. After one condescending barb by a Nobel laureate about immunology as *real* science, Dr. Salk, undeterred, commented on the importance of encouraging the "poets of biology." His efforts at peacemaking had little effect. The bench immunologists, to my surprise, seemed to find him an embarrassment and ignored him.

After the first day, he invited me for a chat. He asked me about my research and my ambitions. I described learned helplessness. I told him about the way that pessimism undermined people's ability to fight off depression. I also told him that pessimism even lowered resistance to physical illness. As chance would have it, it was, to the day, the thirtieth anniversary of the first trial of the polio vaccine, and Dr. Salk was expansive. "That's what I meant by the poets of biology," he said, grinning broadly. "If I were a young scientist today, I would still do immunization. But instead of immunizing kids physically, I'd do it your way. I'd immunize them psychologically. I'd see if these psychologically immunized kids could then fight off mental illness better. Physical illness too."

Psychological immunization. The chord resonated through me. In my earliest experiments we had tried psychological immunization with astonishing success. We first gave animals control over shock to teach them "mastery." Shock went off only if an animal made an active response. They first learned that they could master shock, before they had any experience with inescapable shock. We gave this mastery experience either early in their lives or in adulthood. In either case, these "immunized" animals never gave in to helplessness — when they later got inescapable shock, they did not become passive.[2] We named this phenomenon, pretentiously, and with Dr. Salk's vaccine in mind, "immunization." This was a promissory note on which I had never made good. I felt a circle closing. Could experience with mastery, or acquiring the psychological trait of optimism, immunize children against mental illness? Against physical illness?

There was an epidemic, quite comparable to polio, in full swing, and this epidemic has grown every year since then. The rate of depression had already zoomed to ten times the rate of the 1950s. When an individual has depression, she[3] feels miserable. But that's not the only cost: it markedly hurts her productivity at work or school, and it even undermines her physical health. On a massive scale, an epidemic of depression can compromise the very future of a nation. But if Dr. Salk was right, this was an epidemic against which psychologists could immunize kids.

AN EPIDEMIC OF PESSIMISM

We want more for our children than healthy bodies. We want our children to have lives filled with friendship and love and high deeds. We want them to be eager to learn and be willing to confront challenges. We want our children to be grateful for what they receive from us, but to be proud of their own accomplishments. We want them to grow up with confidence in the future, a love of adventure, a sense of justice, and courage enough to act on that sense of justice. We want them to be resilient in the face of the setbacks and failures that growing up always brings. And when the time comes, we want them to be good parents. Our fondest hope is that the quality of their lives will be better than our own, and our inmost prayer is that our children will have all of our strengths and few of our weaknesses.

All this we should be able to achieve. Parents can teach confidence, initiative, eagerness, kindness, and pride. What's more, most American children are now born into a time of enormous opportunity: they live in a very powerful and wealthy country, where people enjoy unprecedented individual liberties and choices; as the shadow of nuclear war recedes, science and medicine continue to make major advances; and communications networks span a global village of books, music, games, trading, and knowledge. So, if we are good parents and if today's world is a better place for children, we have good reason to expect their lives to surpass ours in every way.

There is, however, a serious obstacle that threatens to dash these hopes. It is eroding our children's natural state of activity and optimism. The unvarnished word for it is "pessimism." It boils down to this: dwelling on the most catastrophic cause of any setback. Pessimism is fast becoming the typical way our children look at the world. A crucial task for you as a parent is to prevent your children from absorbing this trendy outlook, and the mission of this book is to teach you how you can bring up your children so that they will enjoy a lifetime of optimism.

Why would you want your children to be optimists? Pessimism, you may think, is just a posture, a mental costume you can take off at will. If pessimism were simply a ploy for appearing sagacious at cocktail parties, or a "sour grapes" posture to protect yourself from disappointments, I would not have written this book. But pessimism is an entrenched habit of mind that has sweeping and disastrous consequences: depressed mood, resignation, underachievement, and even unexpectedly poor physical health. Pessimism is not shaken in the natural course of life's ups and downs. Rather, it hardens with each setback and soon becomes self-fulfilling. America is in the midst of an epidemic of pessimism and is suffering its most serious consequence, depression.

When Dr. Salk mentioned psychological immunization, my thoughts turned to this epidemic of depression among young people. I knew that newly discovered cognitive and behavioral techniques could markedly relieve depression and pessimism in depressed adults. Might the same skills, if taught to healthy kids, make them resistant to becoming depressed later in life? Would such immunization curtail this epidemic?

I wondered if these skills, taught to healthy kids, would help them achieve more in school and work and sports. Might these kids even get fewer physical diseases? Could the rampant troubles of American teenagers — drug abuse, pregnancy, suicide, feelings of despair or meaninglessness — be alleviated by psychological immunization in childhood? All these questions, and more, tumbled one after another through my mind in the weeks that followed.

This book narrates the story of the resulting immunization program for school children. Again, the specific purpose of this book is to teach parents, coaches, teachers, and entire school systems how to imbue children with a sense of optimism and personal mastery. I will do this by telling you about the studies of optimism and helplessness that my colleagues and I have carried out over the past thirty years. I will tell you about pessimism's sources and its insidious consequences. I will explain how to tell if your child is showing danger signs, and then how to change his pessimism into optimism and his helplessness into mastery.

Unlike most child-rearing or self-improvement books, this book is not just opinion combined with clinical lore. Advice on crucial issues such as breast-feeding versus bottle-feeding, discipline versus freedom, daycare versus full-time mothering, home schooling, androgyny, the impact of divorce, the devastation wrought by sexual abuse, and sibling rivalry has been freely and loosely dispensed to the public by "experts." Worse, many parents have gobbled up this advice and changed their child-rearing practices based on weak evidence, ideology, and mere clinical hunches.

Footless advice is easy to believe when there is little hard data about children. But the situation, fortunately, has now changed. The last decade has seen large-scale, careful research that has reshaped the landscape of child rearing. The advice in this book, the programs I present, the underlying theory of optimism and personal control, and the tests you will be giving your children are based on three decades of painstaking research with hundreds of thousands of adults and children. When my advice is speculation or based just on my own clinical or parental "wisdom" (I *do* have five children), I will so label it.

My book is aimed at all parents, from residents of the wealthiest suburb to the poorest neighborhood, and at all children, from the cradle until the end of adolescence. I have a more ambitious purpose as well. If America's pessimism does not change, our liberty, our wealth, and our power will be of little use. A nation of pessimists will not seize the opportunities that the twenty-first century has to offer. We will lose our economic edge to more-optimistic nations. We will lack the initiative to achieve justice at home, and our children will come to adulthood in a country crippled by sterile self-absorption and mired in passivity and gloom.

If my analysis of what is going awry is correct, the solution lies in our own hands. We can teach our children the skills of a flexible and reality-based optimism. In telling the story of a program proven to prevent depression and pessimism in children, I will give you — parents, teachers, and coaches — a practical, concrete plan of action. At stake is nothing less than the future of your own offspring and the very existence of the next generation of children, that they might be clear-eyed, forward-looking, and confident.

2

From the First Step to the First Date

T HE FIRST TWO YEARS of life mark the emergence from helplessness. The newborn is almost totally helpless, a creature of reflex. When he cries, his mother comes. But he does not *control* his mother's coming. His crying is a reflexive response to pain or discomfort; he has no choice about whether or not to cry. To emerge from helplessness and develop the means to personally control and master his environment, he must develop voluntary responses to bring about desired consequences. The only muscles the newborn can voluntarily control are those he uses for sucking and eye movement. In the first three months of life, he starts to control his arms and legs, though his motions are rudimentary. Soon his arm flailing refines into reaching. Then his crying becomes voluntary, once he learns that he can bawl whenever he wants his mother. The first and second years usher in the two great milestones of personal control: walking and talking. These two years see a titanic struggle toward mastery and achievement. Toddlers kick against obstacles and they persist when thwarted. Thankfully, they do not easily become helpless. Robert is on the right path.*

Eighteen months old, Robert is Jessica and Joe's first child. They are in awe of their son, dumbfounded by the things Robert can do, amazed at what he understands and what he can commu-

*Throughout the book we have changed the names and identifying information in all the examples taken from the experiences of children and parents in our studies. Many examples are collages.

nicate. At dinner, as Robert smushes his head in the applesauce and crams gigantic pieces of cornbread into his mouth, Jessica tells Joe the latest Robert story.

Robert's current fascination is with the small, dusty area behind the couch. He squeezes his body around the end table, nearly bringing the lamp down onto his head, for the pleasure of standing behind the couch where the electric outlets are. Why this so intrigues him is lost on Jessica. Each time Robert makes a dash for the couch, she attempts to distract him. First she tries singing the Barney song. "I love you, you love me. . . ."

It doesn't work. Then she tries making funny noises with the Elmo puppet. It doesn't work. She even lets him bury himself in the sofa cushion. Each time, Robert persists in running behind the couch.

As Robert remains undeterred, his mother's techniques become more creative. She pushes his stroller right up against the side of the couch so he can't get by. This works for two minutes. As soon as she sits down, Robert saunters over, gets down on his belly, and wiggles his way past. To add insult to injury, he stands up and gives his mother a big grin while clapping his hands in victory. It's clear that Robert is proud of himself.

In a final attempt to stop Robert, Jessica moves a box of books in front of the stroller to block his way. Robert waits patiently until she is done and then very confidently approaches her construction. At first he tries to get his leg on top of the box so he can climb over it, but the box is too big. Then he tries to push the box out of his way, but he can't budge it. With his "I can do it" look on his face, Robert pulls himself up onto the box with his elbows and lands on his bum in the stroller. He then rolls out of the stroller and is behind the couch. Robert stands up and excitedly shouts, "Bobby do! Bobby do!"

Through this ordeal Jessica decides that it is the challenge of climbing that Robert enjoys. Still fearing that he may hurt himself in his climb behind the couch, she decides to take him outside and build a fort out of old boxes and pillows. Jessica hides Elmo behind the fort and encourages Robert to find him. Each time

Robert makes it over the mountain of boxes and pillows to find Elmo, he holds the doll out toward his mother and says, "Bobby do! Yay . . . Bobby do!"

Like most parents of young children, Jessica is constantly scanning the world for dangers to Robert. She did not want Robert to play behind the couch because there were too many electric cords. She tried to block his path. Robert, however, saw this as a challenge and, with determination, figured out ways to master the situation. Jessica could have scolded Robert because he would not stop trying to get behind the couch; after all her goal was to keep him from playing there. However, rather than scold Robert, Jessica recognized that Robert was seeing the obstacles as challenges to overcome, so she chose to share in his adventure and pride. She congratulated him on his accomplishment and then re-created the challenge for him in a safer environment. In doing this, Jessica helped her son feel masterful, and abided by her philosophy to constantly create new opportunities for mastery for her child.

Masterful *action* is the crucible in which preschool optimism is forged. Your child's task, aided by informed parenting, is to make a habit of persisting in the face of challenge and overcoming obstacles. Once your child enters school, the tactics for creating the optimistic child shift from masterful action to the way your child *thinks* — particularly when he fails. At school age, children begin to think about the causal skein of the world. They develop theories about why they succeed and why they fail. They develop theories about what, if anything, they can do to turn failure into success. These theories are the underpinnings of their basic optimism or their basic pessimism.

Ian is six and is already beginning to develop a pessimistic theory of himself. His dad, in a recurring effort to boost Ian's self-esteem, is making things worse. Dad comes home from work and shouts, "Come and get it, kids! I've got a big box just waiting to be ripped open!" Ian and his nine-year-old sister, Rachel, stampede toward the door and wrestle the package from Dad's arms. To their delight, they discover the biggest Lego set they've ever seen.

They both plop on the floor and begin reaching for pieces. Rachel quickly settles into building a spaceship. Methodically, she pieces the blocks together: first the body of the ship, then the wings. As she puts the pieces together, Rachel talks to herself about the spaceship's mission: "We've gotta fly to the moon and pick up the astronauts. And then we've gotta look out for Martians and make sure they don't get us."

Ian tries to mimic his sister. If Rachel picks up a blue square piece, Ian picks up a blue square piece. If Rachel snaps it together with a yellow rectangular piece, Ian snaps it together with a yellow rectangular piece. But Ian can't build the spaceship. Rachel builds too quickly and Ian can't keep up. As Rachel goes about her space conquest, Ian becomes more and more agitated. Each time a section falls apart, he gets angry. He starts to throw the pieces at his sister.

Dad sees Ian struggling and wants to make Ian feel better.

Dad: Ian, this is really great! I think the rocket you made is wonderful!

Ian: It is not. Rachel's is great. Mine is stupid. I can't even make the wings stay. I'm a dumbo. I never get things right.

Dad: I like it, Ian. I think you are the best rocket maker around.

Ian: Then how come Rachel's is bigger and has wings that are real long and they don't fall off like mine do? I can't do this. I can't do anything right. I hate Legos!

Dad: That's not true, Ian. You can do whatever you set your mind to. Here, give me the pieces and let me make it for you. I'll make you one that can fly to the moon and Mars and Jupiter. It'll be the fastest rocket ship ever and it will be all yours!

Ian: All right. You make one for me. Mine never work.

Dad's heart is in the right place. He hears how miserable Ian is as he fails to keep up with his older sister, and he wants to help. His approach is to try to bolster Ian's self-esteem directly. He tells Ian that the rocket is great. When Ian doubts his ability, Dad tells Ian that he can do whatever he sets his mind to.

Dad is making three mistakes. First, just about everything Dad says is false. And Ian knows it. No matter how hard Ian tries, he will not be able to build a rocket ship that is as sophisticated as his nine-year-old sister's. And his rocket ship is not wonderful. The wings fall off, the body is misshapen; clearly, it would never make it off the launching pad. Dad should tell the truth. He should explain that when Ian gets to be nine like Rachel is, the things he builds will be sturdier, and that when Rachel was only six, her structures looked like Ian's.

Second, to make Ian feel better, Dad takes over and builds Ian the rocket ship Ian cannot make for himself. Dad is sending the message "When things don't go as you want, give up and let someone else rescue you." In trying to build Ian's self-esteem, his dad has taught him a lesson in helplessness. There is nothing wrong with letting Ian fail. Failure, in itself, is not catastrophic. It may deflate self-esteem for a while, but it is the interpretation your child makes of the failure that can be more harmful. Dad should sympathize with Ian and validate his feelings, making it clear he knows just how bad Ian feels ("When I was seven, I remember how awful I felt the time I built a kite and it blew into fourteen pieces the moment my dad and I tried to fly it."). But Dad should not solve Ian's problem for him.

The third is the most important mistake Dad makes, and this kind of mistake is the centerpiece of this book. Dad must learn to counter Ian's way of interpreting failure. Ian thinks about his setbacks and small tragedies in the bleakest way. "I'm a dumbo," "Mine never work," and "I can't do anything right" are all sweeping causes that will create yet more setbacks. Not only does Ian gravitate to the most pessimistic causes, but his way of reacting to problems is with passivity, giving up, and a whiny inwardness. Ian's learned pessimism is self-fulfilling.

But pessimism is a trait that psychologists have discovered how to change. Cognitive psychology has developed a powerful technology for changing the maladaptive thinking habits that many people fall into when they fail. These techniques can be taught by parents and turn out to work especially well for school-age children. The techniques of changing pessimism into optimism are the fulcrum that I use to immunize children against depression.

Meet Tamara, who unlike Ian is being immunized against depression by her mother. Tamara's mom does not make the mistakes that Ian's dad does, and Tamara is acquiring an optimistic theory of herself. When she encounters setbacks, which she does as often as Ian, she has learned to bounce back. Instead of trying to make Tamara feel better by denying reality, Tamara's mom validates Tamara's disappointment and teaches her perseverance and active problem solving. She also guides Tamara in explaining her failures optimistically and accurately.

At seven, Tamara is much heavier than most girls her age and is less coordinated than the other children in the neighborhood. Her mom enrolls her in a ballet class to help her develop better motor skills. Tamara is thrilled and can't wait to start. The week before the program begins, Tamara and her mom go shopping for dance clothes. Tamara picks out a pink leotard and skirt and white ballerina slippers. Every night, Tamara pulls on her ballerina outfit and dances around the house. "Look, Mommy! I am a pretty ballerina. I can't wait to take my lessons so I can be a real ballerina. When I grow up I'm going to be the best dancer in the world!"

Each night while Tamara pulls on her outfit, Mom puts a record on the stereo for Tamara to dance to. She watches as Tamara twirls. Often Tamara loses her balance and ends up sprawled on the floor. Undaunted, Tamara picks herself up and continues to twirl and leap to the music.

Tuesday afternoon is Tamara's first lesson. Mom brings her to the studio and watches as the other girls, slimmer and more fit, run around the space. Tamara kisses her mom goodbye and walks into the room with the instructor. When Mom returns an hour later, Tamara is tearful.

Tamara: I had a bad day. The other girls did better. I kept falling down and they didn't. Miss Harkum showed us how to skip and move our arms and hands in a real pretty way, but I kept tripping and my hands didn't look the way they were supposed to. It really hurts.

Mom [*comforts Tamara*]: I'm sorry you had such a hard time today. I know it hurts when you feel like you aren't as good as some of the other girls. Lots of times, Mommy feels disappointed too. Like when I'm at work and don't do as good a job as I'd like to. That makes me feel upset. But you know what I do when that happens? I practice more and most of the time after I keep trying, I do a better job. I have an idea. Let's go say hello to Miss Harkum and I'll ask her to teach me the dance step and then you and I can go home and practice it together. I bet if we work hard at it, you'll be better at it for your next lesson. How does that sound?

Tamara: Okay, I guess. Will you practice with me tonight after dinner? I want to get good at it, so that I can be a ballerina when I grow up.

Mom: You bet. Let's go talk to Miss Harkum, and then after dinner, we'll push the sofa back and make the living room into your very own dance studio!

Tamara: That'll be fun! I'm gonna practice real hard!

Tamara's theory of failure is that failure is temporary and local ("I had a bad day" and "the other girls did better," as opposed to "I never do anything right"). Problems for Tamara are just setbacks, temporary and changeable. Sometimes reality will prove Tamara wrong. Tamara will not grow up to be a ballerina any more than I grew up to be a major league catcher. But childhood dreams have great value. Effort and practice often compensate for small talents. Unlike Ian, who will just not try anymore, Tamara will find out that perseverance and good cheer often work. In the course of disengaging from her dreams of becoming a prima ballerina, Tamara will discover that time stops for her when she dances, and classical music will become a joy for life. She will also find out that people admire her grit and that kids revel in her good cheer.

As puberty approaches, your child's theory of the world crystallizes. She may now be pessimistic, passive, and introverted. As the routine but painful rejections and failures of puberty start, depression reaches alarming proportions. Almost one-third of contemporary thirteen-year-olds have marked depressive symptoms, and by the time they finish high school almost 15 percent have had an episode of major depression.[1] Marla is about to go into a tailspin, one that may end in a debilitating depression. This, her first depression, is critical, for it will become the template for how she reacts to bad events for the rest of her life. Here is an excerpt from her diary:

May 12, 1993
Dear Diary,

Today totally sucked. Cory said no, of course. I never should of let my mom talk me into asking him in the first place. Why do I even listen to her?! I did just like she said. He was standing by himself and I went over and tried to joke around a little. Of course, everything I said was stupid. He was looking at me like I was a complete dork. Anyway, then I said, "Would you want to go to the Sadie Hawkins dance with me?" and he just gawked at me for the longest time and didn't say anything. Finally he said no. Just like that. He made some lame excuse about going to stay with his father next weekend, but I know it was a total lie.

Why did I ever listen to my mom?! She doesn't get it. Of course she thinks I'm gonna get a date — she's my mother. But she's living in a fantasy world about her darling twelve-year-old. She doesn't know that I have no friends. She still thinks I'm tight with Joan and Tracy and Leah, but the truth is they barely talk to me anymore. Ever since we got in the seventh grade, they've started hanging out with Betsy and Crystal from Woodside. I bet Leah doesn't even invite me to her party. The other day they were sitting at lunch together and they acted like they didn't see me. I know they saw me. I didn't even bother to say hi and I sat on the other side of the cafeteria with some sixth-graders. I can't take this anymore. I don't ever want to go back to school. I hate it there. Nobody likes me.

I don't blame them. I hate everything about myself. My hair is gross. My nose looks like a ski slope and I'm totally uncoordinated. Yesterday Richard got mad because Mr. Harper put me on his team and told him that he had to let me bat. Some days I wish

I would just not wake up in the morning. I mean it. I don't want to spend the rest of my life like this. I'm like those people Mrs. Applebaum taught us about in social studies. She said that there are these people who live in India and they are called untouchables. They are total outcasts and they are treated like dirt by everyone and they are forced to do the most horrible jobs. Even if they are really smart, they could never be a doctor or something like that. Anyway, that's what I am, an untouchable.

I know this sounds weird, but last night after I turned out the light, I just lay there and made up this whole story about finding out that I was dying of some gross disease and what Mom and Dad and Lynn and Craig would do and who would come to my funeral and what people would say. The saddest part was that I could only think of eleven people who would even come to my funeral besides my family. And I had to think really hard to come up with that many.

Well, I'm gonna stop for now. I'll write more later.

It was 1984 and I had already spent two decades studying the manifestations of optimism and pessimism from birth into adulthood. I knew that pessimism in these early years produced depression and poor achievement. With Dr. Salk's vision in mind, I now hypothesized that the proven techniques for adults' learning optimism, when taught early in life, would immunize schoolchildren and teenagers against the kind of depression that Marla was headed for. I was ready to build a research team to find out.

3

Building the Team

"WHY DOES DEPRESSION ever go away? I mean, given the theories you talked about, depression should stay forever once you get it," queried the dark-haired student in the sixth row.

Questions were rare in this setting. It took courage to stand up in front of three hundred other University of Pennsylvania students in Psychology 162, Abnormal Psychology, and venture a question. This question caught me off guard. I had been lecturing about the three main theories of depression: the biomedical theory, which invoked insufficient brain chemicals; the psychoanalytic theory, which held that depression was anger directed at the self; and the cognitive theory, which held that depression came from pessimistic, conscious thoughts. This student was puzzled, rightly so. Each of these theories explains why depression starts, and why it continues, and each prescribes a therapy. So far, so good.

But it is a commonplace that depression almost always simply goes away in time, on its own, untreated. The time seems agonizingly long to the sufferer, three months to six months, but wane it almost always will. How could each of these theories explain that?

I stopped and thought. And thought some more. The silence was getting embarrassing. "I don't know. I just don't know," I finally muttered.

"What's your name?" I added in tribute.

"Karen Reivich," she said and dropped back into her seat. Karen Reivich. I had heard of her. She was the high school student the *Daily*

Pennsylvanian wrote about a few years before. Penn's admissions committee, for want of some better way of choosing among applicants, mandated an essay about what world problem the student would solve. The result was tens of thousands of grandiose essays about world peace, the ozone layer, racism, and the evils of capitalism. Karen Reivich wrote that she would tackle the urgent, much-neglected problem of static cling. I had the clipping in my files: "War, poverty, disease, static cling. We stand on the brink of chaos. What Spartacus was to slavery, what George Washington was to colonialism, what Gloria Steinem is to sexism, so may I be to static cling." She was admitted anyway.

This one insightful question, her aplomb, and her iconoclasm intrigued me, so I asked her after class to come and see me at my office. I invited her to put her graduate school plans on hold (she was a senior) and work full-time on research with me the next year. At the time, I had begun a project under the auspices of the Metropolitan Life Insurance Company to train pessimistic life insurance sales agents to become optimists. We incorporated the cognitive and behavioral techniques successfully used to fight depression, but we changed them to a preventive mode for adults so they would be useful to the pessimistic, but not depressed, sales agents. Karen soon proved indispensable to this project and became the coordinator. Once we began to find that we could change pessimistic agents into optimistic ones, I asked Karen to expand our horizons.

"I had a talk with Jonas Salk," I told her, "and it has changed my thinking about what psychologists should be spending their time doing. I think it's going to change what I do with my own time." Psychologists, I explained to Karen, had spent 99 percent of their efforts helping troubled people become normal. The National Institute of Mental Health should really be called the National Institute of Mental Illness: almost their entire budget goes to underwriting help for the severely troubled. Almost no effort or money has been devoted to helping normal people reach their fullest potential and live better than normal lives. The Met Life project moved us in that direction. "Now I want to mount a research program in which we teach normal children the skills of optimism, and try to prevent problems that would otherwise come about. I'd like you to join the research team."

Before the conversation was over, she had eagerly agreed. I had found one collaborator, but I needed more.

JANE GILLHAM asked to meet with me shortly after she arrived at Penn. She had just heard me give a talk about the link between pessimism and depression in children. Jane was a first-year graduate student who had come from a distinguished undergraduate career at Princeton. Her teachers raved about her abilities and told me that Penn was lucky to get her. She had done research in developmental psychology and spent two years as a teacher. Jane was also a single mother with a young son, so her commitment to working with children had a special significance.

"Sean had a bad day yesterday," she said. "He came home from school and told me that a bigger kid in his class had been picking on him. He was whining, 'I don't want to go to school. I never have any fun. I used to like school but now I don't have any fun anymore. I want to write to Mrs. Johnson and tell her I'm quitting school.'

"I found myself using cognitive therapy with him," Jane continued. "We talked about how he was feeling and what he hated about school. Then I helped him remember the parts of school he loved. I had him telling me all the fun things they did at recess yesterday. I got him to dispute his own catastrophizing. He realized that school would be fun if he could solve the problem with Gary. He even worked out a plan for winning Gary over."

I knew from Jane's mention of cognitive therapy and "decatastrophizing" that here was a sophisticated young professional with a well-tuned sense of how to use discoveries in psychology in real life. Cognitive therapy was the breakthrough for depression of the 1980s. Its founder, Aaron T. Beck, a psychiatrist at Penn and a mentor of mine, had made an extraordinary theoretical move. The symptoms of depression divide into four classes: low mood, listless behavior, physical problems, and catastrophic thinking. Beck contended that catastrophic thinking was more than just a superficial symptom of depression, rather that it is the root cause of all the other symptoms of depression. The depressive's habit of thinking that the future is bleak, the present unbearable, the past filled with defeat, and the self without the ability to improve matters *creates* the low mood, the lack of zest, and the somatic symptoms of depression.

A new therapy for depression followed: teach the depressive to change her habits of thinking, to decatastrophize, and all the rest of the symptoms should evaporate. This was the essence of cognitive therapy, and Jane apparently had ideas on how to apply it to kids.

Jane told me that she wanted to work with children at Penn and asked if I had thought about trying to use cognitive therapy to prevent depression in children. I told her about my conversation with Dr. Salk and invited her to work with me on developing psychological immunization for children.

SO, JANE AND KAREN and I started to develop a training program for children. We worked on finding creative and engaging ways to teach children the cognitive skills that are essential for preventing depression and overcoming adversity. Things were progressing well and it looked as though the program would be ready to test soon. Then I had lunch with Lisa Jaycox, one of Penn's star graduate students.

She was at loose ends. "Rena's leaving and I just don't know what to do," she complained to me over soup and salad at Kelly and Cohen's, the campus delicatessen. The previous spring Lisa had done a stunningly important master's thesis on how parents' fighting worsens children's conduct problems and lowers their feelings of competence.[1] Her advisor, Dr. Rena Repetti, an expert on families and children, was now leaving Penn to take a job in New York. Losing an advisor often spells academic doom for a graduate student in the middle of a promising research career, and Lisa's career was in jeopardy.

"Are you doing any projects with kids or families, Marty?" Lisa asked. Here was the real agenda of the lunchtime meeting. So I told Lisa about the immunization project, explaining that we were launching a program designed to impart cognitive skills for optimism to preteenage kids at risk for depression. The logic was that the kids could use these skills to combat the pessimistic thoughts that bring depression and failure in their wake.

"What you say makes sense," Lisa offered, "but you are missing something. Just think about your own findings from the Penn-Princeton study."

I had been lucky enough to collaborate for five years with Joan Girgus, professor of psychology and then dean of the college at Princeton, and with Susan Nolen-Hoeksema, who started the Penn-Princeton Longitudinal Study of Childhood Depression as a graduate student with me and then moved to a professorship at Stanford. Susan, Joan, and I had followed four hundred children, starting at age eight, and their parents for five years. We wanted to know when depression began and what made some kids so very vulnerable and others so resilient. Our findings both startled and dismayed us.

We found that more than a quarter of the kids were markedly depressed at any one time, and almost that many experienced a severe depressive episode at least once during the five years. We found that the pessimistic kids did worse than the optimistic kids, and that once a child experienced a bout of depression, her worldview became much more pessimistic. While the depression went away gradually over time, the pessimism did not, and formerly depressed kids now became dyed-in-the-wool pessimists — easy prey to depression once again as soon as another bad event happened. And happen they would, all too often, once the teenage years arrived.

But Lisa was referring to another finding, just as worrisome. Many of the children first became depressed when their parents started fighting with each other. Divorce, separation, and parental turmoil generally are heavy risk factors for the preteenage child.

"This means that merely teaching kids to think more optimistically isn't enough," Lisa bore in. "It's social hassles — parents' fighting and rejection by other kids — that are at the root of so much of kids' depressions. You need to immunize them with ways of handling their social problems as well. Immunization should have two components: a cognitive one and social skills.

"You create the cognitive program and I'll create the social one," Lisa concluded.

THE FOUR OF US worked together throughout the next year. We pilot-tested the program on a group of fifth- and sixth-graders and were encouraged by the results. We then went back to the lab to fine-tune the program before launching a large-scale test of its effectiveness. And now the whole immunization program, just as Dr. Salk had envisioned, was finally in place: cognitive skills for kids to fight depression and social skills to ward off the rejections and frustrations of puberty. So the four of us — Karen Reivich, Lisa Jaycox, Jane Gillham, and I — launched the Penn Prevention Program. We set out to identify the most vulnerable ten- to twelve-year-olds in advance and then to teach them a set of cognitive and social skills that would prevent depression.

When we began teaching children optimism in the schools, we found that what we were teaching was very different from what many baby-boomer parents were conveying to their children. We also found that our approach was radically different from the self-esteem–centered approach of the schools. Baby-boomer child rearing and the self-esteem movement in the schools, we suspected, were not alleviating the ongoing epidemic of depression and might even be creating it.

PART TWO

Where Boomer
Child Rearing
Went Wrong

4

The Self-Esteem Movement

Inside the locket was a mirror, and in the mirror was her very own reflection.

"Why, it's me!" she thought. "It's really me. *I'm* the magic in the locket." From then on, the little girl wore the locket every day. Every day she held the locket tightly and whispered, "I believe in you." The locket was filled with her own special magic and from that day on she was never without it.

— Elizabeth Koda-Callan
The Magic Locket (1988)

WE WERE SURPRISED by what we saw in the public schools, though we probably should not have been, because what we saw just reflects the way most American parents of the boomer vintage are now raising their children. Armies of American teachers, along with American parents, are straining to bolster children's self-esteem. That sounds innocuous enough, but the way they do it often erodes children's sense of worth. By emphasizing how a child *feels,* at the expense of what the child *does* — mastery, persistence, overcoming frustration and boredom, and meeting challenge — parents and teachers are making this generation of children more vulnerable to depression.

Here is a smattering of what we saw in American classrooms:

- "Building Self-Esteem with Koala-Roo" contains an exercise with "YOU ARE SPECIAL" written fourteen times on one page, followed by "I am very glad that I have been your *x* grade teacher. There's no one else quite like you."

- A poster picturing clapping hands announces, "We Applaud Ourselves!"
- A cartoon character admires itself in a mirror and urges, "Make Loving Yourself a Habit."
- Fill-in-the-blank games ask kids to complete "I am special because . . ." with achievements such as "I know how to play," "I can color," and "Everybody makes me happy."

The rationale for this puffery is explicit: ". . . the basis for *everything we do* is self-esteem. Therefore, if we can do something to give children a stronger sense of themselves, starting in preschool, they'll be [a lot wiser] in the choices they make."[1]

The effects of teaching self-esteem are not confined to teachers mouthing self-contradictory slogans (if everybody is special, is anybody special?). Kids soon learn to ignore such flattery as insincere anyway. The self-esteem movement has teeth. It has helped lead to the abolition of tracking, lest those on lower tracks suffer damaged self-esteem; to the abandonment of IQ testing, lest those who score low feel low self-esteem; to massive grade inflation, lest those who earn D's feel bad; to teaching aimed at the very bottom of the class, to spare the feelings of the kids slower to learn (now that they are untracked); to *competition* becoming a dirty word; to the demise of rote memorization of epic material; and to less plain old hard work. Each tactic is used to protect the feelings of self-esteem of the kids who would otherwise be outshone. This gain is deemed to outweigh any benefits lost to the kids who would shine.

Parents, as well as teachers, have been persuaded, and they routinely leap in to try to bolster kids' feelings of self-esteem.

Randy is in the fifth grade at Bywood Elementary School. His teachers describe him as bright, curious, and creative. Randy excels in the basic subjects and enjoys school a great deal. Except for gym class. Gym class for Randy, as for most unathletic children, is a regular dose of humiliation. Bradley, Garrett, and Beth dodge the ball with ease. Randy, in his efforts to escape the line of fire, either gets hit in the bum or on the side of the head. Or worse, he loses his balance and crashes in a heap onto the gymnasium floor.

Tuesday mornings from 10 to 11 provide Randy with a supply of shame that lasts the rest of the week.

Joel is Randy's best friend. Unfortunately for Randy, Joel has been graced with agility and thus is not humiliated in gym class. When the coach drops in to announce that he will be starting a flag-football team to compete against other elementary schools, Joel whispers to Randy that they ought to try out. Randy whispers back that he would rather die. In spite of Randy's apprehensions, Joel is able to persuade him that flag football, unlike the rest of the games they play in gym, really doesn't require much in the way of coordination; you just have to be able to run, which even Randy can do.

Randy's dad, who believes it would be good for him to be an athlete, encourages him to give the tryout a shot. Randy grudgingly starts practicing with Joel after school. In spite of himself, he gets excited and even starts enjoying the practice drills Joel designs. Much to his surprise, he gets a little better.

The fateful day arrives. Randy, his dad, and Joel reach the field to find a mass of boys tossing footballs and wrestling each other to the ground. Immediately, Randy's excitement congeals into dread. Joel grabs a ball and throws it to Randy. Randy jams his finger trying to catch it. Joel runs for a pass and Randy hurls the ball. It wobbles through the air, landing ten feet short of Joel. Dad tries to give Randy last-minute tips, but with his ears ringing, Randy can't hear him.

Randy finishes next-to-last in the running drills, he catches only one ball, and none of his passes lands in the vicinity of the receivers. Dad is pained by the look of humiliation on Randy's face as the tryout breaks up. He turns to Randy and says, "You know, I think you did a real good job out there. Your passes didn't always hit the mark, but you've got a strong arm. You can always work on accuracy. That's not so hard. Really, I think you ought to be proud of yourself, Randy. I'm sure you'll make the team next year. You just got a bad break this time."

"What are you talking about, Dad? I sucked. I didn't make the team this year and I won't make it next year either. I can't believe I even tried out for the team. Let's face it, I'm a spaz."

Undeterred by the response, Dad goes on boosterishly: "That's no way to talk. You can't let yourself think like that. I'm telling you, you did really well out there. As far as I'm concerned, you are just as good as any of the rest of them. I don't want to see you hanging your head like that. You've got to tell yourself you were good and that next time you'll be better."

"Okay, you're right. I was good. Now, can we get outta here, please?"

Randy's dad had the best of intentions. He saw Randy's feelings were really hurt, and he wanted to help him feel better, and to do this right away. Like many parents, he chose to bolster Randy's self-esteem with glib positive thinking. He told Randy "nice" things, words that he hoped would soothe away Randy's pain and replace it with pride. But Dad's approach backfired. Randy is not a simple, gullible creature who hungers to plaster over unpleasant truths. Dad's approach deflated Randy further, and eroded his own credibility in the process.

A BRIEF HISTORY OF SELF-ESTEEM

One of the reasons Randy's dad failed so badly is due to the legacy of the self-esteem movement and its damaging effect on American child rearing. Self-esteem has a venerable provenance. William James, the father of modern psychology, more than one hundred years ago had a formula for it:[2]

$$\text{Self-esteem} = \frac{\text{Success}}{\text{Pretensions}}$$

The more success we achieve, according to James, and the lower our expectations, the higher our self-esteem. We can feel better about ourselves either by succeeding more in the world or by downsizing our hopes.

James bridges two levels of psychological function: First, self-esteem is a *feeling* state: mortification, contentment, satisfaction, and the like define it. But second, such good feeling is rooted in the world, in *the success of our commerce with the world*. The tension between these two aspects of self-esteem — feeling good versus doing well in the world — has provided the theoretical underpinnings of the self-esteem movement ever since. These two aspects — "feeling good" and "doing well" — highlight what is right with self-esteem and, more important, what is wrong and counterproductive with trying to instill self-esteem directly in a child as did Randy's dad.

The notion of self-esteem lay dormant for almost seventy-five years after James proposed it, as America was consumed with fighting wars and overcoming economic depression. Given the specter of such powerful real-world problems creating such misery, American psychology was dominated by theories that had people pushed or pulled by the powerful forces beyond their control. For the Freudians, "conflicts" pushed human action. For the behaviorists, external "positive reinforcers" pulled people toward them and "punishers" pushed them away. For the ethologists, fixed action patterns governed by genes underlay behavior. For the followers of Clark Hull, biological drives and tissue "needs" goaded action. Whatever the details, the worldview of all these theories was that human beings are at the mercy of forces beyond their control.

A sea change occurred in the social sciences of the 1960s. Individual choice became a legitimate explanation of human action, and being pushed or pulled by external forces began to go out of fashion as an explanation. It was more than coincidence that this change occurred just as America moved into an era of unprecedented wealth and power, with individual consumption driving the economy. Choice and control, personal preference, decision, and will became the hallmarks of the new theories. Self-direction, rather than outside forces, became the primary explanation of why people do what they do.[3]

The time was now ripe for the resuscitation of self-esteem, and in 1967 Stanley Coopersmith, a feisty and iconoclastic young psychology professor at the University of California at Davis, proposed that self-esteem was crucial for child rearing.[4] Coopersmith's first goal was to measure self-esteem. He devised a test that emphasized the feeling-good side of self-esteem, defining the concept as the personal judgment of worthiness. "I often wish I were someone else," "I'm pretty happy," "It's pretty tough to be me," and "I have a low opinion of myself" are some of the true-false entries on his widely used test.

He then assessed the child-rearing practices of parents whose children had high self-esteem and came up with a surprising, and uncongenially old-fashioned, finding about the origins of high self-esteem: the clearer the rules and the limits enforced by parents, the higher the child's self-esteem. The more freedom the child had, the lower his self-esteem. Coopersmith's conclusions about the disciplinary origins of self-esteem were soon forgotten, but the idea of self-esteem as a goal of child rearing was embraced widely by the popular culture, particularly the schools, the churches of liberal doctrine, and the inspiration industry.

The most thoughtful of the inspiration psychologists retained both the "feeling-good" and the "doing-well" aspects. Nathaniel Branden, early an Ayn Rand disciple, then a clinical psychology Ph.D., and now a doyen of the self-esteem movement, defined self-esteem as follows:[5]

1. Confidence in our ability to think and to cope with the basic challenges of life (doing well).
2. Confidence in our right to be happy, the feeling of being worthy, deserving, entitled to assert our needs and wants and entitled to enjoy the fruits of our efforts (feeling good).

So widely accepted today is this kind of self-esteem that California has made it official. In "Toward a State of Esteem," a set of recommendations made by a task force under the auspices of the California legislature, poor self-esteem is claimed to cause academic failure, drug use, teenage pregnancy, dependence on welfare, and other ills. Teaching self-esteem is touted as the "most likely social vaccine" to inoculate children against these ills. Every school district in California is urged "to adopt the promotion of self-esteem . . . as a clearly stated goal, integrated into its total curriculum and informing all of its policies and operations." Further, it is recommended that "course work in self-esteem should be required for credentials . . . for all educators." Shirley MacLaine has urged the president of the United States to create a cabinet-level Secretary of Self-Esteem.

The kind of self-esteem California envisions is distinctly on the feeling-good side: "Appreciating my own worth and importance and having the character to be accountable for myself and to act responsibly toward others."[6] But the recommendations for just *how* feelings of self-esteem should be taught are disappointing. On the "doing-well" side, the recommendations are useful, if traditional: teach real-world job skills, encourage community service, and teach the arts. On the "feeling-good" side, however, the recommendations are vague: expand counseling services, get parents involved, be sensitive to the needs of failing students. But what should the counselors counsel? What should the involved parents do? And how should the teachers put their sensitivity to work to help failing students?

With support from educators, inspirational psychologists, the ministry, the California legislature, and movie stars, dare I question the value of self-esteem?

FEELING GOOD VERSUS DOING WELL

The reason the California report is so flabby on the feeling-good side is because there is no effective technology for teaching feeling good which does not first teach doing well. Feelings of self-esteem in particular, and happiness in general, develop as side effects — of mastering challenges, working successfully, overcoming frustration and boredom, and winning. The feeling of self-esteem is a byproduct of doing well. Once a child's self-esteem is in place, it kindles further success. Tasks flow more seamlessly, troubles bounce off, and other children seem more receptive. There is no question that feeling high self-esteem is a delightful state to be in, but trying to achieve the feeling side of self-esteem directly, before achieving good commerce with the world, confuses profoundly the means and the end.

The premium we put on feeling good is peculiarly modern. Aristotle had a timeless view: Happiness is not an emotion that can be separated from what we *do*. Happiness is like grace in a dance, not something the dancer *feels* at the end of a good dance, but an inalienable accompaniment of a dance well done. Happiness is not a separable feeling-state that can be obtained in any other way save as part and parcel of right action.

My skeptical opinion of the feeling side of self-esteem has been formed by twenty-five years of work with depressed adults and children. Depressed people, both young and old, have four kinds of problems: behavioral — they are passive, indecisive, and helpless; emotional — they are sad; somatic — their appetites, for both sleeping and eating, are disrupted; and cognitive — they think living is hopeless and they feel worthless. Only this last half-symptom amounts to the feeling side of self-esteem, and I have come to believe that this is the least important of a depressed person's woes. Once a depressed child becomes active and hopeful, her feelings of worth always improve. Bolstering the feeling side of self-esteem without breaking the shackles of hopelessness or passivity accomplishes nothing. If your child suffers from feelings of worthlessness, hates herself, or feels no confidence, it is a reflection that she believes her commerce with the world is going badly. Once her commerce with the world improves and she realizes it, she will feel good.

This is just what makes the California report on self-esteem so gaseous. It is true that many school dropouts feel low self-esteem, many pregnant teenagers feel sad, many young drug addicts and criminals feel self-loathing, and many people on welfare feel unworthy. But what is cause and what is effect? The California report, with its "vaccine" recommendations, claims that the feelings of low self-worth cause the school failures, the drug use, the dependence on welfare, and other social ills. But the research literature shows just the opposite. Low self-esteem is a consequence of failing in school, of being on welfare, of being arrested — not the cause.[7]

The hundreds of scholarly articles about self-esteem are replete with *correlations* of self-esteem and how children do: homely kids have low self-esteem, high achievers have high self-esteem, depressed people have low self-esteem, good athletes have high self-esteem, children who get F's have low self-esteem, and so on. But does failure cause low self-esteem or does low self-esteem cause failure? This is a

surprisingly easy question to answer with mo_
niques: The researcher needs to look at large grou_
across time, say a year, measuring self-esteem at the beg_
various presumed consequences such as grades, popularity, or d_
sion at the beginning of the year and at the end.[8] If self-esteem _
causal, the prediction is clear: among the kids who have the same
grades at the beginning (this is controlled for statistically), those with
high self-esteem should see their grades rise, and those with low
self-esteem should see their grades fall over the year.[9]

There are, however, almost no findings showing that self-esteem
causes anything at all. Rather, self-esteem is caused by the whole
panoply of successes or failures in the world.[10] If self-esteem is a
consequence of success and failure, not its cause, it should be hard to
teach self-esteem directly. If we, as parents and teachers, promote the
doing-well side of self-esteem, the feeling-good side, which cannot be
taught directly, will follow. What California (and every state) needs is
not children who are encouraged to feel good, but children who are
taught the skills of doing well — how to study, how to avoid pregnancy, drugs, and gangs, and how to get off welfare.

There is a mental state, related to self-esteem, that is considerably
more potent: explanatory style. This state is the key to optimism. I
will discuss explanatory style in chapter 6, but I preview it now
because it underscores the feeling and doing sides of self-esteem.
When a child does badly, she asks herself "Why?" There are always
three aspects to the answer she comes up with: *who* is to blame, *how
long* will it last, and *how much of her life* will be undermined. The
distinctions among these three are crucial because the first question —
blaming the self versus the world — governs the feeling side of self-esteem. The second and third questions — how permanent is the cause
and how pervasive is the cause — govern what she will *do* to respond
to failure. Feeling bad about the self does not directly cause failure. The belief that problems will last forever and undermine everything, in contrast, directly causes your child to stop trying. Giving up
leads to more failure, which then goes on to undermine feelings of
self-esteem.

OING WELL AND THE VAST MIDDLE GROUND

The whole issue of promoting feelings of self-esteem in children, on the one hand, and promoting mastery and optimism, on the other, needs to be seen as a continuum. At one end are those who advocate feeling good as the primary goal, with how the child does in the world a fortunate byproduct. For those at this end of the spectrum, what matters is how the child *feels* about himself. At the other end are those like myself who advocate doing well in the world as the primary goal, with feeling good only a delicious byproduct.

Most theorists, and every practitioner, are someplace in between. Most parents and teachers, regardless of their theories, sometimes intervene just to relieve hurt and make a child feel better. Most parents and teachers sometimes let the child endure frustration to promote perseverance. People guided by the popular "feeling-good" viewpoint are ready to intervene to make the child feel better. People guided by the "doing-well" approach are ready to intervene to change the child's thinking about failure, to encourage frustration-tolerance, and to reward persistence rather than mere success. The feeling-good advocates, in concert with the "power-of-positive-thinking" teachers, have ways to try to make children feel better about themselves. The doing-well advocates have two new technologies: one for changing pessimism into optimism, and one for changing helplessness into mastery. This book will teach you about both of these.

America has seen thirty years of a concerted effort to bolster the self-esteem of its kids. This movement would be justified if it worked and self-esteem were on the rise. But something striking has happened to the self-esteem of American children during the era of raising our children to feel good. They have never been more depressed.

5

The Epidemic of Depression

I N   S P I T E   O F   the self-esteem campaign, in
spite of the natural optimism children have as
toddlers, and in spite of the new opportunities that are now unfolding
in our society, our children are experiencing pessimism, sadness, and
passivity on an unprecedented scale.

How can this be? Is it just a coincidence that during the era when
Americans made feeling good and boosting self-esteem in children a
primary aim, the incidence of depression has skyrocketed and feelings
of self-esteem have plummeted?

Depression until the 1960s was a fairly unusual condition, typically reported by middle-aged women. In the early 1960s, depression
started becoming much more prevalent. Now, after only thirty years,
depression has become the common cold of mental illness and it takes
its first victims in junior high school — if not before.

We know this from four large-scale studies.[1] The first, called the
ECA Study (short for Epidemiological Catchment Area Study), was
designed to find out how much mental illness there is in the United
States. Researchers went door to door and interviewed 9,500 people
who were randomly picked to be a cross section of adults. They were
all given the same diagnostic interview that a troubled patient who
walks into a knowledgeable psychologist's or psychiatrist's office
would get.

Adults of different ages were interviewed in large numbers all in
the same short period. Each person narrated his entire life history,
centered around whether and when in his life he experienced any

mental problems. The study thus gave the first picture ever of mental illness over many years and made it possible to trace the changes in rates of mental illness that had taken place over the course of the twentieth century. The single most surprising change was in the *lifetime prevalence* of depression, that is, the percentage of the population that has suffered from it at least once in their lifetime.

When the statisticians looked at these findings, they saw something very odd. People born around 1925 — who, since they were old, had more time to develop the disorder — hadn't suffered from depression much at all. Only 4 percent of them ever had severe depression by the time they were well into middle age. And when the statisticians looked at the findings for people born even earlier — before World War I — they found something more surprising. Again, the lifetime prevalence had not climbed, as one would have thought; only a mere 1 percent experienced depression by the time they were in old age. But of people born around 1955, who had the least opportunity to develop depression, 7 percent already had been severely depressed by their early twenties.

This means that people born after the feeling-good era and self-esteem movement had gotten under way were suffering from depression roughly ten times the rate of people born in the first third of this century!

The second study looked at 2,289 close relatives of 523 people who had been hospitalized for severe depression. Again, as in the ECA Study, the findings were astonishing. They showed a strong increase in depression over the course of the century — even more than ten-to-one. Consider just the women who were born during the early 1950s and went to school as the feeling-good era was taking hold. By the time they were thirty, more than 60 percent of them had been severely depressed. By contrast, only 3 percent of the women born around 1910, who went to school under the hard-work, dunce-cap ethic, had a severe depression by the time they were thirty. This is a twentyfold difference — as big an effect as is ever observed in social science. The statistics on the males in the study showed the same surprising ratio.

You might wonder if this explosion of depression is just an artifact of labeling. Maybe our grandmothers suffered as much as we do but didn't call it "depression." They just called it "life." Maybe the grinding misery that we call depression used to be an acceptable, inevitable part of the human condition. Now it has become a "disorder," and a treatable one — one that we believe we can and should get rid of.

These factors are valid considerations, but they do not explain the explosion of depression. The interviewers did not just ask "Have you ever been depressed?" They asked about the occurrence of each symptom over a lifetime: "Did you ever have a period in which you cried every day for two weeks?" "Did you ever lose twenty pounds in a short time without dieting?" "Did you ever try to kill yourself?" The more such symptoms in a given period, the more likely the diagnosis of depression would have applied. Nor is this explosion of depression an artifact of old people forgetting their symptoms from early in life; for they remember and report their youthful alcoholic or schizophrenic symptoms at a high rate.

Not only is severe depression much more common now; it also attacks its victims much younger. Statistically, if you were born in the 1930s and later had a depressed relative, your own first depression, if you had one, struck on average between the ages of thirty and thirty-five. If you were born in 1956, your first depression struck on average between ages twenty and twenty-five — ten years sooner.

The third major study warns us that this trend is still accelerating — more depression, beginning younger and younger. Dr. Peter Lewinsohn, an eminent West Coast depression researcher, and his colleagues gave diagnostic interviews to 1,710 randomly selected western Oregon adolescents. By age fourteen, 7.2 percent of the younger adolescents, born in 1972–74 had a severe depression; in contrast, 4.5 percent of the older adolescents, born in 1968–71, had a severe depression. "Severe" means marked symptoms of low mood, cognitive impairment, passivity, and bodily changes.

In the fourth study, the prevalence of full-blown depressive disorder among 3,000 twelve- to fourteen-year-olds in the southeastern

United States was 9 percent. Nine percent of children with depression is unprecedented.[2]

To those of us who work with depression, such a high percentage of kids suffering severe depression and depressive disorder at such a young age is astonishing and dismaying. Since severe depression recurs in about half of those who have had it once, the ten or twenty extra years of depression add up to that many extra years of misery and missed opportunities for every other person.

What is going on here? What can explain this constellation of facts: depression has been markedly increasing since the late 1950s, the increase is still going on, and younger and younger people now suffer from it.

What is going on is a matter of speculation. However, what is not going on is a matter of fact; while a good part of severe depression can have biochemical and genetic causes, this epidemic is not biological. Thirty years is much too short a period for a shift in genetic vulnerability to depression. Nor can anyone identify a biochemical change (e.g., fluoride in the water, ozone-layer breakdown, industrial pollution, birth control pills) that fits the time trends.

But there have been several sweeping social changes since the 1950s that, on their face, fit the facts. The epidemic begins as the baby boomers (people born soon after World War II) become adolescents in the early 1960s, accelerates as they become parents in the early 1970s, and continues as they now become grandparents. What is it about the life and times of the baby boomers? I believe there has been one sea change in the goals of Americans (and most of the "First World") that is to blame.

Our society has changed from an achieving society to a feel-good society. Up until the early 1960s, achievement was the most important goal to instill in our children. This goal was then overtaken by the twin goals of happiness and high self-esteem. This fundamental change consists of two trends. One is toward more individual satisfaction and more individual freedom: consumerism, recreational drugs, daycare, psychotherapy, sexual satisfaction, grade inflation. The other is the slide away from individual investment in endeavors larger than the self: God, Nation, Family, Duty. Some of the manifestations reflect what is most valuable about our culture, but others may be at the heart of the epidemic of depression:

- Family, Nation, and God take a back seat to the Self.
- Consumerism becomes a way of life, shopping an antidote to depression.
- Leaving an unsatisfactory, but not unbearable, marriage for the possibility of a better life after divorce becomes acceptable.
- Daycare, single mothers, and absent fathers become common.
- Duty, formerly the bedrock of adult life, goes out of fashion.
- Depression, a disorder of feeling bad, is separated from manic depression and labeled an illness.
- The study of self-esteem becomes a field in psychology.
- Drug use goes from something only jazz musicians do to the commonplace.
- Psychotherapy becomes usual for "normal" troubled people.
- Entertainers and sports figures command higher salaries and more prestige than captains of industry and politicians.
- Women's magazines feature dieting, looking good, and sexual satisfaction more than cooking, gardening, mothering, and wifery.
- Litigation by ordinary individuals becomes rampant.
- American manufactured goods become flashy and shoddy (in contrast to Japanese goods, which become muted and sturdy).
- Physical punishment of children becomes unusual and illegal.
- Failing students get an "Incomplete" or even a "Satisfactory" instead of an F.
- **Instilling feelings of high self-esteem becomes the explicit goal of education and of parenting.**

I am not against these developments. I am assuredly not against individualism, divorce, feeling good, psychotherapy, daycare, or single parents. But the feel-good society, as it overtook the doing-well society, created new opportunities and new freedoms along with new perils. The new perils are less obvious than the new freedoms, and this book is written to combat the greater risk for depression that these new opportunities bring.

One peril is difficulty finding meaning in life. It would be sophomoric to try to define meaning in these pages, but one truth about meaning is this: the larger the entity to which you can attach yourself, the more meaning you will feel your life has. While some argue that generations that lived for God, for America, for Duty, or for their children were misguided, these same generations surely felt their lives imbued with meaning.[3] The individual, the consuming self, isolated from larger entities, is a very poor site for a meaningful life. However, the bloated self is fertile soil for the growth of depression.

Depression is a disorder of individual helplessness and individual failure. When we find ourselves helpless to achieve our goals, we suffer depression. The more I believe that I am all that matters and the more I believe that my goals, my success, and my pleasures are extremely important, the more hurtful the blow when I fail. And life inevitably brings failure and helplessness. In the same historical moment that the self has become all-important, a new risk factor for depression, the old spiritual consolations that buffer against depression — God, Nation, Community, Family — have lost their powers.

DYSPHORIA

The one element most responsible for the epidemic is the *cushioning of dysphoria*. In the campaign to feel good and to enjoy high self-esteem, Americans began to believe that we should strive to avoid dysphoria — anger, sadness, and anxiety. These feelings were deemed inconveniences to be banished altogether if possible, and certainly to be minimized. In attempting to cushion bad feeling, the self-esteem movement also minimizes the good uses of feeling bad.

Strong emotions, such as anxiety, depression, and anger, exist for a purpose: they galvanize you into action to change yourself or your world, and by doing so to terminate the negative emotion. It is natural to want to avoid feeling bad, and when it comes to our children we instinctively rush in to protect them from negative feelings, an impulse legitimized by the feel-good society. But feeling bad has three crucial uses, and all of them are needed for learning optimism and for escaping helplessness. The states of dysphoria have a long evolutionary history. They are not mere inconveniences, but of crucial use in that each bears a message. Anxiety warns you that danger is around. Sadness informs you that a loss threatens. Anger alerts you that someone is trespassing on your domain. All these messages, of necessity, carry pain, and it is this very pain that makes it impossible to ignore what is going wrong and goads you to act to remove the threat.

Bad feeling, as an alarm system, is far from flawless. Many, perhaps even most, of its messages are false alarms — the kid who elbowed you is not a bully, but just clumsy, the bad grade does not mean your teacher thinks you're dumb, and the sarcastic valentine was not intended to humiliate you. When bad feelings become chronic and paralyzing, and when they set off too many false alarms, we call this state "emotional illness," and we try to dampen it with drugs, correct it with psychotherapy, or both. But dysphoria's primary virtue is that most of the time the system is your first line of defense against danger, loss, and trespass.

FLOW

The second good use of bad feeling is "flow." When does time stop for you? When do you feel truly at home, wanting to be nowhere else? Playing touch football, listening to Springsteen, speaking to a group, painting a fence or a picture, making love, writing a letter-to-the-editor, or engaged in conversation about psychology? This state is called flow, and it is one of the highest states of positive emotion, a state that makes life worth living. Researchers have been studying it — who experiences it, when does it occur, what impedes it — for two decades. Flow occurs when your skills are used to their utmost — matched against a challenge just barely within your grasp. Too little challenge produces boredom. Too much challenge or too little skill produces helplessness and depression. Flow cannot be achieved without frustration. Success after success, unbroken by failure, regrouping, and trying again will not produce flow. Rewards alone, high self-esteem, confidence, and ebullience do not produce flow. The cushioning of frustration, the premature alleviation of anxiety, and learning to avoid the highest challenges all impede flow. A life without anxiety, frustration, competition, and challenge is not the good life; it is a life devoid of flow.[4]

PERSISTENCE

The third good use of bad feeling concerns overcoming helplessness. Any complicated task your child might undertake consists of several steps, each of which is more or less easy to fail at. If he falters at any step, tries again, and then succeeds at that step, he gets to go on to the next step. If the steps are not too numerous, and no one of them insurmountable, he will succeed — but only if he keeps trying after each small failure. If he stops trying after any particular faltering, he will fail at the whole task. In Robert's titanic struggle to get behind the couch in chapter 2, he first failed to get over the box, but he tried again and climbed over it. Then he got to the stroller barrier, faltered but tried again, plopping in and out, and finally got behind the couch. If he had given up after any one of the little failures, he never would have reached his goal.

Every subfailure, as well as every big failure, produces bad feeling — some admixture of anxiety, sadness, and anger. These emotions, when moderate, are galvanizing, but they are also daunting. Your child has one of only two tactics available when he feels bad. He can stay in the situation and act, trying to terminate the emotion by changing the situation. Or he can give up and leave the situation. This tactic also terminates the emotion by removing the situation altogether. The first tactic I call mastery, the second I call learned helplessness.

In order for your child to experience mastery, it is necessary for him to fail, to feel bad, and to try again repeatedly until success occurs. None of these steps can be circumvented. Failure and feeling bad are necessary building blocks for ultimate success and feeling good.

In the struggle to cure syphilis in the first decade of the century, Paul Ehrlich concocted a drug, 606, that worked by poisoning *Treponema pallidum,* the spirochete that causes syphilis. It was called 606 because before it Ehrlich concocted 605 other drugs, none of which worked. Ehrlich, presumably, experienced 605 defeats but persisted.

Almost all of life's most challenging tasks are like 606 in that they abound with subfailure. If they did not, someone else would have gotten there first — high-jumped eight feet, won the big account, or made friends with the arrogant and aloof young man who turns out to be compassionate and loving. On rare occasions, having extraordinary talent or sheer good luck will shortcut many of the subfailures. But for most children, most of the time, little worth doing is accomplished without persistence.

Children need to fail. They need to feel sad, anxious, and angry. When we impulsively protect our children from failure, we deprive them of learning the 606 skills. When they encounter obstacles, if we leap in to bolster self-esteem as Randy's dad did in chapter 4, to soften the blows and to distract them with congratulatory ebullience, we make it harder for them to achieve mastery. And if we deprive them of mastery, we weaken self-esteem just as certainly as if we had belittled, humiliated, and physically thwarted them at every turn.

So I speculate that the self-esteem movement in particular, and the feel-good ethic in general, had the untoward consequence of producing low self-esteem on a massive scale. By cushioning feeling bad, it has made it harder for our children to feel good and to experience flow. By circumventing feelings of failure, it made it more difficult for our children to feel mastery. By blunting warranted sadness and anxiety, it created children at high risk for unwarranted depression. By encouraging cheap success, it produced a generation of very expensive failures.

"You were determined and stuck with it. That was what brought you good luck," said her instructor.

From then on, the little girl wore the Good Luck Pony every time she went riding. The Good Luck Pony was indeed lucky. It reminded her that it was her own effort that brought her good luck. And from that day on she never forgot it.

— Elizabeth Koda-Callan
The Good Luck Pony (1990)

PART THREE

*Is Your Child an
Optimist or a
Pessimist?*

6

The Fundamentals of Optimism

UNTIL RECENT TIMES, America was a nation of optimists. The first half of the nineteenth century was the great age of social reform, whose cornerstone was the optimistic belief that humans could change and improve. The doctrine that all men are created equal was its manifesto. As Andrew Jackson put it,

> I believe man can be elevated; man can become more and more endowed with divinity; and as he does he becomes more God-like in his character and capable of governing himself. Let us go on elevating our people, perfecting our institutions, until democracy shall reach such a point of perfection that we can acclaim with truth that the voice of the people is the voice of God.[1]

Utopias sprang up to achieve human perfection. Waves of immigrants found an endless frontier, and "rags to riches" was not for them an empty dream. Nineteenth-century optimists created the institution of universal schooling, founded public libraries, freed the slaves, rehabilitated the insane, and fought for women's suffrage.

Historians analyzing the rise of American power often emphasize America's vast natural resources and its felicitous geography, with two fortress oceans protecting it from foreign trespass. Purple mountains, amber waves of grain, and alabaster cities are undeniable boons. But rarely mentioned is a common element among Americans of the last century. They were mostly immigrants, who fled Europe and Asia because there one's destiny was determined by one's class and family. They often endured harrowing passage to reach an unfamiliar place whose promise was that their merit, not their genes, would be rewarded. What kind of mentality does it take to feel oppressed by caste and class, to leave family and possessions behind, and to journey in the hope of a better life? Optimism. These men and women had it in abundance and they became a nation of optimists. An aggressive optimism was the theme of the American boardroom, map room, and living room from the time of Andrew Jackson until the end of World War II.

Pessimism came into fashion in America as a reaction to the "whistle a happy tune" boosterism of the 1950s. The optimism of the 1940s and '50s had a more brittle edge than nineteenth-century optimism. It was a forced, self-conscious reaction to the grimness of the Great Depression and to the mass destruction of the war. The media and the political leaders orchestrated a propagandistic attempt to lift the nation's spirits, to divert attention from the sagging quality of life, and most important, to increase production. And as the country leaped into the postwar boom, boosterism seemed to work. Norman Vincent Peale's *The Power of Positive Thinking* was its bible.

The underside of the "accentuate the positive, eliminate the negative" boosterism of the 1950s, however, was "don't mess with Mr. In-Between." While boosterism was energizing, it was footless, almost dishonest. While it increased cheer, it urged the wearing of blinders. It asked people to ignore oppressive reality and even eschew all doubt. This offended the swelling ranks of the college educated. Among educated Americans, blind faith was dying. Skepticism, with its detached weighing of evidence, was taught as the scientific way of looking at the future. The sophisticated American prided himself on looking unpleasantness in the face without having to mouth upbeat slogans.

Among such people, footless boosterism became anathema. Optimism got a bad name. It was commonly paired with the adjectives *false, foolish,* and *unwarranted.* Pessimism escalated in the 1960s from just a fashion of seaboard intellectuals to become the required posture of educated Americans. The gloomy pronouncement, the cynical angle on noble deeds, and the view that the world was sliding downhill all became marks of urbanity and depth. In those days, to say at a social gathering that we do not live in "terrible times," or that technological progress can clean up the mess it creates, or that nuclear holocaust was not inevitable was to mark yourself as shallow — an ignoramus, a Pollyanna, a booster. The social pressure to sound pessimistic was hard to buck.

The 1960s and '70s provided ample fodder for the growth of American pessimism. The assassinations, Watergate, and the Vietnam catastrophe steeped the parents, teachers, and journalists of the current generation in their dour worldview. In a thousand small ways, and a few huge ones, they have passed their pessimism drop by drop to the next generation. This pessimism has now found its way into many of our children's hearts. Have you ever heard a young person say that racism and sexism might not be forever, or that both Fascism and Stalinism were defeated in this century, or that fewer soldiers are dying on battlefields than at any time in this century, or that the danger of nuclear holocaust is more remote today than at any time since atomic weapons were invented?

The pessimism of our children is not inborn. Nor does their pessimism come directly from reality. Many people living in grim realities — unemployment, terminal illness, concentration camps, the inner city — remain optimistic. Pessimism is a *theory* of reality. Children learn this theory from parents, teachers, coaches, and the media, and they in turn recycle it to their children.

It falls to us to break this cycle.

Why should we bother? Isn't pessimism just a posture with no effects in the world? Unfortunately not. I have studied pessimism for the last twenty years, and in more than one thousand studies, involving more than half a million children and adults, pessimistic people do worse than optimistic people in three ways: First, they get depressed much more often. Second, they achieve less at school, on the job, and on the playing field than their talents augur. Third, their physical health is worse than that of optimists. So holding a pessimistic theory of the world may be the mark of sophistication, but it is a costly one. It is particularly damaging for a child, and if your child has already acquired pessimism, he is at risk for doing less well in school. He is at risk for greater problems of depression and anxiety. He may be at risk for worse physical health than he would have if he were an optimist. And worse, pessimism in a child can become a lifelong, self-fulfilling template for looking at setbacks and losses. The good news is that he can, with your help, learn optimism.[2]

WHAT OPTIMISM IS

The commonsense view is that optimism is seeing the glass as half full, or always seeing the silver lining, or habitually expecting a Hollywood ending to real troubles. The "positive thinking" angle on optimism tells us that optimism consists of repeating boosterish phrases to ourselves, like "Every day in every way, I'm getting better and better," or visualizing the ball dropping into the cup when we putt. These may be manifestations of optimism, but optimism goes much deeper than this. With twenty years of research, investigators have come to understand what is fundamental to optimism. The basis of optimism does not lie in positive phrases or images of victory, but in the way you think about *causes*. Each of us has habits of thinking about causes, a personality trait I call "explanatory style." Explanatory style develops in childhood and, without explicit intervention, is lifelong. There are three crucial dimensions that your child always uses to explain why any particular good or bad event happens to him: *permanence, pervasiveness,* and *personalization.*

PERMANENCE: SOMETIMES VERSUS ALWAYS

Children who are most at risk for depression believe the causes of the bad events that happen to them are permanent. Since the cause will persist forever, they reason, bad events are always going to recur. In contrast, children who bounce back well from setbacks and resist depression believe that the causes of bad events are temporary.

BAD EVENTS

Permanent (Pessimistic)	*Temporary (Optimistic)*
"No one will ever want to be friends with me at Bywood."	"It takes time to find a new best friend when you move to a new school."
"My mom is the crabbiest mom in the entire world."	"My mom is in the crabbiest mood ever."
"Tony hates me and will never hang out with me again."	"Tony is mad at me today and won't hang out with me."

The differences between permanent and temporary causes may appear subtle at first, but so important is this dimension to the well-being of your child that you must learn to tune your ear in to this nuance. In the first example ("No one will *ever* . . ."), the pessimistic child believes the cause of being friendless will last indefinitely, but the optimistic child believes that if she keeps at it long enough ("It takes time . . ."), good friends can eventually be made. In the second example ("the meanest mom"), the pessimistic child sees the cause as stemming from lasting character, but the optimistic child blames a bad mood ("the crabbiest mood"), and moods are transient. The pessimistic child thinks about bad events as coming from abiding flaws in his personality, whereas the optimistic child thinks about moods and other temporary, changeable states.

If your child thinks about her failures, rejections, and challenges in terms of "always" and "never," she has a pessimistic style. If she qualifies and thinks about bad events in words such as "sometimes" and "lately," she has an optimistic style. The next chapter contains a questionnaire that will tell you just how worrisome is your child's explanatory style.

Optimistic and pessimistic children also respond differently to good events in their lives. Children who believe good events have permanent causes are more optimistic than children who believe they have temporary causes (just the opposite of the optimistic style for bad events).

GOOD EVENTS

Temporary (Pessimistic)	*Permanent (Optimistic)*
"The only reason I won the spelling bee is because I practiced hard this time."	"I won because I'm a hard worker and I study my lessons."
"I was voted captain of the safety patrol because the other kids wanted to do a nice thing for me."	"I was voted captain of the safety patrol because the other kids like me."
"Dad has been spending time with me because he's been in a good mood lately."	"Dad loves to spend time with me."

Optimistic children explain good events to themselves in terms of permanent causes. They point to traits and abilities that they will always have, like being hard-working, likable, or lovable. They use "always" when they describe the causes of good events. Pessimists think in terms of transient causes. "I was in a good mood," or "I practiced hard this time." Their explanations of good events are qualified with the words "sometimes" and "today," and they often use the past tense and limit it to time only ("I practiced hard this time."). When children who believe their successes have permanent causes do well, they will try even harder next time. Children who see temporary reasons for good events may give up even when they succeed, believing their success was a fluke.

PERVASIVENESS: SPECIFIC VERSUS GLOBAL

If you believe a cause is permanent, you project its effects across time. If you believe a cause is pervasive, you project its effect across many different situations in your life. The underlined phrases in the next two examples show the stark difference between interpreting failure from a global versus a specific point of view.

Jeremy and Melissa are both in seventh grade. Their school, along with nine others nationwide, is chosen by the White House to send a boy and a girl to Washington, D.C., to talk with the vice president about ways children can help conserve the planet's resources. Every seventh-grader wants to be selected.

The principal holds an essay contest to choose which two children will represent the school. Jeremy and Melissa spend weeks working on their essays: They both go to the library to read about natural resources; Jeremy makes a poster showing all the things children his age can do to help out; Melissa even takes a poll of the other seventh-graders to find out what her classmates are already doing to help the planet. The project, and the prospect of going to the White House, consumes their energy for weeks.

The seventh-grade teachers select the four best essays, from which the principal is to choose the two winners. Melissa and Jeremy can hardly contain their excitement when they find out that their essays have made it to the final four.

The principal announces the winners over the PA system at the close of the school day. Neither Melissa nor Jeremy is selected. Both are crushed. Jeremy and Melissa, however, have very different reactions.

JEREMY'S REACTION: "*I'm a loser*! I worked as hard as I could on that essay and I still lost. *I stink* at writing, just like *I stink at everything else*. I mean, *nothing ever goes right for me*. I might as well stop trying, because no matter how hard I try, *I always end up doing badly* anyway. I just want to be by myself. I know everyone thinks *I was stupid* for even thinking I might have a shot at going to the White House. I know my friends are laughing at me behind my back!"

Jeremy goes home after school and retreats to his bedroom. He refuses to talk to his parents about how he is feeling. At dinnertime, he comes to the table only after his mother demands that he join the family. Jeremy picks at his food and remains sullen. After dinner, Jeremy's father tries to get him to play ball, but Jeremy is unwilling. He won't go bike riding with his friends when they come to the door.

Jeremy's withdrawal lasts for several days. School, family, and friends no longer interest him. Nothing brings him pleasure. His depressed mood doesn't lift.

The italicized phrases in Jeremy's reaction exhibit his global explanations of failure. Melissa, on the other hand, attributes her failure to more specific causes (italicized here).

MELISSA'S REACTION: "*I blew it*! I guess *I'm not a good writer* after all. I worked as hard as I could on that project but *Mrs. Bailey still thought Betsy's and Josh's were better.*"

Melissa goes home after school and cries. She tells her mother how disappointed she is and that she never wants to try hard like that again. Her mother spends an hour comforting Melissa, and by dinnertime Melissa is able to tell her father about the results without bursting into tears. Melissa eats less than usual, but she perks up when her parents suggest going out for sundaes. Though she remains downcast for the rest of the evening, Melissa calls her girlfriend on the phone and they talk about the essay contest and going to the mall together over the weekend.

Whenever Melissa thinks about the essay contest, she gets upset, but she does not withdraw from the other areas of her life. She still enjoys food and friends, and she is interested in planning activities for the weekend.

Jeremy and Melissa have opposite ways of understanding failure. Their immediate reaction was the same: They both felt devastated. They both believed that the loss meant that they were not good writers — identical explanations as far as permanence goes. But they were opposite on pervasiveness. Jeremy was a catastrophizer; he believed that the reason he was not selected (in addition to being a poor writer) was that he was also a total loser ("I stink at writing, just like I stink at everything else"). Melissa found local causes, which she spelled out to herself in detail. She believed she was not chosen because she was not a good writer and because her essay wasn't as good as Josh's and Betsy's.

Some children can put their troubles neatly into a box and go about their lives even when one important part crumbles. Others catastrophize. When one thread of their life snaps, the whole fabric unravels. It comes down to this: Children who latch on to global explanations for their failures give up on everything when they fail in just one realm. Children who believe specific explanations may become helpless in that one realm yet march stalwartly on in the rest.

Here are some examples of global and specific explanations of bad events:

BAD EVENTS

Global (Pessimistic)	Specific (Optimistic)
"Teachers are unfair."	"Mrs. Carmine is unfair."
"I'm a total clod at sports."	"I stink at kickball."
"Nobody likes me."	"Jamal doesn't like me."

When it comes to good events, the optimist believes that their causes will enhance everything he does, but the pessimist believes that they are caused by specific factors.

GOOD EVENTS

Specific (Pessimistic)	Global (Optimistic)
"I'm smart at math."	"I'm smart."
"Erica invited me to her party because she likes me."	"Erica invited me to her party because I'm popular."
"I got to play Oliver because I'm a good singer."	"I got to play Oliver because I've got a lot of talent."

Being smart is more global than being smart at math; being popular is a trait that implies many people liking you, not just Erica; having talent is a more global blessing than just being a good singer. As far as accuracy permits, children who think about good events as having more global causes do better across more walks of life.

PERSONAL: INTERNAL VERSUS EXTERNAL

There is a third dimension of explanatory style, beyond permanence and pervasiveness: personalization, deciding *who* is at fault. When bad things happen, children can blame themselves (internal) or they can blame other people or circumstances (external). Self-esteem is governed by whom you blame. Children who habitually blame themselves when they fail have low self-esteem. They feel guilty and ashamed. Children who blame other people or circumstances feel better about themselves when bad events strike. On the whole, blamers of others feel less guilt and shame and they like themselves better. They are also angrier children.

Does this mean we should teach children to be external about bad events? If my only concern were self-esteem, I would advocate this approach. But it is not. Teaching children to blame others whenever things don't go their way is like teaching children to lie. I urge two other goals for your child's habits of blame.

The first goal is not to let children off the hook for the things they do wrong. The last thing I want to do is to help create a generation of children who cannot say, "I'm sorry. It was my fault. I'll do better next time." Children must hold themselves accountable when they are to blame for their problems, and then go on to try to rectify the situation. On the other hand, I do not want to see a generation of children who blame themselves whenever things go wrong whether it was their fault or not. Depressed children and adults are forever blaming themselves and feeling guilty over things that are not at all their fault, and being a chronic self-blamer increases a child's risk for depression. My goal is to teach children how to see themselves accurately, so that when problems are their fault, they take responsibility and try to correct their behavior, whereas when the problem is not their fault, they still feel worthwhile.

Andrea and Lauren have been best friends for years. This year they started the ninth grade at Northern Burlington High School. Andrea and Lauren have few classes together and have separate lunch periods. They don't see much of each other during the school day. After school they still hang out together, but Andrea spends a lot of time with new friends. By the end of the first marking period, Andrea has become good friends with two girls in her math class. Lauren feels left out and tries to get Andrea to do things without the other two. But more and more, Andrea spends her time with her new friends and excludes Lauren.

Lauren [approaching Andrea as they wait for the bus]: Hi! What are you up to? Tonight is the first new episode of *90210* and I thought maybe we could watch it together at my house. What do you think? I could order some pizza and stuff. It would be fun.

Andrea: Well, thanks. I'm going over to Shira's with Leslie. So, I really can't.

Lauren: Oh. Well, how about we do something on Saturday? We could go to the mall or something.

Andrea: I can't. I'm going to do something with Shira and Leslie.

Lauren: I don't get it. We used to be such good friends. Now I never see you. You never call me anymore and whenever I call you, you act like I'm getting on your nerves or something. Why are you doing this to me? I know you like Shira and Leslie a lot, but I don't see why we can't all be friends.

Andrea: Look, Lauren, I'm sorry, but things have changed and it doesn't seem we have as much in common now.

Lauren: I can't believe you are doing this to me. We've been best friends since third grade. How can you just drop me like this?

Andrea [*coldly*]: I said I'm sorry. You must have other friends in your classes. Why don't you start spending more time with them.

Lauren: I don't have friends like you. I know things can work out if we started doing more together. I could invite Shira and Leslie over and we could all hang out together. How about that?

Andrea [*angrily*]: Lauren, look, I'm sorry. I still think you are nice and everything, but now that we're in high school, we just aren't going to be friends in the same way. Shira and Leslie and I have a lot more in common. So you gotta stop trying to tag along all the time. Okay?

Here is what Andrea thinks to herself afterward (the italicized words reflect her locus of blame):

I feel horrible that Lauren still wants to hang out the way we used to and I don't. *I've really hurt her feelings.* I know I'd hate to be in her shoes. She thought we would be best friends forever and *now I'm telling her that I've got new friends that I like more.* I *wish I didn't hurt her like that. I could have handled this better.* I shouldn't have been so mean to her today. *Maybe I should have talked to her more about it and explained how I feel.* But it's really hard to tell someone that you like other people better and that it just isn't going to be the same anymore. Maybe I ought to call her tonight and apologize. I don't want her to feel bad, but the truth is *I just don't want to be her best friend anymore.* What a horrible situation!

Changing friendships is difficult. The person being dropped feels rejected and hurt; the person doing the dropping feels guilty. There are kind and unkind ways of making this transition, but they are all unpleasant. Andrea feels bad that she no longer wants to be close friends with Lauren, but she does not see this as a reflection on her own character. She is able to own up for the way in which she handled the situation ("I shouldn't have been so mean to her today") without beating herself up about it. Andrea didn't think, "I'm a horrible person. I'm the world's worst friend." And Andrea is mercilessly accurate both about her impact on Lauren ("I've really hurt her feelings") and about her own desires in the matter ("I just don't want to be her best friend anymore"). Because she takes responsibility, Andrea can correct her trajectory and form a plan of action that may help a bit ("I ought to call her tonight"). Andrea will probably do a better job in parallel situations in the future ("I could have handled this better" and "explained how I feel"). This *is* a horrible situation, one that most children experience from both sides. As parents, we want our children to react like Andrea. We want them to take responsibility (Andrea *is* causing Lauren pain), but we don't want our children to be overwhelmed with guilt and shame whenever they do something that displeases someone else.

SO THE FIRST GOAL as you work toward improving your child's explanatory style is to make sure he takes realistic responsibility. The second goal is to get your child to use *behavioral* rather than *general* self-blame. Read the following examples and notice the difference in how each child blames himself.

Luke D. is a fifth-grader. Lately his parents have been fighting a lot about taking care of the house and the children. Luke's mother is going back to work and she expects her husband to help pick up the slack. Saturday mornings Luke's family always has breakfast together. While his parents are planning the weekend, Luke reminds his mother that he has Little League practice and needs her to drive him. Mrs. D. asks her husband to take him instead. Mr. D. says he can't because he needs to prepare for a meeting on Monday. A bitter fight erupts about who will take Luke to practice. Luke slips away from the table unnoticed and walks to the ball field.

Luke thinks to himself: "I did it again! I'm always making them fight. When am I ever going to learn to keep my mouth shut. Mom and Dad have been fighting so much lately. It's always because of me. I'm spoiling everything. If they get divorced, it's going to be all my fault. I'm the world's worst kid. I'm always ruining everything!"

Contrast Luke's style of self-blame to Rodney's.

Rodney is about to have his twelfth birthday. He lives with his mother, stepfather, and two younger brothers. Over dinner, Rodney is helping his mother plan his birthday party. Rodney's stepfather, Steve, suggests having a "Schwarzenegger Birthday." He says that Rodney could invite his friends over and they could start out by watching *T2* or *Predator* and then go out back and play capture-the-flag. Rodney thinks it sounds great. He and his stepfather immediately start planning the details: they can make invitations with a camouflage design, the boys can come dressed in army gear, they'll watch a couple of Arnold movies, and then the kids will be divided into teams and will be given plastic guns and all the trimmings for a great game of capture-the-flag.

Rodney's mother listens in horror. She bursts into the planning and tells her husband that she thinks a "war birthday" is disgusting. She will not allow it. Rodney's mother and stepfather launch into a fight about his party.

Rodney thinks to himself: "That was dumb of me. I know how

much Mom hates all that war stuff and she really hates those kinds of movies. She hardly ever lets me watch them. The two of them fight about these kinds of things a lot. I should have told Steve that I didn't want that kind of party, then they wouldn't be fighting now. It's my fault!"

Luke and Rodney both blame themselves for their parents' fighting. They both are making internal ("It's my fault") explanations. However, their explanations differ along the other two dimensions of explanatory style. Luke's explanation is not only internal, but it is also permanent ("I'm always spoiling everything") and pervasive ("I'm the world's worst kid"). Self-blame that is also permanent and pervasive is called *general self-blame*. Most often the general self-blamer believes that the problem is an unchangeable flaw in his own character. General self-blame, because it is permanent and pervasive, not only damages self-esteem (because it is internal) but produces long-lasting (because it is permanent) and global (because it is pervasive) passivity and despair.

Rodney, on the other hand, believes the fight is the result of an internal, temporary, specific factor ("I should have told Steve that I didn't want that kind of party"). Self-blame that is temporary and specific is called *behavioral self-blame*. The child blames a particular action rather than indicts his character. Unlike general blame, behavioral blame, because it points to a changeable cause, motivates a child to try harder to change the behavior so that he can prevent the problem or overcome the setback. While the child's self-esteem may suffer, just as it does when the child blames his character, he is not helpless to change what needs changing.

Here are examples of general self-blame and behavioral self-blame.

General Self-Blame (Pessimistic — permanent, pervasive, and internal)	*Behavioral Self-Blame (Optimistic — temporary, specific, and internal)*
"I got a C on the test because because I'm stupid."	"I got a C on the test because I didn't study hard enough."

"I got picked last in gym class again. No one likes me."

"I got picked last in gym class again. I'm no good at soccer!"

"I got grounded because I'm a bad kid."

"I got grounded because I hit Michelle."

In chapters 10–12, I will show you techniques for teaching your child realistic responsibility and behavioral self-blame.

THE RIGHT WAY TO CRITICIZE YOUR CHILD

Not surprisingly, children learn some of their explanatory style from parents, teachers, and coaches. They listen to how adults criticize them and absorb the style of the criticism as well as the substance. If you criticize your child as being lazy, rather than as not trying hard enough today, your child will believe not only that he is lazy, but that his failures come from permanent and unchangeable factors. Also, children listen closely to the way parents interpret their own misfortunes and model their style. If you are a pessimist, your child is learning pessimism directly from you.

You must therefore be thoughtful when you criticize your child, or yourself in front of your child, for you are shaping his explanatory style about self-blame. The first rule is accuracy. Exaggerated blame produces guilt and shame beyond what is necessary to galvanize the child to change. But no blame at all erodes responsibility and nullifies the will to change.

The second rule is that whenever reality allows, you should criticize with an optimistic explanatory style. When parents unthinkingly criticize their child with permanent and pervasive messages, the child begins to acquire a pessimistic style himself. When they blame changeable and specific causes of the problem, the child begins to learn optimism. Any time you find your child to be at fault, it is important to focus on specific and temporary personal causes, if truth allows, and avoid blaming the child's character or ability. Here are a few examples of good and bad criticism of a preschooler.

CRITICIZING A PRESCHOOL CHILD

Permanent (Pessimistic)

"Tammy, what's wrong with you? You are always such a monster!"

"Wendy said you cried the whole time I was out. You're such a sensitive child."

"Cory, I asked you to pick up your toys. Why don't you ever do what I ask?"

Global (Pessimistic)

"You are a bad boy."

"That's okay, Tanya. You've got your mom's knack when it comes to sports. I'm horrible at sports, too."

"She never likes to play with the other kids. She's so shy."

Internal and General (Passive)

"You're not athletic."

"You kids are so selfish."

"Another C-minus?! I guess you just aren't an A student."

"This room is a pig sty! You are such a slob!"

Changeable (Optimistic)

"Tammy, you are really misbehaving today. I don't like it at all."

"Wendy said you cried the whole time I was out. You've been having a hard time being away from me lately."

"Cory, I asked you to pick up your toys. Why didn't you do what I asked?"

Specific (Optimistic)

"You tease your sister too much."

"That's okay, Tanya. You've got to learn to keep your eye on the ball."

"She has a hard time joining groups of kids."

Internal and Behavioral (Active)

"You have to work harder on watching the ball meet the bat."

"You kids must share more."

"Another C-minus?! You need to spend more time on your studies."

"This room is a pig sty! You need to start picking up after yourself."

Elena W. is ten years old. She lives with her parents and her three-year-old brother, Daniel. Mrs. W. takes the children to the petting zoo for the afternoon. From the moment they get in the car, Elena begins tormenting her brother. She tells Daniel that their father is really only her father and that Daniel's real father is a gorilla. She tells him that the lion at the zoo is going to bite off his willy. She tells him that right next to the zoo is a prison and that if he does anything wrong, they are going to send him there to live for the rest of his life. Elena is in rare form and Mrs. W. is in no mood for it.

Mrs. W: Elena, *the teasing has got to stop. What has gotten into you today?* You are such a *wonderful big sister.* You teach Daniel games. You share your toys. You really make him feel special. But *today you haven't been nice* to him at all. Zoos can be scary for little kids and your teasing him is not helping. You know I don't like *this kind of behavior,* Elena. I want you to apologize to Daniel and *if you tease him again today,* you will not be allowed to play outside after dinner. Is that clear?

Clearly, Elena needs to be reprimanded. She is making her brother miserable. Mrs. W. holds her daughter accountable for her behavior so that Elena can change what she is doing wrong. Mrs. W. points out the specific and temporary problem behavior ("teasing . . . today"), while also pointing out how this behavior is not typical of Elena ("wonderful big sister"). Mrs. W. uses concrete evidence that the problem is not general ("You teach Daniel games. You share your toys") so that Elena can feel proud of herself. She tells Elena specifically what she should do ("apologize to Daniel") and what the consequences of further teasing will be ("you will not . . . play outside after dinner"). Mrs. W. does not bluff about these consequences, by the way.

Criticism of this sort is ideal. From it Elena absorbs this: "Mommy thinks I'm usually a good big sister, but she thinks that I have been mean to Daniel today. I can apologize to Daniel for being mean and then Mommy and Daniel will feel better." Thus, Mrs. W.'s criticisms, while internal, are specific and changeable. They direct Elena toward right action rather than condemn her character.

Imagine that Mrs. W. said this instead:

> Elena! I am sick of this! Why are you *always* such a *brat*? Here I plan a nice day for the three of us, and *you go and ruin it*! I don't know why I even bother trying to do fun family things, when *without fail, you pull some stunt* that *spoils everything*!

This criticism is toxic. Here Mrs. W. denigrates Elena's character. Elena is called a brat (characterological) and is accused of *always* ruining her mother's plans (permanent and unchangeable) and *always* causing the family misery (pervasive and permanent). Children absorb criticism of this sort and take away this message: "I'm a horrible person. Mommy wishes I wasn't her daughter. I always ruin everything she does. She's right. I ought to run away. They'd be better off without me." Elena feels worthless, and the only action possible is to withdraw emotionally from the family.

Your child's fundamental optimism or pessimism is forming now. Your child is acquiring it not only from the realities of his world but also from listening to the way you criticize him and yourself. If his style is becoming pessimistic, he is at risk for depression and lowered achievement. As our depression-prevention program showed, depression is not inevitable and parents and teachers can do a great deal to prevent it. Your first step is to assess whether or not your child is depressed and where he falls on the optimism–pessimism continuum.

7 | *Measuring Optimism*

You PROBABLY BELIEVE that it is easy to tell whether your child is an optimist or a pessimist. Not so. Indeed, some aspects of personality are readily apparent and require no fancy measurement. You can, for example, talk to a person for ten minutes and guess quite accurately if she is extroverted or introverted, anxious or calm. Such traits are called "transparent." Other aspects of personality are less transparent, and you can be grossly wrong in your guesses even about people you know well. Optimism is one of these traits. It is hard to intuit because everyone has both optimistic and pessimistic thoughts. Optimism as a trait depends not on a few salient examples but on the day-in-and-day-out frequency of making optimistic interpretations and your readiness to do so. On a scale from 1 to 100, where 100 is most optimistic, try to estimate how optimistic your child is. Write the number here: _____

TEST YOUR CHILD'S OPTIMISM

To measure optimism accurately requires a standardized questionnaire like the one reprinted on the following pages. After your child takes it, you can see how far off your guess was. The Children's Attributional Style Questionnaire, or CASQ, was created fifteen years ago by two of my students, Drs. Nadine Kaslow and Richard Tanenbaum. Since then, many thousands of children have taken it, so it can give a valid reading of where your child stands.

To give your child the questionnaire, set aside twenty minutes, sit down at a table with him, and say something like this:

> Different kids think in different ways. I've been reading a book about this, and I've been wondering how you think about some things that might happen to you.
>
> Look at this. It asks you a bunch of questions about what you think. Each question is a little story, and for each story, there are two ways you might react. You're supposed to choose one way or the other, the one that's closest to the way you'd really feel if that particular thing happened to you.
>
> So here's a pencil. I want you to give it a try. Imagine that each of these little stories happened to you, even if they never have. And then check either the A answer or the B answer — the one that best describes the way you would feel. But the great thing about this is that there are no wrong answers! Now, here, let's take a look at number one.

Once you get him going, your child can probably complete the questionnaire without any assistance. But for younger children who are not skilled readers, you should read each item aloud at the same time the child is reading it to himself. Eight to thirteen is the target age for the questionnaire, and it takes about twenty minutes for a child of that age to complete. If your child is somewhat younger, say six or seven, you can still give her the questionnaire by reading each item aloud to her twice. Her answers will be first approximations of what her optimism level is. The younger a child is, the harder it is for her to think about her own thinking ("metacognition" is what psychologists call this ability), and all the items require that the child tell you what she would think if a certain event happened. Children younger than age eight likely have an explanatory style, but it is difficult to measure.

CHILDREN'S ATTRIBUTIONAL STYLE QUESTIONNAIRE[1]

Score

1. You get an A on a test.
   PVG
   A. I am smart.   1
   B. I am good in the subject that the test was in.   0

2. You play a game with some friends and you win.
   PSG
   A. The people that I played with did not play the game well.   0
   B. I play that game well.   1

3. You spend a night at a friend's house and you have a good time.
   PVG
   A. My friend was in a friendly mood that night.   0
   B. Everyone in my friend's family was in a friendly mood
      that night.   1

4. You go on a vacation with a group of people and you have fun.
   PSG
   A. I was in a good mood.   1
   B. The people I was with were in good moods.   0

5. All of your friends catch a cold except you.
   PMG
   A. I have been healthy lately.   0
   B. I am a healthy person.   1

6. Your pet gets run over by a car.
   PSB
   A. I don't take good care of my pets.   1
   B. Drivers are not cautious enough.   0

7. Some kids you know say that they don't like you.
   PSB
   A. Once in a while people are mean to me.   0
   B. Once in a while I am mean to other people.   1

Score

8. You get very good grades.
   PSG
   A. Schoolwork is simple.   0
   B. I am a hard worker.   1

9. You meet a friend and your friend tells you that you look nice.
   PMG
   A. My friend felt like praising the way people looked that day.   0
   B. Usually my friend praises the way people look.   1

10. A good friend tells you that he hates you.
    PSB
    A. My friend was in a bad mood that day.   0
    B. I wasn't nice to my friend that day.   1

11. You tell a joke and no one laughs.
    PSB
    A. I don't tell jokes well.   1
    B. The joke is so well known that it is no longer funny.   0

12. Your teacher gives a lesson and you do not understand it.
    PVB
    A. I didn't pay attention to anything that day.   1
    B. I didn't pay attention when my teacher was talking.   0

13. You fail a test.
    PMB
    A. My teacher makes hard tests.   1
    B. The past few weeks, my teacher has made hard tests.   0

14. You gain a lot of weight and start to look fat.
    PSB
    A. The food that I have to eat is fattening.   0
    B. I like fattening foods.   1

15. A person steals money from you.
    PVB
    A. That person is dishonest.   0
    B. People are dishonest.   1

Score

16. Your parents praise something that you make.
    PSG
    A. I am good at making some things.   1
    B. My parents like some things I make.   0

17. You play a game and you win money.
    PVG
    A. I am a lucky person.   1
    B. I am lucky when I play games.   0

18. You almost drown when swimming in a river.
    PMB
    A. I am not a very cautious person.   1
    B. Some days I am not a cautious person.   0

19. You are invited to a lot of parties.
    PSG
    A. A lot of people have been acting friendly toward me lately. 0
    B. I have been acting friendly toward a lot of people lately.   1

20. A grown-up yells at you.
    PVB
    A. That person yelled at the first person he saw.   0
    B. That person yelled at a lot of people he saw that day.   1

21. You do a project with a group of kids and it turns out badly.
    PVB
    A. I don't work well with the people in the group.   0
    B. I never work well with a group.   1

22. You make a new friend.
    PSG
    A. I am a nice person.   1
    B. The people that I meet are nice.   0

23. You have been getting along well with your family.
    PMG
    A. I am easy to get along with when I am with my family.   1
    B. Once in a while I am easy to get along with when
       I am with my family.   0

Score

24. You try to sell candy, but no one will buy any.
    PMB
    A. Lately a lot of children are selling things, so
       people don't want to buy anything else from children.   0
    B. People don't like to buy things from children.   1

25. You play a game and you win.
    PVG
    A. Sometimes I try as hard as I can at games.   0
    B. Sometimes I try as hard as I can.   1

26. You get a bad grade in school.
    PSB
    A. I am stupid.   1
    B. Teachers are unfair graders.   0

27. You walk into a door and you get a bloody nose.
    PVB
    A. I wasn't looking where I was going.   0
    B. I have been careless lately.   1

28. You miss the ball and your team loses the game.
    PMB
    A. I didn't try hard while playing ball that day.   0
    B. I usually do not try hard when I am playing ball.   1

29. You twist your ankle in gym class.
    PSB
    A. The past few weeks, the sports we played in gym
       class have been dangerous.   0
    B. The past few weeks I have been clumsy in gym class.   1

30. Your parents take you to the beach and you have a good time.
    PVG
    A. Everything at the beach was nice that day.   1
    B. The weather at the beach was nice that day.   0

Score

31. You take a train which arrives so late that you miss a movie.
PMB
    A. The past few days there have been problems with
       the train being on time.   0
    B. The trains are almost never on time.   1

32. Your mother makes you your favorite dinner.
PVG
    A. There are a few things that my mother will do
       to please me.   0
    B. My mother likes to please me.   1

33. A team that you are on loses a game.
PMB
    A. The team members don't play well together.   1
    B. That day the team members didn't play well together.   0

34. You finish your homework quickly.
PVG
    A. Lately I have been doing everything quickly.   1
    B. Lately I have been doing schoolwork quickly.   0

35. Your teacher asks you a question and you give the
wrong answer.
PMB
    A. I get nervous when I have to answer questions.   1
    B. That day I got nervous when I had to answer questions.   0

36. You get on the wrong bus and you get lost.
PMB
    A. That day I wasn't paying attention to what was going on.   0
    B. I usually don't pay attention to what's going on.   1

37. You go to an amusement park and you have a good time.
PVG
    A. I usually enjoy myself at amusement parks.   0
    B. I usually enjoy myself.   1

Score

38. An older kid slaps you in the face.
    PSB
    A. I teased his younger brother.   1
    B. His younger brother told him I had teased him.   0

39. You get all the toys you want on your birthday.
    PMG
    A. People always guess right as to what toys to buy
       me for my birthday.   1
    B. This birthday, people guessed right as to what toys
       I wanted.   0

40. You take a vacation in the country and you have
    a wonderful time.
    PMG
    A. The country is a beautiful place to be.   1
    B. The time of the year that we went was beautiful.   0

41. Your neighbors ask you over for dinner.
    PMG
    A. Sometimes people are in kind moods.   0
    B. People are kind.   1

42. You have a substitute teacher and she likes you.
    PMG
    A. I was well behaved during class that day.   0
    B. I am almost always well behaved during class.   1

43. You make your friends happy.
    PMG
    A. I am a fun person to be with.   1
    B. Sometimes I am a fun person to be with.   0

44. You get a free ice cream cone.
    PSG
    A. I was friendly to the ice cream man that day.   1
    B. The ice cream man was feeling friendly that day.   0

Score

45. At your friend's party the magician asks you to help him out.
PSG

A. It was just luck that I got picked.   0
B. I looked really interested in what was going on.   1

46. You try to convince a kid to go to the movies with you,
but he won't go.
PVB

A. That day he did not feel like doing anything.   1
B. That day he did not feel like going to the movies.   0

47. Your parents get a divorce.
PVB

A. It is hard for people to get along well when they
are married.   1
B. It is hard for my parents to get along well when
they are married.   0

48. You have been trying to get into a club and you don't get in.
PVB

A. I don't get along well with other people.   1
B. I can't get along well with the people in the club.   0

SCORING KEY

PMB: _____   PMG: _____

PVB: _____   PVG: _____

HoB: _____

PSB: _____   PSG: _____

Total B: _____   Total G: _____

G − B: _____

To score the questionnaire, start with the PMB (permanent —
bad events) items. Total the numbers following the chosen A and B
answers — the ones and the zeros — for the following items: 13, 18,
24, 28, 31, 33, 35, and 36; enter that total in the scoring key, next to
PMB. Then total the PMG (permanent — good events) numbers for

these items: 5, 9, 23, 39, 40, 41, 42, and 43; enter that total in the scoring key next to PMG.

Total and enter the PVB (pervasive — bad events) results for items 12, 15, 20, 21, 27, 46, 47, and 48. Then score and enter the PVG (pervasive — good events) numbers for items 1, 3, 17, 25, 30, 32, 34, and 37.

Total the PMB and PVB scores and enter the result next to HoB (the hopelessness score) in the scoring key.

Next, total and enter the results for PSB (personal — bad events), items 6, 7, 10, 11, 14, 26, 29, and 38. Then do the same for PSG (personal — good events), items 2, 4, 8, 16, 19, 22, 44, and 45.

Compute the total score for bad events (PMB + PVB + PSB) and record it in the key next to Total B. Then total the scores for good events (PMG + PVG + PSG) and record it next to Total G.

Finally, compute the overall score for the scale, G − B (subtract Total B from Total G). Write it on the bottom line of the key.

Here's what your child's scores mean and how your child compares to the many thousands of children who have taken this test. First, you should know that girls and boys score differently. Girls, until puberty, are noticeably more optimistic than boys. The average eight- to twelve-year-old girl has a G − B score of 6.5 (the higher the G − B score, the more optimistic the child), whereas the average eight- to twelve-year-old boy has a more pessimistic overall G − B score of 5.05. I have yet to hear a good theory about why. At any rate, if your girl scores less than 5.0, she is somewhat pessimistic. If she scores less than 4.0, she is very pessimistic and at marked risk of depression. If your boy scores less than 3.0, he is somewhat pessimistic; if he scores less than 1.5, he is very pessimistic and at marked risk of depression. Table 1 shows the norms for eight- to twelve-year-olds. Use this table to compare the guess you made at the beginning of the chapter with the level of optimism your child actually turns out to have.[2]

As for the Total B (bad events) score, the average girl's is 7.1 and the average boy's is a more pessimistic 8.7 (the higher the Total B score, the more pessimistic is the child). A Total B score at least 1.5 points *higher* than the average is very pessimistic. This Total B score

TABLE 1: G–B SCORES

Percentile	Girls	Boys
90th (most optimistic)	11.31	10.30
80th	9.67	8.16
70th	8.35	7.14
60th	7.22	6.07
50th (average)	6.50	5.05
40th	5.86	4.04
30th	5.00	2.86
20th	3.80	1.46
10th (most pessimistic)	2.27	0.43

tells you how your child reacts to bad events in his life. A pessimistic score indicates that your child does not bounce back from setbacks, generalizes his setbacks from one realm to another, and blames himself too much when things go wrong.

The individual bad-event dimensions (PMB, PVB, and PSB) each average about 2.4 for girls and 2.9 for boys (the higher the bad event score, the more pessimistic is the child). A score of 3.5 or *higher* suggests risk of depression. A pessimistic PMB (permanent — bad events) score characterizes a child who becomes passive and does not bounce back when defeated. A child with an optimistic PMB score rolls up her sleeves and comes back from setbacks, seeing them as challenges. A child with a pessimistic PVB (pervasive — bad events) score catastrophizes, generalizing from a single bad event. Such a child starts to do badly at school when things go wrong at home or with peers. An optimistic PVB score indicates a child who can build walls around her problems: she still gets on well with her friends even when her grades plummet. A pessimistic PSB (personal — bad events) score indicates a child who is a self-blamer: he feels guilt, shame, and low self-esteem when something goes wrong, even if it is not his fault. After a defeat he feels worthless. An optimistic PSB score characterizes a child who blames others; his self-esteem does not go down

TABLE 2: GIRLS

Score	Value	Interpretation
PMB (permanent — bad events)	Optimistic: <1.5	Is resilient, comes back for more
	Average: 1.5–4.0	Becomes demoralized briefly
	Pessimistic: >4.0	Collapses after setbacks, brittle
PVB (pervasive — bad events)	Optimistic: <1.5	Does not generalize setbacks
	Average: 1.5–4.0	
	Pessimistic: >4.0	Becomes generally helpless, catastrophizes
PSB (personal — bad events)	Optimistic: <1.5	Blames others, has high self-esteem
	Average: 1.5–4.0	
	Pessimistic: >4.0	Blames self, feels guilty, has low self-esteem
PMG (permanent — good events)	Optimistic: >6.0	Is energized by success
	Average: 3.0–6.0	Can take advantage of success
	Pessimistic: <3.0	Is de-energized by success

when he fails, and he often gets angry at people he perceives as causing his failure.

The average Total G (good events) score for both girls and boys is 13.8 (the higher the Total G score, the more optimistic is the child). A Total G score at least 2.0 points lower is very pessimistic. An optimistic score for good events indicates a child who is energized by victory and takes credit for successes.

The individual good-event dimensions (PMG, PVG, and PSG) each average about 4.6 for both girls and boys, with a score of below 4.0 being very pessimistic. An optimistic PMG (permanent — good events) score indicates that your child will get on a roll with one or two successes. A pessimistic PMG score indicates that your child does

TABLE 2 (CONTINUED)

Score	Value	Interpretation
PVG (pervasive — good events)	Optimistic: >6.0	Successes generalize widely
	Average: 3.0–6.0	
	Pessimistic: <3.0	Successes evaporate
PSG (personal — good events)	Optimistic: >6.0	Glories in success
	Average: 3.0–6.0	Takes credit readily
	Pessimistic: <3.0	Resists credit taking
HoB (hopelessness — bad events)	Optimistic: <3.0	Is resilient and upbeat
	Average: 3.0–8.0	
	Pessimistic: >8.0	Brittle, catastrophizes
Total B (bad events)	Optimistic: <6.25	Is almost invulnerable to depression
	Average: 6.25–8.10	Is somewhat depressive
	Pessimistic: >8.10	Is at marked risk for depression
Total G (good events)	Optimistic: >15.27	Is active, success prone
	Average: 12.84–15.27	
	Pessimistic: <12.84	Is passive, failure prone

not capitalize on success: one success does not augur more successes. An optimistic PVG (pervasive — good events) score indicates generalization across successes: when such a child does well with her friends, her schoolwork goes better too. A pessimistic PVG score, in contrast, characterizes a child who doesn't benefit in other realms from success in a single realm. An optimistic PSG (personal — good events) score characterizes a child who readily takes credit for successes and feels high self-esteem. A child with a pessimistic PSG score, however, often has self-esteem problems even when he does well, but sees success as coming from luck or circumstances.

Tables 2 and 3 summarize the meaning of your child's scores.

The most worrisome consequence of pessimism in your child is

TABLE 3: BOYS

Score	Value	Interpretation
PMB (permanent — bad events)	Optimistic: <1.5	Is resilient, comes back for more
	Average: 1.5–4.0	Becomes demoralized briefly
	Pessimistic: >4.0	Collapses after setbacks, brittle
PVB (pervasive — bad events)	Optimistic: <1.5	Does not generalize setbacks
	Average: 1.5–4.0	
	Pessimistic: >4.0	Becomes generally helpless, catastrophizes
PSB (personal — bad events)	Optimistic: <1.5	Blames others, has high self-esteem
	Average: 1.5–4.0	
	Pessimistic: >4.0	Blames self, feels guilty, has low self-esteem
PMG (permanent — good events)	Optimistic: >6.0	Is energized by success
	Average: 3.0–6.0	Can take advantage of success
	Pessimistic: <3.0	Is de-energized by success

depression, for pessimistic children are at much higher risk for becoming depressed than optimistic children. This was the main result of our five-year study of more than five hundred children in the Penn-Princeton Longitudinal Study of Childhood Depression.[3] Our central aim was to find out what put children at risk for getting depressed. All the children began with the study in the third grade. At that time, and then every six months for the next five years, we measured their optimism level with the CASQ, the major events that occurred in their lives, their popularity, their grades, and their tendency to become helpless in academic and social situations, among many other variables. Most important was our target: we measured how depressed each child was every six months.

Because it is prospective (going forward over time) and longitudi-

TABLE 3 *(CONTINUED)*

Score	Value	Interpretation
PVG (pervasive — good events)	Optimistic: >6.0	Successes generalize widely
	Average: 3.0–6.0	
	Pessimistic: <3.0	Successes evaporate
PSG (personal — good events)	Optimistic: >6.0	Glories in success
	Average: 3.0–6.0	Takes credit readily
	Pessimistic: <3.0	Resists credit taking
HoB (hopelessness — bad events)	Optimistic: <3.0	Is resilient and upbeat
	Average: 3.0–8.0	
	Pessimistic: >8.0	Brittle, catastrophizes
Total B (bad events)	Optimistic: <7.26	Is almost invulnerable to depression
	Average: 7.26–10.0	Is somewhat depressive
	Pessimistic: >10.0	Is at marked risk for depression
Total G (good events)	Optimistic: >15.0	Is active, success prone
	Average: 12.5–15.0	
	Pessimistic: <12.5	Is passive, failure prone

nal (measuring the same children repeatedly), a study of this sort is uniquely able to pick out risk factors for depression. For example, investigators had noticed that depressed children are often unpopular with other kids, and so a theory arose that being unpopular puts a child at risk for becoming depressed. This is just a theory, however, because it is based on a mere correlation, a mere co-occurrence of unpopularity and depression. It is entirely possible that depression causes the children to become unpopular (misery loves company, but company doesn't love misery), rather than the other way around. It is even possible that some other factor (called a "third variable"), like getting failing grades, causes both depression and unpopularity.

A prospective, longitudinal study untangles all of this. A hypothetical example shows how: Of the five hundred children who started the study in third grade, twenty-five are now depressed when fourth grade starts. How do these children differ from the other four hundred seventy-five who are not depressed? Perhaps being unpopular in third grade made them depressed. If this was so, these twenty-five should have been more unpopular in third grade, on average, than the other four hundred seventy-five. This turns out to be so. So far it looks as though unpopularity causes depression.

But wait. Maybe they were unpopular in third grade because they were already depressed in third grade. When we look more closely, we find that of the twenty-five, ten were already depressed when they began third grade and these ten were also quite unpopular at the start of third grade. Fifteen of the kids who became depressed later were not depressed when they started third grade and they were popular. This shows that unpopularity does not put a child at risk for depression; it merely correlates with, or "marks," depression. The same logic when coupled to powerful statistical procedures can apply to finding out if other possible factors, such as pessimism, parents' fighting, the tendency to become helpless, and bad grades contribute to becoming depressed or merely mark depression.

So by taking into account each child's earlier depression score and then looking at the child's movement in and out of depression over five years, we were able to separate out risk factors for depression from markers of depression. Out of the welter of possible causes, we found two that stood out: First, bad life events, like parents' fighting, a pet's death, or a sibling's illness increase a child's risk of becoming depressed. This is particularly so when the child is in the third or fourth grade. Second, pessimism. Kids who believe bad events are permanent, pervasive, and personal while good events are temporary, local, and externally caused were at heightened risk for getting depressed. This is particularly so with those in fifth or sixth grade. The age shift from the importance of bad events in younger children to the importance of pessimism in producing depression among older children probably reflects the increasing importance of the way children *interpret* events as they mature. As we grow up, depression resides more and more in our head, not in the world.

So we established that pessimism in a child puts him at risk for depression. And once depression sets in, the biggest risk factor for later depression is prior depression. A vicious circle has started, and children now react to each new setback by getting depressed again.

What does depression in a child look like and how can you tell if your child is depressed?

RATE YOUR CHILD'S DEPRESSION

Short of a diagnostic interview with a psychologist or psychiatrist, there is no completely conclusive way to tell if your child is depressed. But you can get a good first approximation by asking your child to fill out the following questionnaire, devised by Drs. Myrna Weissman and Helen Orvaschell, working through the Center for Epidemiological Studies of the National Institute of Mental Health. It is called the Center for Epidemiological Studies — Depression Child (CES-DC) test.[4] You should probably not overload your child by giving the depression questionnaire on the same day as the CASQ. Wait at least a day and then introduce the second questionnaire to your child:

> I've been reading a book about how kids feel, and I've been wondering how you feel lately. Sometimes it's hard for kids to find the words to describe how they feel. Here's something that gives you different ways to say how you feel. Each sentence has four choices. All you need to do is read each sentence and pick out the choice that describes best how you have been feeling or acting *for the past week*. There are no right answers or wrong answers, because it isn't a test. Just pick the one that describes you.

Scoring the questionnaire is simple. Each "Not at all" counts as 0, each "A little" counts as 1, each "Some" counts as 2, and each "A lot" counts as 3. Just total these numbers. If your child checked two boxes for one question, give him the higher of the two scores.

If your child scored 0 to 9, he is probably not depressed. If he scored 10 to 15, he is probably mildly depressed. If he scored more than 15, he is showing significant levels of depression: 16 to 24 puts him in the moderately depressed range, and if he scored more than 24, he is probably severely depressed.

An important caveat is in order, however: no questionnaire is as good as a professional diagnosis. There are three mistakes a questionnaire like this can make, and you should be alert to each of them: First, many children hide these symptoms, particularly from their

DURING THE PAST WEEK . . .

1. I was bothered by things that don't usually bother me.
   Not at all _____ A little _____ Some _____ A lot _____

2. I did not feel like eating; I wasn't very hungry.
   Not at all _____ A little _____ Some _____ A lot _____

3. I wasn't able to feel happy, even when my family or friends tried to help me feel better.
   Not at all _____ A little _____ Some _____ A lot _____

4. I felt that I was not as good as other kids.
   Not at all _____ A little _____ Some _____ A lot _____

5. I felt like I couldn't pay attention to what I was doing.
   Not at all _____ A little _____ Some _____ A lot _____

6. I felt down.
   Not at all _____ A little _____ Some _____ A lot _____

7. I felt like I was too tired to do things.
   Not at all _____ A little _____ Some _____ A lot _____

8. I felt like something bad was going to happen.
   Not at all _____ A little _____ Some _____ A lot _____

9. I felt like things I did before didn't work out.
   Not at all _____ A little _____ Some _____ A lot _____

10. I felt scared.
    Not at all _____ A little _____ Some _____ A lot _____

11. I didn't sleep as well as I usually sleep.
    Not at all _____ A little _____ Some _____ A lot _____

12. I was unhappy.
    Not at all _____ A little _____ Some _____ A lot _____

13. I was more quiet than usual.
    Not at all _____ A little _____ Some _____ A lot _____

14. I felt lonely, like I didn't have any friends.
    Not at all _____ A little _____ Some _____ A lot _____

15. I felt like kids I know were not friendly or that they didn't want to be with me.
Not at all _____ A little _____ Some _____ A lot _____

16. I didn't have a good time.
Not at all _____ A little _____ Some _____ A lot _____

17. I felt like crying.
Not at all _____ A little _____ Some _____ A lot _____

18. I felt sad.
Not at all _____ A little _____ Some _____ A lot _____

19. I felt people didn't like me.
Not at all _____ A little _____ Some _____ A lot _____

20. It was hard to get started doing things.
Not at all _____ A little _____ Some _____ A lot _____

parents. So a few children who score less than 10 may actually be quite depressed. Second, some children with high scores may have problems other than depression which are producing the high scores. Third, a child sometimes scores high one day because she is in a bad mood or is feeling crummy, but she didn't feel that way yesterday and won't feel that way tomorrow. If your child scored more than 15, wait a week and have her fill it out again.

So if your child scores more than 15 across a two-week span, you should arrange for professional help. If your child scores more than 9 and also talks about committing suicide, you should arrange for professional help. A "cognitive" or "cognitive-behavioral" therapist would be ideal. Look in the Yellow Pages under "psychologist," "psychiatrist," or "psychotherapist" or ask your pediatrician for a referral. If you can't find a therapist who specializes in cognitive or behavioral therapy for children (you will see why this is important in chapters 10–13), write a note to me at the Department of Psychology, 3815 Walnut Street, University of Pennsylvania, Philadelphia, Pennsylvania 19104 or write to DART (Depression Awareness, Recognition, Treatment Program) at the National Institute of Mental Health, 5600 Fishers Lane, Rockville, Maryland 20857. If you need a quick answer, send e-mail to me at "seligman@cattell.psych.upenn.edu". One way or another, I will try to let you know the name of a well-qualified therapist near you. For parents, teachers, and school districts who want more than this book contains, we give training seminars at the University of Pennsylvania that offer intensive supervision in how to teach optimism techniques. You can send regular mail or e-mail to me at the addresses above for information.

This questionnaire tells you what depression in a child looks like because it measures the intensity of each of the four clusters of symptoms. The first set of symptoms consists of a change in your child's *thinking*. The way a child thinks when he is depressed differs from the way he thinks when he isn't. When depressed, he has a grim picture of himself, the world, and his future. He attributes his hopeless future to lack of ability ("I'm not good at anything, so nothing will ever work for me"). Small setbacks seem like insurmountable barriers. He believes everything he touches turns to ashes, and this state of mind provides an endless supply of reasons why each success is really a failure.

Gary is in eighth grade at Eagle Rock Middle School. He usually has fun at school and his teachers think he has a lot of pluck. Lately, however, Gary hasn't been himself. He rarely raises his hand in class, and he hasn't been doing his homework. After school, instead of hanging out with his friends, he goes home and locks himself in his bedroom, where he listens to Guns N'Roses until his parents force him to join them for dinner. No matter what his parents say, he denies that anything is wrong.

Several months ago, Gary entered a picture he painted in a city competition sponsored by the Art Alliance. When Gary arrived at school, his art teacher, Mrs. Hilbert, told him that she had just heard that his painting made it to the finals. Four pieces were chosen, and each student will be asked to come to the Art Alliance and discuss his or her work. A famous local artist will then select the winner. That student will receive a scholarship fund for college and will be enrolled in a special art program for a few selected children statewide.

Mrs. Hilbert expected Gary to be excited by this news. She knew how hard he had worked on the painting and that winning the contest meant a lot to him. To her surprise, Gary was uninterested.

Mrs. Hilbert: Hey, Gary! Come here a minute, I've got some great news to tell you.

Gary: Yeah? What?

Mrs. Hilbert: Looks like you are on your way to artistic stardom. Watch out, Andy Warhol!

Gary: What are you talking about?

Mrs. Hilbert: The painting you did for the contest has made it to the finals. You and three others are going to discuss your work at the Art Alliance and then a famous local artist will choose the winner. You — and I do mean you, Gary — will get a scholarship fund and you get a chance to participate in the governor's art program they are starting this fall.

Gary: Really? That can't be right. My painting looked like something a third-grader would do. Anyway, I don't want to do it.

Mrs. Hilbert: What are you talking about? You worked so hard on that painting. I know this means a lot to you. What's the matter?

Gary: Nothing. I know I'm not going to win, so why even bother. Anyway, who cares? It was just a stupid contest.

Mrs. Hilbert: Gary, I've got to say that I'm really surprised. This just isn't like you. I don't get it. What is going on with you?

Gary: Nothing, Mrs. Hilbert. I just don't want to waste my time. That painting wasn't good, so I sure don't know why it made it this far. It must have been a fluke. And anyway, I can't discuss it in front of a bunch of people. I don't have anything to say. I'll just end up sounding like a moron in front of everyone.

Mrs. Hilbert: Gary, Gary, Gary, what is going on here? You and I both know that the painting was real good. You are a real artist. It's not like this is the first time you've won awards for your stuff. What about the prize you won for the mural you painted at the Y? Was that luck too?

Gary: A lot of people helped with that. That's why it won, not because of anything I did.

Mrs. Hilbert: Hold on. Let me finish. I've never seen you put yourself down like this. I can understand being nervous about talking about your work. I'd be nervous too. But we can practice it together. You could even present it to our class to give you a chance to practice before a big group of people. Let's meet after school and plan your talk.

Gary: That's nice of you and everything, but I really don't want to, Mrs. Hilbert. I'll just flub it, so let's forget it.

Mrs. Hilbert: Come on. I've heard you speak in public before. You didn't flub your lines in *The King and I.* And for that you had to sing. You dazzled the audience.

Gary: That doesn't count. Anyone could have done it. And anyway, I remember Mr. Davico telling me that I was off key a few times. Let's just forget it, okay?

No matter how many successes Mrs. Hilbert recalls, Gary trots out why the successes were really failures. Gary is not being modest or shy, nor is Gary engaged in a random litany of complaints. At this moment, he truly believes that nothing will work out and it is because he has no talent. This is the standard thinking pattern of a depressed child. A pessimistic explanatory style is at the core of this kind of thinking. The bleak view of the future, the self, and the world stem from seeing the causes of bad events as permanent, pervasive, and personal, and seeing the causes of good events in the opposite way.

Aisha was a depressed sixth-grader. One week she got a B-minus on her science test. This grade, for Aisha, was great. She usually failed her science tests or barely managed to eke out a D. When Aisha came to gym class, the gym teacher, having heard the good news, congratulated her on her test: "Hey, Aisha, I hear you did real well this week on your science test. Mr. Meisel told me that he was real proud of you. How do you feel about it?"

Typical of depressed children, Aisha was unable to see her success. The B-minus, instead of meaning improvement, was just another mark of failure. "Nah, I didn't do good. I don't know what he's talking about. Shawana got an A on that test, an A, that's good. Me, I can't ever do those science problems. I never can keep all those numbers and words in my head. I go to start working on a problem and my head is just empty. I just got to face it — I'm too stupid for school."

While the first symptom cluster of depression is a change in a child's thinking, the second is a negative change in her *mood*. When she is depressed, she feels awful. Sad, discouraged, in a pit of despair. She may cry a lot, or even be beyond tears. Life goes sour. Formerly enjoyable activities become empty-wastes-of-time. She never laughs and rarely smiles.

On her worst days Aisha would refuse to come out of her room. For hours she would lie in her bed, slowly rocking from side to side while cradling her favorite stuffed animal in her arms.

Sadness is not the only mood symptom of depression in children; anxiety and irritability, which can express themselves as bad conduct, are often present as well.

Jocelyn, a thirteen-year-old, has suffered from bouts of depression since she was eleven. As Jocelyn's depression increases, she becomes more and more difficult to be around. A "spirited" child in the best times, Jocelyn's crabbiness, complaining, and hostility make it impossible to console her when she is depressed. In contrast to Aisha, when Jocelyn is depressed she goes on a "fight-picking" rampage. No matter what anyone says to her, it is wrong. When in the greatest pain, she lashes out fiercely, and family, friends, and classmates have learned that it's just better to steer clear of her.

For Tory, feelings of anxiety rather than irritability accompany his sadness. Situations that normally do not faze Tory now trigger dread. When he is depressed, Tory often worries that someone is going to hurt his parents. The feeling is unshakable. If his parents go out for the evening, he can't fall asleep until he hears the front door close behind them when they come back. Worse, at night Tory is afraid of windows. He feels certain that if he looks out the window, he will see a face there, staring in, watching him. To avoid the faces Tory positions himself in the family room, so that he cannot see out any windows. He doesn't move. He keeps his eyes focused on the TV screen, never glancing around. If he needs to walk to another room, he first considers which route will take him by the least number of windows and then darts by with his head down, his heart ready to explode.

The third symptom cluster in childhood depression concerns three *behaviors:* passivity, indecisiveness, and suicide. A depressed child often cannot get started on any but the most routine tasks, and he gives up easily when thwarted.

Carmen makes extra money for himself delivering newspapers. He's had his route for over a year and by now the whole process runs seamlessly. Carmen knows each of his customers personally; he knows the best time to collect for each of them; he enjoys the responsibility of the job. When Carmen feels depressed, the seams start to show. Even the most basic and simple parts of the job begin to feel too heavy. Carmen explained to us what happens:

> It's just crazy. I mean, delivering newspapers isn't the most complicated thing in the world. Don't get me wrong, you've got to stay on top of things and you've got to be careful and all, but it really isn't hard or anything. When I feel good, it's no problem. I pick the papers up, I fold them, and then I go make the rounds. I really sort of even get a kick out of it. Not to mention that I make some good money. But the thing is, when I'm feeling really down — *bam!* — the whole thing seems to fall apart. Like last month. I remember it was a Sunday, so it is a big-paper day. On Sundays, you've got to pick the papers up extra early. And I kept looking at my clock thinking, "Come on, Carmen, you've got to go now. If you don't go now, you're going to screw everything up." But, you know, I just couldn't get myself to go. No matter what, I just kept lying there thinking how much I hated delivering papers.
>
> Finally my mom got me out of bed. She could tell I was feeling bad so she offered to drive me down to pick up the papers. She even said she'd help me put them together. But I didn't want her to help me. Well, I did, but I also didn't. I know that sounds weird,

but it's that part of me wanted her to come with me, but another part of me just kept on complaining and wanted to be alone. When I finally got down there, my boss was pretty mad, because I was so late. And then, once I got the papers, all I could do was just sit there and look at them. I couldn't even pick them up and load them into my cart. It's like it took all my energy just to get down there and now I had none left over to do the next part of the job. I really hate when it gets like that for me. It scares me.

A depressed child cannot decide among alternatives.

Jason, eleven, is an avid collector of stamps. He has three big books filled with stamps from all around the world. His stepdad works in a big office and asks all the secretaries to save any interesting-looking stamps for Jason. As a special treat, Jason's stepdad takes him to a local stamp show and tells him that he can pick out five stamps for his collection. His stepdad hopes that this will help cheer up Jason, who has been in a funk for the last three weeks. At the show, Jason wanders through the stalls, looking at the stamps. He finds many that he really likes, but he can't decide which to buy. Each one would be a great addition to his collection, but Jason can't make a decision. Finally his stepdad selects eight and tells Jason to pick the five he wants. Jason stares listlessly at each stamp. He selects one, then changes his mind. He selects another, and then wonders whether it really is a good one to pick. It's as if Jason believes that there are a correct five to choose and doesn't want to make a mistake. Jason's stepdad tries to help him see that there is no wrong decision, but Jason remains stuck. Finally, exasperated, Jason's stepdad buys all eight. Jason looks embarrassed and quickly stuffs the stamps into his pocket.

Many depressed children think about suicide. James, twelve, had been thinking of killing himself. This is how he describes it:

I was feeling really low. Things were just horrible for me. My father split on us a few years back, and ever since then I sometimes feel real bad — you know, sad and mad all mixed together. A couple months after he left, things got really bad. I just couldn't stop thinking about my dad. I couldn't understand how he could just leave like that. I mean, he didn't give us no warning or nothing. That day he just left for work like it was any other day, but it wasn't, 'cause he never came home. I was nine at the time and I remember that night perfectly. My dad wasn't the greatest guy in the world or nothing. I mean, I knew that, but I never thought he would just up and leave us. Anyway, I remember sitting watching TV and my mom kept coming in the room and looking out the window to the street. She did that about a hundred times. I could tell she was upset, but my parents used to fight a lot, so I figured that there was just going to be a big blowout when he came home.

Anyway, my mom asked me like ten times whether he had called and I kept telling her no. Finally she called him up at his job and they said that he came in that morning and quit, just like that. After that, my mom ran up to their bedroom and she just started screaming — like, cursing and crying all at once. I got real scared and didn't want to move, but I thought maybe she got hurt or something, so I ran on up. She was just sitting on the floor holding the box where she keeps her jewelry and she kept saying over and over again, "He took my wedding ring. He took my ring. He took my ring." Then she made me go to bed.

Anyway, it wasn't until a few days later that she explained to me that my dad had left. After that, things just started to get real bad. I started getting into a lot of trouble at school and I used to stay out real late. I know I was making my mom real worried, but I didn't care. I just hated to be around that house 'cause everything made me think about my dad, and thinking about my dad made me feel horrible. So I got into more and more trouble, you know, like stealing things and fights and that kind of stuff. Inside I just felt like I was going to explode I was so mad and lonely and stuff. More and more I started thinking about what it would be like to be dead. At first I started thinking about people I knew who had died and what happened to them, but then I started thinking about what it would be like if I was to die. I would sit in class a lot of times and just think up ways to die, like hanging myself or jumping in front of the subway or getting a gun and shooting myself. I know this sounds weird, but I liked to think like that. It made me feel a little better. But after a while, it was like that was all I could think about. No matter what I was doing, I'd be thinking up ways to kill myself.

Everyone always asks me why I wanted to die. And all I can say is that it just seemed like the only way I could ever stop feeling the way I was feeling. I didn't want to hurt my mom, but I just knew that I had to stop those feelings and I knew that the only way to stop them for good was to kill myself.

When depressed children think about suicide, they generally have one or both of two motives. The first is surcease: the prospect of going on like this is intolerable, and they want to end it all. The other is manipulation: they want to get love back, or get revenge, or have the last word in an argument. In spite of frequent suicidal thoughts, depressed children, unlike depressed adolescents and adults, rarely commit suicide. While children's suicides are often publicized, in actuality there are probably fewer than two hundred suicides a year by children under the age of fourteen in the entire United States. This is less than a tenth of the rate of suicide among adults and adolescents.[5] With depression striking younger and younger children, however, this low rate may be on the rise. While children have as many depressive symptoms as adults, evolution seems to have buffered children somewhat against killing themselves.

The fourth and final cluster of symptoms of depression in children is *physical*. Often a child's appetite changes. Many children simply can't eat. Other times, however, the opposite happens, and children will overeat even if they don't feel hungry. Sleep disturbance is very common. A depressed child may start sleeping much more than usual. For example, it is not uncommon for a depressed child to come home from school and go up to his room and sleep until dinner. Other times, a depressed child has difficulty getting to sleep, especially if he is also feeling anxious. The normal aches and pains that many children experience are exaggerated. A depressed child may complain of stomachaches and headaches and make many more visits to the school nurse than is usual for her.

YOU HAVE NOW measured your child's level of optimism and you have learned to recognize the faces of depression in your child. Pessimism, as we have seen, puts your child at risk for depression, even if your child is not depressed now. Depressive symptoms, by themselves, put your child at risk for more depression. Where does pessimism in a child come from? The answer to this question is found in the next chapter. In our study, the discovery of the sources of pessimism provided the major clue about what parents and teachers can do to change a child's pessimism into optimism.

Where Optimism Comes From

IN TWINSBURG, OHIO, there is a national convention every August. Five thousand pairs of twins (and a handful of triplets) come to celebrate the special benefits of growing up twinned. One such benefit has been not to the twins themselves but to science. Studying twins offers scientists a unique opportunity for a rigorous examination of the influence of genes versus experience (nature versus nurture) in shaping personality.

THE GENETICS OF OPTIMISM

Aggressive parents tend to have aggressive children; musical parents have musical children; alcoholic parents have children who tend to become alcoholic; the children of geniuses are usually very clever. Optimistic parents tend to have optimistic children, and pessimistic parents, pessimistic children. There are two overarching hypotheses: The first is that these children inherit their parents' genes, and somehow combinations of genes code for aggression, musical talent, alcoholism, genius, and optimism. The second is that the parents create environments for their children that somehow teach aggression, music, alcoholism, genius, and optimism. Twins, looked at carefully and in large numbers, allow these two possibilities to be teased apart.

Identical twins have entirely identical genes. Fraternal twins, in contrast, share on average only 50 percent of their genes. They are just like any two siblings genetically, but they happen to be born at the same time. Consider the similarity, or "concordance," of pairs of identical twins as opposed to the concordance of fraternal twins for a trait such as height. Identical twins are much more similar to each other in height than are fraternal twins, and it is on this basis that we know that height has genetic underpinnings.

We can even find out *how much* genetics, as opposed to environment (plus everything else), contributes to a trait by looking at how much more concordant identical-twin pairs are than fraternal-twin pairs. So, for example, identical twins are much more similar in IQ than are fraternal twins. The size of the difference (in their similarity) tells us that between 50 and 75 percent of IQ is heritable, leaving the remainder (between 25 and 50 percent) contributed by nongenetic factors such as child rearing, school experience, childhood illnesses, error of measurement of IQ, and fetal hormones.

Perhaps the most astonishing finding that has emerged from the twin studies is that between a quarter and a half of each of the major personality traits is inherited from your parents: depression, job satisfaction, religiosity, liberalism, authoritarianism, exuberance, to name just a few, and even the amount of television watching and the likelihood of divorce are almost 50 percent heritable.[1] How can this be, you might wonder: divorce and television watching have not existed long enough for evolution to select for them. True, but personality characteristics — like aggression or lust or need for action or passivity — are vastly more ancient and form part of the basis for divorce or television watching. Since such a large slice of personality and complex behavior is heritable, we began to wonder how much of optimism might be heritable? To find out, we drove to Twinsburg, Ohio, in August 1990.

The Twinsburg twins, knowing their unique position in science, have been very cooperative with researchers. We set up a booth and got 115 identical-twin pairs and 27 fraternal-twin pairs to take the adult version of the test of explanatory style your child took in the last chapter. We then looked at how similar identical-twin pairs were to each other when compared with the fraternal-twin pairs. The pairs of identical twins were much more similar to each other for optimism and pessimism than the fraternal pairs. When one of an identical pair was a strong pessimist, the other was almost sure to be a strong pessimist. This was also true for optimism. In contrast, the score of one fraternal twin did not predict the score of his co-twin at all. When we computed the heritability of optimism, it turned out to be a shade under 50 percent.[2]

But this finding is not watertight. Perhaps it means only that identical twins are treated more similarly to each other than fraternal twins, and the greater similarity of the life experiences of identicals produces a greater similarity of optimism. This is a cogent objection, and there is a clever way of surmounting it: study identical twins who are reared apart. When identical twins are separated early in life and raised in different families, it is hard to argue that any striking personality traits they share come from common treatment, rather than from common genes. So if the identical twins reared apart still have more similar explanatory style than fraternal twins, that leaves only genetics.

You might think it is hard to get enough twins reared apart to test this, but the yeoman Swedish Adoption/Twin Study of Aging has done just that. Seventy-two pairs of identical twins who were reared apart filled out an optimism questionnaire in 1987, as did 126 pairs reared together (with 178 pairs of fraternal twins reared apart and 146 pairs of fraternal twins reared together thrown in for good measure). This study produced similar results to our Twinsburg study: around 25 percent of the optimism and pessimism scores were heritable.[3] Indeed the difference between our estimate of 50 percent heritability and the Swedish estimate of 25 percent may reflect the similarity of rearing for the identical twins who grow up together.

This convinced most scholars that optimism is partly caused by genes, but frankly it doesn't convince me. There is a flaw in the argument, rarely recognized, which casts doubt on the conclusions of the entire genetics of personality, but the problem is writ large for optimism. I wish to distinguish between a trait being "heritable" and a trait being directly caused "genetically." Make the reasonable assumption that the more success in life a person has, the more optimistic she becomes. What characteristics cause lots of success? Handsomeness and beauty, high verbal intelligence, athletic ability, motor skills, visual acuity, to name a few. Each is highly heritable: identical twins are more concordant for each of these than fraternal twins. So identical twins may be more similar for optimism because they have more similar amounts of success (and failure) in life, and the more success, the more optimism (the more failure, the more pessimism). The similarity of their success (or failure) is caused by more similarity of genetically controlled traits, like motor skills, beauty, and intelligence.

In general, the studies of twins (whether reared apart or together) can tell us a trait is "heritable," but they cannot tell us that it is directly "genetic." These studies all leave open the possibility that the trait is caused by particular kinds of experience, rather than controlled directly by genes. The genes control physical factors that tend to produce the crucial experience. All of the following are hypothetical paths, but they illustrate the point: Athletic ability is heritable because tallness (genetically controlled) leads to devoted basketball coaches (the crucial experience), which leads to athletic stardom. Self-esteem is heritable because beauty (genetic) leads to doting parents (the crucial experience), which leads to self-esteem. Depression is heritable because poor coordination (genetic) leads to lots of rejection for clumsiness (the crucial experience), which leads to feelings of insecurity and vulnerability. Obesity is heritable because liking sweet tastes enormously (genetic) leads to eating more sweets (the crucial experience), which leads to obesity.[4]

Even though optimism is unquestionably heritable in minor (less than 50 percent) part, this does not mean that optimism genes exist, or that the right childhood experience is not crucial to forming optimism. As parents and teachers, you should remain alert to the likelihood that lots of success for your child will lead to optimism. You should go out of your way to help your child follow up one success with another, and another. The right coaching from you will support and maintain his optimism, and the right crucial experiences will set his optimism in concrete. We now turn to the roles that parents, teachers, and crucial experiences play as sources of your child's optimism.

PARENTS

When you become emotional, your child's antennae go up. Your daughter uses your display of emotion, whether subtle or glaring, as a sign to take seriously whatever you are responding to. Much of emotional learning occurs this way. I had a close friend, otherwise quite normal, who had an unusual phobia. She was a telephone phobic. When people called her, this sociable person broke into a flop-sweat and could barely utter a word. She was aware of her problem and ashamed of it. It was especially puzzling because she could recall no origin — no phone trauma, no childhood prohibitions about talking on the phone, or the like. At one Thanksgiving dinner, I was helping in the kitchen when a social phone call came in for her father. To my astonishment, he broke into a sweat and, usually voluble, was completely tongue-tied. I made the connection. Throughout her childhood, my friend had seen her father react with anxiety to phone calls and had learned this unusual phobia at his knee.

When you are upset, you find yourself explaining the disturbing events to whomever is around: the car got dented because that inconsiderate wretch cut you off; Daddy slammed the door because he is in a bad mood; you can't get a job because the economy stinks; Granny is sick because she's so old. Your own explanatory style is on display and your child is listening intently. She is learning not only the specific content of your explanations but also the general style, and she is making your style her own.

Tori is nine years old and lives with her mother, Jody, her stepfather, Jacob, and her stepbrother, Alex. Before giving birth to Tori, Jody worked for a large real estate agency as the office administrator. She enjoyed the work, especially managing other office personnel. Jody could successfully mediate conflicts, and since office conflicts were common, she quickly became a prized member of the team.

When Jody decided to leave the agency before the birth of Tori, she negotiated coming back half time after three months and then returning to full time after a year. Though her employers wanted her to return sooner, they agreed to this arrangement because they didn't want to lose her.

After Tori was born, Jody decided that she didn't want to go back to work so soon. She was surprised by how much she enjoyed being a mother, and the thought of leaving Tori with someone else made her uneasy. Tori's father never liked the idea of his wife working, so he supported her decision to stay at home. Jody dreaded telling her employers about her change of plans. They had been so reasonable with her that she felt embarrassed about backing out. So, rather than arrange to meet with them to discuss it, she sent them a letter that tersely said she would not be coming back. When her employers phoned her, she avoided their calls. It was a bad ending to a good career.

Now that Tori is older, Jody wants to enter the job market again. She has been thinking about it for a while, but each time she makes plans, she feels overwhelmed by anxiety and decides that it really isn't a good time to go back to work after all. Her husband broaches the subject with her at dinner. (Jody's explanations of why she can't get a job are italicized.)

Jacob: So, I haven't heard you mention the job hunt in a while, what's going on with that?

Jody: Oh, well, I don't know. *I'm always so swamped* I haven't had time to get moving on it. I will.

Jacob: That wasn't very convincing. Are you still feeling nervous about it?

Tori: Why are you nervous, Mom?

Jody: Oh, well, I guess I am feeling a bit nervous about the whole thing. I mean, *it's been almost ten years since I've had a real job. I can't even see myself in that environment anymore.*

Jacob: It'll certainly be a transition, but from the stories you've told me about when you worked at Providence, you were very good at what you did and really liked it a lot. Why don't you start by giving them a call? Maybe they have some openings.

Alex: What was your job, Mom?

Jody: Oh, I worked at a company that helped people buy and sell houses and I was in charge of making sure everything got done in the office. *It wasn't anything special.* Anyway, even if I was okay at that job, I certainly couldn't call them now. *I really blew it when I left there. I doubt they'd even remember me, and if they did, it sure wouldn't work in my favor.* I don't want that kind of job again, anyway. *It was always one hassle after another.*

Jacob: Well, maybe a good way to think about it is to think about what your strengths are and what things excite you and then maybe we could brainstorm about jobs that fit those things.

Jody: Strengths. That's a tough one.

Tori: You're a great mom. Does that count as a strength?

Jody: Thanks, hon. That's real sweet, but I'm afraid being a great mom isn't real marketable.

Jacob: Well, hold on a second. That's not true. It is marketable. How about checking into daycare places? Or, better yet, the reason you are a great mom is because you are patient and creative and have lots of energy — those are your strengths — so how about looking —

Jody: Jake, I appreciate all your help, but I just can't see it happening. No matter what job we come up with, the fact of the matter is that *I will be competing against people a lot younger, who have a lot more education, and who haven't been out of the work force for a decade.* Why hire a middle-aged housewife when you can have someone with better training and better qualifications?

Jacob: Boy, Jody, you really are feeling nervous. Maybe you just need to get started on this. You know, a jump-start. Why don't you make it your goal to go through the help-wanted ads or fix up your résumé or something like that for this week? I know that works for me.

Tori: Yeah, like when I don't want to clean my room, you always tell me that I should just start by picking up all the clothes that are yellow, or all the socks, or all the clothes that start with the letter *S* or something. That makes it go faster for me and it's even a little fun sometimes.

Jody: Oh, well, I'm afraid this is a little more complicated than that, Tori. This isn't a matter of me needing a kick to get started. *It's a matter of me not having what it takes to get hired* and no matter how many cute little gimmicks we try to motivate me, the bottom line is going to stay the bottom line.

Jody is a brooding pessimist and she is broadcasting her style in capital letters to her children. Look at the style of her explanations of why she can't get a job:

- It's a matter of me not having what it takes (permanent, pervasive, personal).
- No matter what job we come up with, the fact of the matter is that I will be competing against people a lot younger, who have a lot more education, and who haven't been out of the work force for a decade (permanent, pervasive, personal).
- I'm always so swamped (permanent, pervasive, personal).
- It was always one hassle after another (permanent, pervasive).

Her family, in trying to counter her negativity, displays a much better explanatory style than she does. They make the arguments that Jody, were she a skilled disputer of her own catastrophic thoughts, would spontaneously be giving herself.

- It'll certainly be a transition (temporary, local, impersonal).
- Maybe you just need to get started on this (changeable, local).
- You really are feeling nervous (temporary).

Our data tells us that Jody's kids are learning, drop by drop, her pessimistic theory of why bad things happen to her and making it their own. We find a strong correlation between a mother's optimism or pessimism and her children's, whether boys or girls.[5]

Zach's dad, unlike Jody, is teaching his son an optimistic explanatory style — even in the face of a family tragedy:

It's always the same. Each Sunday, not long after the sun rises, seven-year-old Zach explodes into his parents' bedroom and pounces on the bed. He lands atop his father's belly and laughs as his father is jolted out of sleep. The routine has officially begun. With fake grumpiness, Zach's father slowly works his way out of bed and slips into his Sunday costume: shorts, Bruins T-shirt, and Knicks cap. Once properly attired, the two return to Zach's room, where he changes out of his pajamas and into a size-six version of his father's outfit. Then they are off.

Within twenty minutes of the pounce, Zach and his father are in the car, heading to Joelle's Diner for their usual "Noah Special": two eggs, two pancakes, two strips of bacon, and two slices of toast for $2.22. Zach eats one special, his dad eats three. During breakfast they talk about a variety of things, but first they recap the sporting events of the week. After lamenting Stark's temporary but fatal inability to hit the three-pointers, the conversation turns to Zach's mother.

Zach: Mommy always slept late on Sundays.

Dad: Yeah, she liked to sleep until at least ten-thirty. Whenever the sun started to shine through the window, she would steal my pillow and bury her head under it. You missing her this morning?

Zach: Yeah. I miss her a lot. Last night I dreamt about the day we all went to that boring museum and she started saying all those funny things about the pictures. Except, in my dream, she had blond hair, not brown hair. How come?

Dad: Hmm. I don't know, Zach. I dream about her too, you know.

Zach: Did you dream about her last night?

Dad: No. Last night I dreamt about . . . hmmm . . . I don't remember. Oh, no, I do remember. I dreamt about a kid I grew up with on Olney Avenue. Gosh, I haven't thought about him for years. He was my best friend when I was about your age. I remember that day at the musuem. You just did not want to go, but me and Mom were on that "at least two hours of culture a week" kick. The things we put you through! You were so bored, the only way we could keep you in the place was to make fun of all the artwork — a real cultural experience!

Zach: I miss Mom a lot. We used to have a family and now we don't. You've been meaner to me since she died.

Dad [*explanations italicized*]: *It has been a real bad time for us,* Zach. I never thought we'd have to go through something like this. As hard as this is, we're going to make it. I want you to know that. Okay? I really want you to know that. It may not feel like it right now, *but slowly there will be more days when*

we feel good than days when we feel really horrible. It's going
to take time, but it's going to happen.

Zach: I guess.

Dad: Sometimes I know I have been short with you and sometimes I haven't listened real well. That's not fair to you. I can't
promise that things will go back to how they were. There are
going to be times when I don't treat you as well as I should, as
well as I want to, but *it isn't because I am mad at you or that I
don't love you. Sometimes when I miss Mom a lot, it's hard for
me to put that aside and focus on being Dad,* but just like the
good days are going to increase, the times when I don't listen
right or am cranky with you are going to decrease. And I'm
really sorry when I act in ways that hurt you, Zach. Okay,
Zeezer?

Zach: Okay. Sometimes I get mad too. I'm sorry. You know,
Joey's mother moved to San Diego and his dad got a girlfriend.
You'd never do that, would you?

Dad: I don't feel like meeting other women right now, but sometime later I will, and when I do, I'll start to go on dates with
women. Your mom and I were together for a long time, so it's
going to feel strange to start getting to know someone else, but
eventually I will. That'll take a lot of getting used to for the
both of us.

Zach: I wonder if she'll have blond hair.

To explain why he has treated Zach crankily, Dad does not shirk
his responsibility, and he gives explanations as consistently optimistic
as grim reality allows — temporary, changeable, and specific explanations. Dad is teaching hope in the face of what seems to Zach,
hopeless.

- It has been a real bad time for us.
- But slowly there will be more days when we feel good.
- It isn't because I am mad at you or that I don't love you.
- Sometimes when I miss Mom a lot, it's hard for me to put that
  aside and focus on being Dad.

Since children learn their own explanatory style, in part, from their parents, it is important for you to change your style if you are a pessimist. In chapters 10, 11, and 12, when we present the cognitive skills program for changing your child's explanatory style, we will teach you how to change your own pessimistic talk as well.

TEACHERS AND COACHES

Parents are not the only adults who unwittingly impose their explanatory style on children. Teachers and coaches are enormously influential. Their day-to-day material is the success and, more important, the failure of your child, and when they criticize him, they influence your child's theory of the way his world works. A child soon begins to criticize himself using the explanatory style of the criticism he gets from respected mentors.

Jamel and Rachel are both in Mrs. Fitzwater's seventh-grade English class. Mrs. Fitzwater is known for her hard tests, for making her students memorize and recite passages from the classics, and, of course, for "Come As Your Favorite Couplet Day," when each student is asked to personify his or her favorite poem. No one would dispute Mrs. Fitzwater's creativity and passion for teaching. For the most part, her students leave the seventh grade imbued with her enthusiasm for reading, writing, and, most important, thinking. In spite of Mrs. Fitzwater's skill as a teacher, at times she makes a common mistake. Notice the differences between the way she talks with Rachel and the way she talks with Jamel during their one-on-one midterm conferences.

> *Mrs. Fitzwater:* Come on in, Rachel. Let's talk about how you've been doing so far this report period. How have you been feeling about things so far?
>
> *Rachel:* Well, I really liked the stuff about satire and irony. My parents are always telling me that I'm too sarcastic — now I can tell them about other famous sarcastic people. They'll love it.
>
> *Mrs. Fitzwater:* Great! I'm making a sarcastic monster out of their

little girl! I'm glad you liked that unit, but your grades are poor, especially in writing. So far you've made mostly midsixties on your writing assignments and some low seventies. Writing doesn't seem to be your thing. Some people really have the flair and others don't. But your spelling and recitation grades are better — you certainly have the knack for those things.

Rachel: I guess you're right. I'm not good at writing. I guess I take after my dad — he says he's horrible at writing and all the other English stuff. He's a math man.

Mrs. Fitzwater: Well, hey, everyone has his or her strengths and weaknesses. I'd be happy to read over your next assignment and give you some help before it's due. How does that sound?

Rachel: Thanks!

Now notice what she says to Jamel, who also has poor marks in writing.

Mrs. Fitzwater: Let's go over your grades, Jamel. Sit down.

Jamel: Ugh. I hate this part.

Mrs. Fitzwater: Well, there is some good news and some bad news. Which do you want first?

Jamel: Oh, hit me with the bad news first, I guess.

Mrs. Fitzwater: Okay, well, your marks on the writing assignments are poor. You've been getting low seventies on most of them. It seems to me you haven't been putting very much time into these assignments. Is that true?

Jamel: Well, writing isn't my thing, you know. I don't express myself that way.

Mrs. Fitzwater: What are you talking about? I've heard you with the girls. It sure sounds to me that when you want to, you know how to use words pretty effectively! I'm sure if you put your mind to it, you could be making eighties and nineties.

Jamel: Maybe. It's just that these topics don't grab me. I don't have anything to say about Boo Radley.

Mrs. Fitzwater: Okay. Well, what do you have something to say about?

Jamel: Girls. I've got a lot to say about girls.

Mrs. Fitzwater: Okay then, why don't you write your essay this week about girls and we'll see how it goes. Put your heart into it. I know you've got the words, just put them down on paper. Now, the good news is that your grades have gotten steadily better in spelling. See, I was right — it was just a matter of focus. You put a little effort in, and your grades went up. Do the same thing in writing!

Teachers criticize different children in different ways. Sometimes the criticisms mirror reality ("you are too short to high-jump six feet"), but other times they reflect the biases and bad habits of the teacher. One documented bias concerns girls versus boys. Carol Dweck, the leading investigator of helplessness in the classroom, monitored third-grade classes to see how teachers criticize children when they fail. She found a striking difference between the criticisms of boys as opposed to girls. When a girl flounders, as Rachel does in writing, the teacher criticizes her lack of ability, as Mrs. Fitzwater does:[6] "Writing doesn't seem to be your thing. Some people really have the flair and others don't." And the criticized child internalizes the criticism, the way Rachel does: "I'm not good at writing. I guess I take after my dad — he says he's horrible at writing and all the other English stuff."

Notice that blaming failure on poor ability is very pessimistic — ability is permanent — and grade-school girls are bombarded with criticisms of ability. In contrast, when boys do badly, third-grade teachers criticize them for lack of effort, rowdiness, and not paying attention. (There is, of course, some truth in these criticisms.) These kinds of criticism, however, are more benign — effort, attention, and conduct are temporary and changeable. Mrs. Fitzwater criticizes Jamel in just this way: "You haven't been putting very much time into these assignments." "If you put your mind to it, you could be making eighties and nineties." "It was just a matter of focus."

Jamel looks at his poor grades in writing using an optimistic explanatory style. He invokes factors that, unlike poor ability, are temporary and changeable: "Writing isn't my thing." "It's just that these topics don't grab me."

This subtle sex difference is of considerable moment. Remember that pessimistic explanations of failure undermine trying. They produce hopelessness and passivity in the face of failure, whereas optimistic explanations are the underpinnings of seeing failures as challenges, reacting with activity, and harboring hope. Jacques Barber, a personality researcher, studied how grown men and women explain their interpersonal failures versus how they explain their failures of achievement. On average, men and women do not differ in overall optimism. But when researchers looked at the two realms separately, important discrepancies appeared. Men are optimistic about work, attributing failure to temporary, local, and external causes; they are pessimistic about interpersonal failures, invoking permanent, pervasive, and personal causes. Women are just the reverse: they are optimistic about social setbacks but pessimistic about achievement.[7]

In this generation, women have entered the job market in unprecedented numbers and — to the surprise of many — have achieved much. But plenty of barriers remain: the so-called glass ceiling, the systematically lower salaries, the slower pace of promotion. Some of these barriers may be external, but others, more insidious, may be internal. All the high school valedictorians in Ohio in the early 1980s were followed through college and beyond. After college, the male valedictorians, by and large, went on to ambitious careers; the female valedictorians began to fall by the wayside by the end of college, choosing less-ambitious careers or dropping out altogether. Perhaps part of the explanation is that when girls fail in achievement situations, they hear pessimistic explanations about their lack of ability and they have been socially conditioned to believe them; boys hear and believe that failure can be overcome if they just try harder, behave, and pay attention. As the girls become women, they carry the burden of an explanatory style that sees failure at work as permanent; boys, maturing into men, learn a style in which such failure can be conquered by working harder, and become consumed with work.[8]

THE HOVING EFFECT

Thomas Hoving, the formidable curator of the Metropolitan Museum of Art in New York, was known for not only his exquisite taste but also his ability to sniff out fraud and his unshakable confidence in his own artistic judgment. But he was not always full of such confidence.[9]

He tells of being nineteen at Princeton University, flunking out, anxious, low of self-esteem, and unsure of judgment. Before dropping out, Hoving decided to venture one more course, an upperclass sculpture seminar. On the first day, the professor placed on the podium a gleaming metal object with streamlined fingers.

"Gentlemen," the professor instructed the eight Princetonians, "comment on the aesthetic merits of this piece."

"Mellifluous fluidity," asserted the Ivy Club senior.

"Harmony of the spheres," agreed a junior in plummy tones. On and on went the plaudits around the room, until only the sophomore, pimpled, quaking Hoving remained.

"Well, this is too well tooled, too mechanical, too cold, and too streamlined. It's too functional. This isn't art," mumbled Hoving apologetically.

The object was an obstetrical speculum.

"After that," Hoving tells us, "there was no stopping me!"

HOVING'S TRANSFORMING event was a positive one, but I am convinced that a single, crucial event that shatters the routine of childhood or adolescent life — for better or worse — can markedly alter pessimism or optimism by changing the child's theory of who he is and what he is worth. It is deucedly hard to study such rare events, precisely because they are rare, so the evidence for the Hoving effect is weaker than for parental or teacher or genetic influences on optimism. One line of evidence comes from a tragic event that is, unfortunately, common enough to study carefully: the death of mother.

George Brown is a tireless and eccentric professor of sociology in London who has, for more than thirty years, studied the antecedents of depression among poor London housewives. He finds that adults whose mothers died before they were eleven are at heightened risk for depression for the rest of their lives. Their mother's death, permanent (she never comes back) and pervasive (so much of a child's repertoire depends on her mother) as it is, becomes their template for thinking about loss from that day forward. All setbacks are soon catastrophized into permanent and pervasive losses. In one case, a woman who lost her mother at an early age is confronted with the news that her adult son is immigrating to New Zealand. Instead of thinking that he has gone off to make his living and will return, she sees him as dead.[10] Adults who report having been abused physically or sexually as children also have a pessimistic explanatory style.[11] An even more common trauma for children is parents' fighting, separating, and divorcing. Children of parental turmoil become pessimistic and are at high risk for depression.[12]

In contrast, as this account illustrates, an unexpected challenge that results in mastery can become a fulcrum for a dramatic tilt into optimism that will last a lifetime.

By 1950, when I was fifteen years old, I was daydreaming in Unk's potato field about succeeding Pee Wee Reese as shortstop for the Brooklyn Dodgers. I worked hard developing my rather modest baseball skills, but it was hard to hide from myself that I was nearsighted, overweight, slow and clumsy. The ball usually managed to find its way past my outstretched glove or curved past my outstretched bat. I spoke a language girls did not understand. I blushed easily. No wonder the series of girls with whom I was lovestruck never even looked at me. . . .

And that was the summer I met my rattlesnake. . . .

He was looking to my right and although his forked tongue flicked the air, it had not yet tasted my approach. . . . I stopped after only a few steps. I couldn't blow this one, couldn't let this fly ball drop at my feet, couldn't let this repulsive serpent laze unchallenged almost in my back yard. . . . I had the stick and I had the rattlesnake: all I lacked was the outcome — the death of one of us. . . .

When I struck, I missed completely, tearing the stick into the ground inches short of its mark, striking only with the tip, just as my grandfather had warned me not to do. His turn of the head registered only annoyance, as if he were insouciantly deciding whether or not to kill me, but his eyes glittered with emerging hatred, and he hissed sharply. He uncoiled in my direction, his rattles thrilling in rage. He showed me the hollow fangs in which he stored his venom, his mouth white and wide. I crouched and struck at him again and again as he approached, and the blows told. He stopped only inches away.

I waited until his convulsions ceased, then picked him up near the rattles and walked, arm outstretched, with my snake dangling before me. "By gosh," my grandfather said, "the boy's got himself a rattler." . . .

Fifteen pounds evaporated from my frame that summer. When I returned to school in the fall, I was trim and walked with grace. I ran faster. I went to school dances and learned to flatter. . . .

At my parents' house, I recently found a 1950 black-and-white snapshot of a chubby bespectacled warrior holding a three-and-a-half-foot freshly killed rattlesnake. The boy's smile is ecstatic.[13]

The reverse is true as well: extraordinary helplessness and failure — the death of a mother, or physical abuse, or severe parental strife, or a crude rejection of the first adolescent gropings toward sexual love — can undo an optimistic worldview. An inchoate theory that "things will never work out for me," or "the world is unjust," or "I am unlovable" that begins in this way is self-fulfilling. Once pessimism gains a foothold, confirmation abounds. Every further rejection or defeat has at least a few real elements that are permanent and pervasive. The developing pessimist seizes on these elements as *the* explanation and ignores the more optimistic ones. All a developing pessimistic child has to do is turn on the television or read the newspaper to have her pessimism reinforced. Pessimism then can become her way of life.

There are, in summary, four places pessimism can originate:

- Genetics
- Parental pessimism
- Pessimistic criticism from parents, teachers, or coaches
- Mastery and helplessness experiences

The most important questions become "How can you intervene? How can you change pessimism into optimism? How can you strengthen and maintain optimism in your children?" You cannot now do much about your child's genes, but so much, even of this, depends on how much failure and success he experiences. You can, however, change your own pessimism, you can change the way you criticize your child, you can provide mastery experiences for your children at just the right time, and you can teach your child the skills of optimism directly. This is the agenda of Part Four.

*How to Raise
Children to
Optimism and
Mastery*

9

The Penn Prevention
Program

ENCOURAGED BY THE RESULTS of our pilot study with a small group of fifth- and sixth-graders, we were now ready to find a school district to launch the full-scale project. We decided to target Abington, a tree-lined, middle-class suburb outside of Philadelphia, as our first choice. At a lecture I have given to eastern Pennsylvania's leading school superintendents, Dr. Louis Hebert, Abington's superintendent of schools, impressed me enormously with his bold questions and his eagerness to be part of a major change in the education of young teenagers. Abington's location was also convenient for Karen, Lisa, and Jane, the key players. We arranged to meet with Dr. Hebert and Dr. Amy Sichel, the director of pupil services, to discuss the details of the project.

Conducting research in schools, with the often-conflicting agendas of teachers, principals, an elected school board, and parents, is exponentially more difficult than conducting research in the controlled environment of a laboratory. Community-based research often requires as much diplomacy and negotiation as it does solid science. Because of the complexity of this type of research, first meetings can be rough. As researchers, there are certain requirements that we must push for in order to ensure that the project, once successful, can be reproduced by others and disseminated widely. As school officials, Drs. Hebert and Sichel have to be very careful that the risk of harm to the children is low and that parents and students do not feel like rats in a laboratory. To our good fortune, Drs. Hebert and Sichel think like scientists. They knew that the integrity of this program and its large-scale application would rest on how well we evaluated its effects.

The initial piece of business, then, was to agree upon the methods for measuring the results of the program. We agreed to give questionnaires to the children, their parents, and their teachers before and after the training segment. Not only would we be able to evaluate the changes, but so would the parents and teachers. We explained that we were not looking to develop a "quick fix" that would help the children in the short term. Instead, we were committed to following these kids through high school, coming to the school every six months for the next several years to assess the participants, and to see if the program, over the long term, could prevent depression.

Next we tackled the thorniest of issues, establishing a control group. A random-assignment control group is the best way to evaluate any program's effectiveness. As researchers, we wanted to give screening questionnaires to every fifth- and sixth-grade child whose parents agreed. Then, of the kids who tested at greatest risk for becoming depressed, we would randomly form two groups: half the kids would participate in the coping skills course and half would form a control group. When researchers use random assignment, there will be no systematic differences, such as a difference in parents' education, between the groups. The only systematic difference between the groups is that one group of children participates in the course and the other doesn't. Then all the children selected for the two groups, no matter which group they are assigned to, take the same set of questionnaires. Since the children are assigned to either the coping skills group or the control group by chance, any differences in depression between the two groups after the end of the program — differences that would be revealed by their answers to the questionnaires — would tell us if the program worked. If the children who participated in the coping skills groups are significantly less depressed than the children in the control group, we could conclude that it was the program that prevented depression.

As administrators of an entire school system, Drs. Hebert and Sichel understandably worried about what parents and members of the school board would think of our identifying kids at risk for depression and then offering to help only half of them — leaving the other half to fend for themselves. Finally, we reached a compromise. We agreed to use a "wait-list" control group. We would include seventy children in the coping skills course and thirty children in the wait-list control group. After one year, the children who were assigned to the control group would participate in the same course the seventy children participated in the year before. Instead of being denied the opportunity to participate in the coping skills course, the control children would be given delayed entry into the program after one year. This solution satisfied the Abington officials, but not us.

Our concern was long-term prevention, and if we had a comparison group for only one year, we could not find out if we brought about long-term prevention of depression. The results of school-based programs, and of therapy, usually fade — sometimes they fade fast. It was our mission to develop a program that changes the trajectory of these kids' lives, and we needed a long-term control group that we could follow through high school. Research shows that the rate of depression rises dramatically as children traverse puberty. Without being able to make the critical comparisons across puberty, any prevention claims we might make would be easy to challenge.

We decided to form a long-term control group from another district that closely matched Abington in income, education, and racial composition. This was not a perfect solution, but it was a good second choice. Another nearby school district signed up. We agreed to run the program, improved by its trial run in Abington, for children in this district after the Abington phase of the project was completed.

THE PROGRAM

We designed our program not to sound like or feel like school. Many of the children we would be working with had developed negative attitudes toward school. As children slip into depression, they begin to withdraw from the important people and experiences in their lives; school and its social connections are prime candidates. As children begin to withdraw, their academic performance declines. When children are depressed, activities that used to bring them pleasure leave them feeling flat. Wendy, when she was not depressed, couldn't wait for social studies class, especially when the subject was the battles of the Civil War. As Wendy describes it, when she became depressed "it was like I didn't even care anymore. I knew I liked that stuff, but I would just feel bored all the time and I stopped liking even my favorite classes and teachers." Not surprisingly, her classwork suffered.

Even if a depressed child remains interested in school, it is often difficult for him to pay attention. One important symptom of depression is a marked decrease in concentration. The normal attention span of school children is short, and for children who are already experiencing low-level depression, it is even shorter. For these children, not only does the classroom environment seem rich with distractions — children making jokes, noises from the hallway, the sounds of recess outdoors — but also their minds provide them with a barrage of negative thoughts that make it difficult to concentrate: "I'll never get this right," "Jamie doesn't like me anymore," "I hate school." As concentration weakens, these children's grades begin to slip, especially since depression drains them of their ability to buckle down and try harder.

Given this special set of circumstances, we knew that the program had to incorporate the central antidepression skills in a format that was gripping and interactive. So by the summer we had developed a twelve-week, twenty-four-hour program that used comic strips, role-playing, games, discussions, and videos to teach each core concept. We also created two "Coping Skills" characters, Hopeful Holly and her brother Hopeful Howard. This optimistic pair became known as the "Silvers" because they could find the silver lining in even the darkest cloud. The Silvers, always liking a challenge, took on Gloomy Greg and Pessimistic Penny. They taught the Despairing Duo to challenge their negative thoughts and helped them find ways to cope with their problems. Say-It-Straight Samantha helped Bully Brenda and Pushover Pete learn assertiveness skills. Each concept was brought to life through a character, and throughout the program they appeared in skits and stories that presented the antidepression skills.

The two main components of the Penn Prevention Program were the cognitive one and the social problem-solving one. By adapting the central elements of cognitive therapy for normal, elementary-aged children, we aimed to teach children that thoughts are verifiable and changeable, that they do not need to believe the first thought that pops into their head. "Automatic thoughts," which we all have, occur just on the edge of awareness. They are the fleeting, barely perceptible statements that we say to ourselves throughout the day. Although such thoughts are fast, and thus hard to detect, they directly bring about sadness, anxiety, and anger. Our first step, then, was to teach children to monitor the things that they say to themselves.

Laurie, a sixth-grader, talks about learning to catch her automatic thoughts:

> You know how sometimes you have the words of a song running in your head over and over again? Like one time, my parents took me to see a show called *The Music Man* and I couldn't get the words from one of the songs out of my head for a whole week — and I didn't even like the show that much. Well, anyway, Karen taught us that we also have words, sentences, things that we say to ourselves, that run through our heads too. At first, I thought she was crazy, but she helped us to sort of pay attention to those things and she was right. Karen did this neat thing where she set a timer and whenever it beeped we had to write down whatever it was we were thinking right then. Sometimes I was thinking things like "My hair is so ugly" or "No boys like me." Sometimes I was thinking happy thoughts, but most of the time I wasn't.

With practice, Laurie was able to listen in on her automatic thoughts. Once children can capture their automatic thoughts, they need to learn how to evaluate their accuracy. Judging the accuracy of accusations is a skill that most children already have, but they do not use it when the accusations issue from inside. When accused of being lazy or selfish or boorish by, say, a friend, most children and adults will counter the criticism by rattling off a list of concrete examples that prove it false: "Lazy?! What are you talking about?! So there are a few dishes in the sink — I got up at six-thirty this morning, worked out until eight, stayed at the office from nine until six, and then stopped on the way home to pick up *your* dry cleaning! Lazy! You've got to be out of your mind, calling me lazy!"

Usually, however, we do not use this skill when we hurl the accusations at ourselves. We act as if what we say to ourselves is always incontrovertibly true. The tendency to accept their own self-critical thoughts as facts is especially pronounced in people who are depressed.

To combat this tendency, our program teaches children to adopt the role of a detective whose job it is to judge the accuracy of their own pessimistic thoughts and accusations. Stories about Sherlock Holmes and his misguided counterpart, Hemlock Jones, are used to introduce the concept.

Once upon a time, in a town very much like Abington, a ten-year-old girl rode her brand-new shiny red bicycle to school. She locked it to the bike rack and skipped merrily off to class. When the final school bell rang, the girl excitedly ran for her bike. She couldn't wait to do wheelies and pedal as fast as she could all the way home. But wait! What is this? When she got to the spot where she had left her bike, she found that it was gone.

"Oh, my brand-new shiny red bicycle!" she cried. She was very, very upset. "I am very, very upset." Just then, a very strange looking man wearing a great big hat appeared by her side. She did not recognize this man. She had never seen him before. "I do not recognize this man," she thought. "I have never seen him before."

"Please don't be alarmed, small child. I am the famous, the great, the famous — Detective Hemlock Jones. At your service."

"I never heard of a detective called Hemlock Jones. Don't you mean Sherlock Holmes?" the girl asked.

"No, I am Hemlock Jones," the detective replied, with a hint of annoyance in his voice. "Why does everybody confuse me with that guy? Anyway, I know who stole your bike. It was that dreadful Dangerous Danny!"

"Wow!" cried the girl. "That was fast. How did you figure out who stole my bike so quickly?"

"Oh, no big deal. His was the first name that popped into my head, so it must be him!" And with that, Hemlock Jones turned on his heels, tripped over his feet, and disappeared into the late afternoon sun.

But our story is not over, because just then onto the scene appeared the dashing, the daring, the famous Sherlock Holmes. He threw off his cape, adjusted his cap, and declared, "I don't agree with that silly Hemlock Jones. I am the dashing, the daring, the famous, not to mention the one they write books about, Sherlock Holmes!"

The girl thought he seemed a little arrogant, but she needed his help. Sherlock Holmes continued, "Now there, my friend, I do not agree with that silly Hemlock Jones. What kind of detective is he? Real detectives do not believe the first name that pops into their head. A good detective makes a list of suspects and then looks for evidence to catch the thief. I am off to search for clues and evidence, and when I return I will tell you who stole your bike." And with that, Sherlock Holmes twirled his cape, straightened his cap, and charged off down the block.

"That's a strange man," the girl thought, "but he seems to take his job seriously."

Later that day while the girl was playing outside of her home, she heard a strange noise. She turned around and standing before her was none other than Sherlock Holmes.

"Hi there, little missy. It is I, the dashing, the daring, the one they write books about, the famous Sherlock Holmes."

"This is getting old," thought the girl. "Did you figure out who stole my bike?"

"Yes, I did. First I thought perhaps it was Dangerous Danny. But when I searched for evidence I realized that Danny was in detention for cutting class when your bike disappeared. It couldn't have been him. Then I thought perhaps it was Slippery Fingers Steve. But when I searched for evidence I found that Steve was gambling away his allowance at the local arcade when your bike was lifted. It couldn't have been him. Then I decided to check out Bad Betty. When I searched for evidence I found a couple of telling clues. First, I found a monogrammed hair ribbon next to the bike rack, and the initials on the ribbon were 'BB.' Then I went to Bad Betty's home, and her mother told me that Betty was out bike riding on a brand-new, shiny red bicycle that she won at school for being the best behaved. Finally, I searched the neighborhood high and low until I found Bad Betty. And sure enough, there she was, scaring the little kids on *your* bicycle."

"Oh, Sherlock Holmes," cried the girl, "you're wonderful! You're so much smarter than that silly Hemlock Jones. Please, Detective Holmes, may I have my brand-new, shiny red bicycle now?"

Sherlock Holmes looked down at his feet and began to stammer. "Uh, well, um, um, I didn't exactly *get* your bike. That Betty is awfully big and, well, she's really pretty scary. I think you had better get your parents to retrieve your bike for you." And with that, the famous Sherlock Holmes twirled his cape, adjusted his cap, and disappeared into the sunset.

The End.

In chapters 10, 11, and 12, we will teach you how to apply the key concepts and do the activities from the cognitive component of the Penn Prevention Program with your child.

The second component of the program teaches children how to handle interpersonal conflicts and solve social problems. Children prone to depression often display one of two interpersonal styles. They are either bullies who explode when they do not immediately get what they want, or they are pushovers who allow themselves to be taken advantage of and withdraw because they don't want to cause any problems. Not surprisingly, the passive child is easy prey for the bully.

The bully sees hostility and aggression everywhere and counters with the same. His credo is "The best defense is a strong offense." He needs to learn to slow himself down, turn down the sensitivity of his "aggression detector," and learn other strategies for dealing with frustration. The passive child, whose credo is "Lay down and play dead," feels helpless to assert himself, so he withdraws whenever conflicts arise. This child needs to recognize that he isn't helpless and learn how to become more assertive. Chapter 13 will teach you about imparting social and interpersonal skills to your child.

CHILDREN AT RISK

The first step in our program was to identify children who were prone to depression. There are a number of factors that increase a child's risk: having a depressed parent, undergoing the death of one's mother, exhibiting low-level depressive symptoms, and living with a family that fights a lot, among others. Since it is hard to find out about parental depression and there were, fortunately, not many maternal deaths in Abington, we focused on the last two factors in order to include as many children as possible.

The actual screening process was quick and simple. Two questionnaires, one that measured symptoms of depression and one that measured the child's perceptions of family conflict, were given to each child whose parents consented. Because our screening method did not require lengthy interviews, we could administer the questionnaires to a group of twenty children in twenty minutes.

THE GROUPS BEGIN

In the winter of 1990 the Penn Prevention Program officially began. Lisa, Jane, and Karen screened two hundred fifth- and sixth-grade children in the Abington school district and offered spots in the program to seventy children who were at greatest risk for depression. The seventy children were divided into six groups; Lisa, Jane, and Karen each taught two. To ensure that each group was being taught the same material, we developed a minute-by-minute manual that scripted each session. We also videotaped each session so that we could monitor how closely we followed the manuals and evaluate our teaching.

Over dinner before the first day, the research team talked about our work and shared our excitement and nervousness over being in the classroom with the kids at last. We had spent two years developing the program; the following day marked the first time we would actually run the program from start to finish with a group of children at risk for depression. Bringing science to the community is a thrilling endeavor. It is also an awesome responsibility. As we thought about entering the lives of these seventy children, I recalled my conversation with Jonas Salk and hoped that these first-ever trials of psychological immunization would live up to his noble legacy.

We continued to run our groups throughout the winter and spring of that year. Each group had a slightly different personality. One was particularly cohesive and outgoing. This group threw Karen a surprise birthday party, complete with handmade gifts and home-baked cookies. It was a complete surprise, since her birthday wasn't for another four months. Another group was quiet but learned the skills with great precision. A third group could be biting and treated one another roughly. The assertiveness skills were particularly helpful for them. We had hoped that we would become a part of their lives, and we were unprepared for how much they became a part of ours.

Many of the children shared similar family experiences. Since one of our screening criteria was family conflict, many of the children lived with separated or divorced parents who fought a lot. Each child, however, also had his or her own story. The mother of one fifth-grade boy was badly hurt in a car crash and his father, bitter about this ugly turn of fate, was often unavailable to his son. Toby entered our program believing that he had done something to make his father hate him. He constantly ruminated about what it was that he had done, hoping that if he knew his wrongdoing he could make amends.

It's horrible at my house. My mom is real sick and can't get out of bed. We set up this bed in the living room so that she can see more people and everything but it's still really hard on her. My older sister is thinking of coming home from her college to help out, but my mom doesn't want her to miss out on school. The thing that really bothers me is that my dad won't hardly even talk to me anymore. I know sometimes I get into trouble and that makes Mom and Dad mad, but I can't even figure out what I did this time. Usually I know when I did something wrong, like picked a fight with Mark or got a bad grade in Mr. Bowman's class, but I really don't know this time. I even asked my dad a couple times, but he just says I didn't do anything, but I know I must have. He wouldn't be so mad at me if I didn't do anything.

Toby's home life was in crisis. While our program could not change the dreadful reality of his situation, we could help Toby learn to stop blaming himself for the chaos and strengthen his mental resources for dealing with loss and pain. Toby describes the changes he saw in himself:

> Things are still pretty rotten at home. My sister took the semester off from Beaver and that's helping a little. And I guess things are a little better between Dad and me, but not much. But I learned how to stop blaming myself for it all the time. The detective games we played helped me to figure out if I'm blaming myself too much. Sometimes when I start thinking that everything is all my fault, I remember to do the things we did in class and that helps. Like a couple of nights ago I was in my bed and I kept thinking that I must have done something bad, 'cause why else would all this bad stuff be happening to my family. I kept thinking about all the bad things I had ever done and then I really started to feel bad. So anyway, I remembered Karen showing me how to look for evidence like Sherlock and I started to do that. I was gonna turn on my light and try to write it down, but I just did it in my head instead. And it really helped. I could think up lots of good things I do, ways I help Mom out around the house and help Dad cook and things, and that made me feel a lot better. Sometimes I forget to do the Sherlock thing when I'm feeling really bad, but it helps a lot when I remember to do it.

A sixth-grade girl in the program had recently found out that she had been adopted. Miriam felt as though her whole world had changed. Nothing seemed the same and she was furious at her parents for not telling her sooner.

> I can remember everything perfectly about the day they told me. I was over at Glenn's house playing with his guinea pigs when my

mom called me and told me to come home. Her voice sounded a little weird and I thought she had found out that I had been making crank calls to Danielle Davis. I figured I was going to get grounded or something. Anyway, when I went inside, both my mom and dad were there and they told me to come into the living room and sit down. Now I got really scared, because they both looked so serious, and usually when I get caught doing something wrong, they just start yelling at me right away. They never have me sit down or anything. So anyway, we all sit down in the living room and my mom starts off by saying, "Miriam, your father and I love you very much and we want to talk to you about something important."

I was expecting them to say that they were getting a divorce or something. I mean, it's not like they fought a lot, but a couple of my friends' parents got divorced, and the way they were talking — it just sounded like it had to be something like that. When they told me I was adopted, I almost died. I didn't even believe them for the longest time. I just kept sitting there thinking, "Man, they've lost it. I can't believe they're playing such a sick joke on me." Finally, it kind of just sunk in and I knew it must be true and then I was really, really, really mad. I mean, definitely the maddest I have ever been. The only reason they even told me was that Jonathan had been snooping around in my father's office and found some papers in the back of his big black filing cabinet that said something about me being adopted and they were afraid that I might find out and so they wanted me to hear it from them and everything. If it wasn't for Jonathan, I'd still be thinking that I was a real Cooper.

During the course of the program, Miriam's primary focus was on the fact that her parents had kept the information from her until recently. She believed that they had conspired together to keep her in the dark and that they would never have told her if her brother hadn't happened to find out. Miriam was so furious at her parents that she refused to talk to them about it and spent as much of her time as she could in her bedroom or at a friend's house.

Throughout the program, we helped Miriam to take a more flexible view of her parents' motivations. This reduced her anger at them and enabled her to talk to them about how she was feeling.

. I really liked coming to the program. Jane was really nice and she helped me a lot. The biggest thing she helped me with was this whole adoption thing. I was so mad at my parents I didn't even want to be in the same room as them. I would come home from school and either go over to Sarah's house or just go into my room and close the door. I guess I was kind of giving them the silent treatment. I know that is pretty childish but I couldn't help it. I mean, I would sit at the dinner table and I would have to keep telling myself over and over and over, "Don't do anything stupid. Just eat your food and keep your mouth shut." I tell you, I really wanted to pick up the food and hurl it at them.

Jane helped me to slow my thinking down so that I could find out what I was saying to myself about the whole thing. I thought that if they really loved me that they would have told me right away, and that since the only reason they did tell was 'cause of Jonathan, that they probably weren't even planning to ever tell me. But Jane helped me think up lots of different reasons why they didn't tell me earlier and reasons why they might have decided to wait until I was even older. You know, like maybe they wanted to make sure I was old enough to understand, or maybe they were scared that I would feel bad if I knew and so they didn't want to tell me. There were, like, seven different reasons I could come up with. After I started thinking about these different things, I didn't feel so mad and I even started asking them some questions about it.

After spending twenty-four hours with these children over twelve weeks, hearing their stories and helping to improve their coping abilities, it was hard to say goodbye. It would have been nice to call the kids every once in a while to say hello and find out how they were doing. But because this was a research project designed to assess whether the twelve-week course could have lasting antidepressive effects for the children, we knew that once the program ended, we could not treat the children who participated in the course any differently than the children who were in the control group.

THE RESULTS

For the next two years, we returned to the schools to take measures of the children's symptoms of depression. The program had a clear and immediate effect on depression. Before the program started, 24 percent of the children in both the control group and the prevention group had moderate-to-severe depressive symptoms. Immediately after the program ended, the prevention group was down to 13 percent but the control group stayed at 23 percent. Since our program was designed to prevent depression, it was the long-term data that we were most interested in, not the immediate relief the program brought about. If we found that our program reduced depression immediately but did not lead to lasting changes, we would have failed. Our aim was to teach the children a set of skills that they could use throughout their lives. We believed that once the children started using these skills, they would begin to have more mastery and fewer failures, which would improve their mood and reinforce the use of the skills. We wanted to create the upward spiral of a self-reinforcing system.

Every six months we analyzed our data and each time we found that prevention worked. Two years after the program ended, only 22 percent of the children who participated in the coping skills course reported moderate-to-severe depressive symptoms. In contrast, 44 percent of the control group was experiencing this level of symptoms. Two years after saying goodbye to the children, with the only intervening contact being our regular six-month assessments, the children in the prevention groups were half as likely to be depressed.

There are two facts you need to know to put these results in perspective. First, it is nearly a universal finding that the positive effects of all psychological treatments wane over time. This is hardly surprising. People forget what they have learned. They return to environments that aggravate their problems. They no longer get the support and encouragement of their trainers. While we hoped that our program would lead to lasting change, based on the literature, the most reasonable expectation was that our program would peak early and then fade. The second fact is that depression steadily increases as children go through puberty, and the rate of depression is higher in adolescence than it is in childhood. So we expected that the number of children with depressive symptoms would go up across the follow-up period. We hoped that our program would reduce this trend.

Now let's revisit our results. Immediately after the program ended, we had reduced by 35 percent the number of children experiencing strong depressive symptoms. Two years later, we had reduced the number of children with strong depressive symptoms by 100 percent. But the overall trend of depression as the children went through puberty was upward. Over time, however, children in the control group showed a much greater increase in their depressive symptoms than the prevention group. The Penn Prevention Program markedly slowed the natural increase in depression. Our program was the exception to the rule: the prevention effect of our program got bigger over time.

The first question we asked was "Did our program prevent depression?" The answer was yes. The next question we asked was "Did our program increase children's optimism?" Again, the answer was yes. Each time the children completed their depression test, they also completed the test of optimism and pessimism in chapter 7. We found consistently that the children in the prevention groups were much less likely to explain bad events pessimistically. In particular, the program helped them undercut their tendency to attribute their problems to permanent causes. Shawanna noticed this change in herself.

When I started, I was like Pessimistic Penny. I always felt really crummy and thought that I always messed things up. Like when my stepdad moved out, I thought it was because of me. Just like when my dad died when I was real little — I thought I had made him die because I was really mad at him right before he died because he didn't let me sleep at Kiona's house. It doesn't seem like I do that anymore. The people from Penn came to our school and helped us be less gloomy all the time. We would do these cartoon worksheets that had a picture of something, like two kids fighting, on the first part of the page, and then on the last part of the page it would say how one of the kids was feeling, like really sad or really mad or something. Then we would have to think up what the kid was thinking and write it in the thought bubble in the middle of the page. You know, like those bubbles you see on the funny page. We did a lot of those cartoons and sometimes we would draw something that happened to us instead of there being a picture there already.

I think the cartoons were really good because it helped me to think of more Hopeful Holly ways of thinking about bad things when they happen to me. Lisa taught me the difference between thinking something is going to last forever and you can't change it and thinking that you can change maybe at least a part of it. And she would make us practice it a lot. She even made us do things for homework. Sometimes I didn't like that too much. I hate homework. But she didn't give us too much, so I guess it was okay.

We have since run the Penn Prevention Program in schools in the Wissahickon, Pennsylvania, school district with similar success. We then modified the program for inner-city children in Philadelphia, changing the language and the stories to reflect the travails of inner-city life. We got good short-term results there as well, and we are now following these children to see if the results are long-lasting. In total, around three hundred fifty children from four school districts in the Philadelphia area have participated so far.

While we are proud of these results, an important question remains unanswered. We had established that Karen, Lisa, and Jane, who were then advanced doctoral students in clinical psychology, could teach children skills that lastingly reduced the risk for depression. But unless others could also do so, the scope of our work would be quite limited. We could personally do hands-on teaching of no more than about a hundred children a year, yet there are hundreds of thousands of children who could benefit from this program. Not even a small army of Ph.D.-level psychologists would be enough. Psychologists are expensive and school budgets are tight.

For our program to be used widely, we needed a two-pronged approach, with one prong involving teachers as the frontline providers, and the other prong, parents. So first we needed to train schoolteachers to teach the skills as effectively as psychologists. We selected a group of teachers from the Upper Darby school district in the suburbs of Philadelphia to be the first teachers to deliver the program directly to their students. These teachers agreed to participate in extensive training and then to devote one afternoon a week to run groups of children at their schools. As I write this chapter, six middle-school teachers are each teaching groups of seventh- and eighth-graders and we are comparing the sessions' depression prevention to that of groups being led by Ph.D. candidates in psychology from Bryn Mawr College. Other children, with similar levels of risk, form the control group. Just as we did in Abington, we will follow these children as they make the transition from middle school to high school.

The second prong of wide dissemination is to show parents how to teach their own children. By teaching parents the skills that their children are learning, we surround the child in an optimistic environment and the parent can continue to reinforce the skills long after the child's program has ended. In this program, the parents learn about and practice the techniques that we are teaching to their children in the depression prevention program.

To date, thirty parents from the Wissahickon school district have participated. The parents met for seven two-hour sessions. We compared the children whose parents were involved in the parent program to children who had direct training from us but whose parents were not trained. Right after the program ended, we did not find significant differences between these groups. This was not a surprise, because the period of reinforcement at home had not yet really begun. We are currently collecting follow-up data to see if group differences have emerged over time.

In the meantime, we have been flooded with "success" stories from the parents. In feedback forms, letters, and phone calls, the parents who participated in the program told us about the changes they saw in their children and themselves. One parent talked about feeling connected to her son in a way that she had not experienced before: "The best part of this program for me has been a deepening of the connection between me and my son. When things go wrong, he now sees me as a resource, as a person he can rely on to help him sort through the problem. Before, I'd be just about the last person he'd ever come to."

Another parent talked about an increase in "family time": "We used to spend Sunday afternoons together as a family, but that was about it. But since we were part of the program, I've started to notice that we're around each other a lot more. My daughter doesn't try to escape the dinner table within minutes of gulping down her food. And the communication between her and my husband has really improved."

The next four chapters contain the central aspects of the parent and teacher training programs, with lots of practice for both you and your child.

10

Changing Your Child's
Automatic Pessimism

Because the penn prevention program worked well at preventing depression when we taught it to children in their schools, we created a way of teaching it to parents so they could teach their own children at home. In the next four chapters you will learn how to impart to your children the core techniques of optimism, the skills that immunized children against depression in the Penn Prevention Program. In this chapter you will learn how to teach your child to see the link between his thinking and his emotional reactions. Chapter 11 will teach you the skills that nurture an optimistic explanatory style, and chapter 12 will teach you how to make your child an expert disputer of his own pessimistic thinking. The social skills that children can learn to use to fight depression make up chapter 13.

In order for you to teach your child the cognitive skills of optimism, you must first incorporate them into your own way of thinking. Children learn their pessimism, in part, from their parents and teachers, so it is very important that you model optimism for your children as a first step. Therefore this chapter takes a two-pronged approach. It teaches you how to use each technique in your own life and then how to teach the same technique to your child. Until you feel comfortable using the skill yourself, it is very difficult to teach it to someone else.

Before you dive into this chapter, understand that there is nothing magical about the strategies you will learn. If you are a pessimist, able to find a hidden criticism in every compliment, a bad omen in all that goes right, you will not lay down this book and see every glass as half-full. With practice, however, you will learn to challenge your pessimistic assumptions. But it will take work. Remember, the children in the Penn Prevention Program spent a total of twenty-four hours in the course learning and practicing the skills of optimism, and they were asked to practice the skills in homework assignments as well. The best way to use these four chapters to teach your child is as follows: Read each chapter all the way through first. You will see that some of the sections are for you and others are for your child. Return to the first adult section and practice the technique described there. Set aside an hour of uninterrupted time so that you can practice each skill without distraction. And be patient. This learning takes time, but these skills may change your life. Once you feel comfortable with your skill level, go on to the next section, where you teach the skill to your child.

OVERVIEW

The techniques you will learn in this chapter and the next two are the main tactics that cognitive therapists use to treat depression, but we have adapted them for people who are not depressed. Cognitive therapy is a short-term treatment and is roughly as effective as medication for treating depression. That is, when patients who have equally severe levels of depression are randomly assigned to either cognitive therapy or the most effective drug treatment, roughly equal numbers of patients (about 70 percent) markedly improve. With time, however, an important difference emerges. If we follow the "responders" (those for whom the treatment worked) across time, assessing depression every six months, we find that the patients who were treated with drugs are twice as likely to relapse as patients who had cognitive therapy. Cognitive therapy lowers the future risk of depression by teaching new skills of thinking that the patient uses the next time something bad happens. So while initially both drugs and cognitive therapy work well, cognitive therapy has twice the preventive effect.[1]

There are four basic skills of optimism that both cognitive therapy and the Penn Prevention Program teach. First, you learn to recognize the thoughts that flit across your mind at the times you feel worst. These thoughts, although often barely perceptible, profoundly affect your mood and behavior. This technique is called *thought catching*.

Lydia has learned to catch the negative things she says to herself. As a mother of three young children, the youngest in the first grade and the oldest in the fifth grade, mornings are not her favorite time of day. Getting the kids ready for school each morning can be tough. Sometimes the last thing the children hear as they are hurried out the door is Lydia screaming something she later regrets. As a consequence, Lydia feels depressed. With thought catching, she recognized that right after these screaming incidents she always says to herself, "I'm a terrible mother — a real shrew. My kids are going to hate me and I'm sure all my screaming has messed them up real bad."

The second skill of optimism is *evaluating* these automatic thoughts. This means acknowledging that the things you say to yourself are not necessarily accurate. Lydia is taught to view her beliefs about herself and the world as hypotheses that need to be tested. She learns how to gather and consider evidence in order to determine the veracity of her beliefs.

When Lydia was asked to support her theory that she is a bad mother, she was able to rattle off a long list of offenses. Lydia, learning optimism, was then asked to make a list of things to indicate that she is not such a bad mother, a task that was much harder for her than listing the offenses. The list seemed very short, so Lydia was urged to consider behaviors that she had not mentioned. Soon the list grew longer than the first: she prepares their meals, washes their clothes, plays football with them after school, tutors them in fractions, soothes their worries, teaches them how to play the guitar, and talks to them sympathetically about their problems. After marshaling this evidence, Lydia was less certain that she is horrible mother.

The third skill is generating *more accurate explanations* when bad things happen and using them to challenge your automatic thoughts. Lydia learned to say: "I'm fine with the kids in the afternoon, but not so great in the morning. I've never been a morning person. I guess I need to learn to contain my morning irritability better." "I've never been a morning person" is a much less permanent explanation for screaming at the kids, and Lydia learned to substitute this explanation when she caught herself thinking, "I'm a horrible mother." With practice, Lydia could interrupt the chain of negative explanations that went, "I'm a terrible mother, I'm not fit to have kids, therefore I don't deserve to live," by inserting the new explanation. Now she is able to say to herself, "It's completely illogical to conclude that I don't deserve to live because I'm not a morning person." When Lydia was able to see that she had trouble in the morning instead of being a complete failure as a mother, her mood improved. As her mood improved, Lydia had more energy and found that mornings were more tolerable.

The fourth skill is *decatastrophizing*. Reflect on a time when something went wrong: You planned an elaborate dinner party and the guest of honor had an allergic reaction to the peanut sauce and the chocolate mousse was lumpy. Or your spouse asked when you were going to start working out again. Or you caught your son smoking pot behind the shed. Or your boss told you that he was disappointed in your performance. When things go wrong, do you ruminate on the worst possible consequences? Do you find yourself fantasizing about the most dire implications? Although thinking about the worst case — catastrophizing — can be productive in some situations, it is counterproductive when the worst case is actually very unlikely. In these cases, planning for the worst is a bad use of your time. It is a drain on your energy, and it ruins your mood.

Lydia was a catastrophizer. When her friend, Eileen, told her that she was feeling frustrated by the number of times Lydia had canceled plans, Lydia believed that this meant not only the end of their friendship but also that all her other friendships would suffer. "When Eileen told me how she was feeling, I immediately thought: 'This is it. I've ruined it. Eileen is too nice to say it, but she doesn't want to have anything to do with me anymore. I know what's going to happen. She's going to tell Sharon, and

Lynn, and Toni and they're going to start withdrawing from me too.'"

Lydia learned to evaluate more accurately the likelihood of the catastrophes she feared. So instead of being bogged down by fantasies of unrealistic horrors, she was able to direct her energy toward correcting problems.

Catching your automatic thoughts, looking for evidence, generating alternatives, and decatastrophizing are the central cognitive skills of the Penn Prevention Program. In the rest of this chapter, I will show you how to teach the first two to yourself and then to your child. In the next two chapters, we will work on generating alternatives and decatastrophizing, the skills that make up effective disputing.

THE ABC MODEL

Many people believe that feeling bad is determined by the "stressors" or adversities that happen to us. We feel angry when someone transgresses against us. We feel depressed when we lose something we cherish. Certainly, the events in our lives are connected to our emotions, but the connection is much weaker than commonly believed. This becomes obvious when you imagine two people in the same situation.

Consider Jennifer and Tara, close friends and neighbors for the last twelve years. Jennifer and Tara have witnessed each other's triumphs and failures. Last year they decided to take a vacation together, without their husbands, without their children. They did not have much money, so they wanted to find a low-cost vacation. Neither had done much camping before, but both thought it would be a challenge. They researched different spots along the East Coast and decided to drive to North Carolina to camp on the Outer Banks. In a car overflowing with gear that they had borrowed from friends, they waved to their families as they pulled out of Tara's driveway.

Three days later, Tara and Jennifer were ensconced in their tent when the rain started. At first a mere patter, the rain soon began to pound. The winds grew strong, ripping the stakes from the ground and sending the tent into convulsions. They had forgotten to bring a tarp, so within minutes Jennifer and Tara began to feel the mud seep into their temporary home. As the sound of the storm became deafening, fear replaced humor and the women decided they needed to find shelter. They got to the car as quickly as possible. They would return for their gear in the morning. The storm raged for eighteen hours.

Because of the flooding and damage from the storm, Jennifer and Tara weren't able to return to the campsite for three days. They spent these days in a cheap motel — no phone, a TV that made everything sound like it was under water, and a desk clerk with a picture of a slain deer and the phrase BORN TO HUNT tattooed across his chest.

When they returned to their campsite, their belongings were in shreds. The tent was gashed in several places. Their sleeping bags and cooking equipment were missing. The glass of the lantern was shattered. They had little to return to their friends.

Though the trip was a fiasco for both women, Tara and Jennifer reacted quite differently to this shared experience. Initially, both were upset. They were horrified by the extent of the damage and sickened by the thought of how much it would cost them to replace the gear.

The car ride home was long, and as they began the drive, both women felt glum. A couple of hours into the trip, Jennifer started to giggle. The irony of their misadventure sent her into fits of laughter. "Oh, yeah, we sure saved a lot of money on this vacation. . . . No four-star hotels for us, no sir. We're going on a low-cost vacation! Two women in the wild. Just you, me, and the great outdoors!" The more Jennifer laughed, the more sullen Tara became.

By the time they pulled into Tara's driveway, Jennifer was bursting with the story of "the city girls lost in the wild." She couldn't wait to tell her family about their harrowing experience, but each time she began the story, she would start to laugh and have to begin again. Tara got out of the car as quickly as possible and told her family that she wanted to rest and would catch up with them in the morning.

Albert Ellis, who along with Aaron Beck founded cognitive therapy, developed the "ABC model."[2] The A stands for adversity. An adversity can be any negative event: a failed vacation, a fight with a close friend, the death of a loved one. The C stands for consequences: how you feel and behave following the adversity. Often it seems that the adversity immediately and automatically produces the consequences. Ellis, however, argues that it is the B — the beliefs and interpretations about A — that cause the particular consequences.

Jennifer and Tara shared the same adversity, a rotten vacation, but the consequences were wholly different. The differences followed from the interpretations they made. Here is what Jennifer believed:

Adversity: Oh, what a trip! I can honestly say it was the worst week I've had since our apartment trauma. In a nutshell, we drove three days only to have one of the worst storms in recent Carolinian history ravage the campsite, destroying most of Bill's and Roger's camping gear. Tara and I ended up spending all of our time in a roach-infested, decrepit motel. I'm telling you, this place made that motel we stopped at last summer look like the Taj Mahal.

Beliefs: I just couldn't believe it was happening. What miserable luck. At first I was thinking we were stupid for even trying to go camping. I mean, it's not like Tara and I have a lot of experience in the rugged outdoors. The closest we ever come to nature is when we take the kids to the "Endangered Species" exhibit at the Please Touch Museum. So I was thinking we were real fools for going on this trip. But then I kept thinking that it must be a joke of some kind. I mean, everything that could go wrong, did. I'm telling you, we ought to be the official "Murphy's Law" mascots. You know, it's not like our inexperience with camping made the storm happen. I guess it was just really, really bad luck!

Consequences: The first couple of days afterward I was pretty miserable. I felt almost embarrassed and I didn't even want to talk about it with Tara. I was feeling really bad about myself. The worst was when we finally got back to the campsite and saw that all the stuff was ruined. I just wanted to get in the car and keep on driving. I didn't want to have to explain it to Roger and Bill. But after the initial shock, I just started laughing about it. I mean, it really was humorous in a twisted kind of way! Once I started laughing about it, it just seemed funnier and funnier. Tara was taking it pretty hard, so I kept trying to cheer her up, but she wasn't in the mood. Maybe I'll write this up. Too bad the paper doesn't have an "Anti-Vacation and Leisure" section!

At first Jennifer felt embarrassed and down about herself. Her fantasy was that she would flee and not have to tell anyone. These consequences make sense in light of the way in which she first viewed the fiasco. Jennifer's initial beliefs were that she was "stupid" and "a complete fool." Most of us would feel embarrassed and down if we believed that the trip flopped as a result of our foolishness or stupidity — personal, permanent, and pervasive explanations. Jennifer's embarrassment was temporary. Once she started viewing the situation as the result of bad luck, her mood improved and she was able to turn a frustrating situation into a source of humor.

Tara's beliefs about this event, as told to her husband, were different, generating different consequences.

Adversity: We were there all of six hours before this huge storm hit. I've never seen anything like it. It just laid waste to the entire place. As soon as we realized what was happening, we jumped into the car and looked for a place to stay. We thought we'd just be there for the night, but the park rangers wouldn't let us back in for three days.

Beliefs: You know, I hate to say, but I should have known better. I mean, I can't get over how dumb I am. Sure, there was nothing I could have done about the storm, but there were about a million ways in which I made a bad situation worse. Like leaving the gear behind. What a stupid thing to do. I mean, we borrowed that stuff and I should have packed it all up before leaving. I just left it there to get stolen or destroyed. And, you know, I should have done better research into where we were going. I mean, I remember thinking that I ought to call down there and ask about the conditions this time of year, but of course, I didn't follow through. That was just so typical of me. Everything I do is half-baked. That's the kind of person I am. I'm lazy and sloppy and this time my laziness cost us a lot of money.

Consequences: It was horrible. We had the worst time imaginable. Jen and I both felt really depressed for the first day or two afterward, but then she started to laugh about it. I don't know how she could see it as funny. She kept trying to cheer me up, and I know she was only doing it to help me, but it really got on my nerves. I mean, I still don't see how she can laugh about it. I know you were mad last night 'cause I wanted to be alone, but I just felt too bad. I hate having to tell you about it. I mean I just feel so guilty and horrible. It might not seem like that big a deal to you, but I still feel really stupid. I just want to forget it ever happened.

There was nothing funny about this trip for Tara. She felt guilty and depressed because she believed that the fiasco was caused by her dumbness, laziness, and lack of forethought. These causes are permanent ("Everything I do is half-baked. That's the kind of person I am."). Jennifer was able to change her interpretation of the trip, which enabled her to feel better. Tara, in contrast, could not see the problem from any other vantage point. For her, the failed vacation was yet another indication of her inadequacy. Tara's set of beliefs is typical of a pessimist. When things go wrong, the problems stem from things about herself that she cannot change.

Tara's pessimism is not just a quirky style or a surface feature without much influence on her life. Pessimistic beliefs, in general, shape experience through two powerful mechanisms: the self-fulfilling prophecy and the confirmation bias.

Denise is thirty-three years old. She is a single woman who feels lonely without an intimate relationship. Stephanie is her housemate and is also single. Stephanie decides that they have to get out more and start meeting people, that they can't just sit back and wait for the men of their dreams to miraculously appear at the breakfast table. "Look, Denise, we've been lamenting our singlehood for long enough," Stephanie begins. "If we have another one of our 'all the good men are taken' conversations, I'm going to puke. How would we know if all the good men are taken? We're such couch potatoes that the only datable men we ever see are on the tube."

Stephanie tries to convince Denise to go to Thursday's, a local club. Denise replies: "Nah. I don't want to. I'm horrible at that kind of thing. I never know what to say, so even if someone would talk to me, I'd just blow it. Really, I'm just a bore. Within five minutes I can see the other person's eyes start to roll back into his head and I swear I've caught at least two people snoring. Then I'd start stammering and hemming and hawing and that would be the end of it. I'll just end up sitting there feeling pathetic." Denise is not easily swayed, but after much cajoling, she agrees to go.

Denise believes that she is a deadly conversationalist. This belief itself changes the way that she relates to people and is self-fulfilling, bringing about the very outcome that Denise most wants to avoid — that she will not meet anyone. When Denise gets to Thursday's she is so convinced that she will blow every conversation that she begins to feel nervous. When she sees a man smiling at her, her anxiety spikes.

Denise thinks, "Oh, great. That man is smiling at me. He's walking over here. Oh, here we go. I'm going to blow it. I have nothing interesting to say. He is going to run for the hills as soon as I open my mouth." It is very difficult to carry on a spritely conversation when your head is filled with such negative thoughts. Not surprisingly, when Denise attempts to start a conversation with this man, her anxiety causes her to stammer and her mind goes blank — she really does have nothing to say. But the reason Denise's mind goes blank is not because she is a bore, but rather because her pessimistic thinking created intense anxiety, one symptom of which is trouble concentrating.

Besides the self-fulfilling prophecy, the confirmation bias is the other mechanism through which our beliefs shape our experiences. Imagine that Denise does meet a man and they strike up a conversation. Stephanie sits on the other side of Denise and listens to the exchange. Later, when Denise and Stephanie are telling a friend, Jason, about the evening, two quite different stories emerge.

Jason: So, how'd it go? Did you get your hooks into anyone last night?

Denise: Yeah, right. I got my hooks into a man all right — and killed him within two minutes.

Jason: It couldn't have been that bad.

Denise: Oh, it was. It was pathetic. That poor guy. He says "Hello" and I barely get a "Hi" out before you see the regret in his eyes.

Stephanie: Come on, Denise. I was sitting right there. You guys were talking for at least twenty minutes. I know, because no one was talking to me, so I didn't have anything better to do but listen to your conversation.

Denise: Okay, maybe he hung around for a while, but who cares. I mean, the pauses were so big, you could drive a truck through them. He got out of there fast enough.

Stephanie: You are such a piece of work. Don't believe a word of this, Jason. From my perch, I could have sworn he only left because his buddy was all but begging to get out of there. He must have told him at least three times that he'd be ready to go in ten minutes.

Jason: It sounds like he was interested.

Denise: Oh, come on. He just didn't want to seem rude.

Stephanie: Is that why he asked for your number?

Jason: He did? Did you give it to him?

Denise: Yeah, but who cares. I'm telling you, I couldn't think of anything to say. He's not going to call.

Stephanie: Wrong again. Okay, there were a few awkward pauses. But that's par for the course. I seem to recall a lot of laughing. It seems like our girl here has found herself an architect. You should have heard the questions Denise was asking. And I quote, "I just saw Wright's Waterfall home. Do you think his use of light and space have influenced the direction of contemporary architecture?"

Denise: All right. I've had just about enough of this conversation. What's up with you, Jason?

A confirmation bias causes people to see only the evidence that confirms their view of themselves and the world. They dismiss evidence that refutes it. Denise focused on the aspects of the conversation that supported her view that she was a bore; Stephanie, as an onlooker, was able to evaluate the conversation more evenhandedly. The confirmation bias reinforces pessimistic beliefs. If left unchallenged, Denise would use the previous night's experience to say, "See, I was right. I am a bore." This in turn reduces the likelihood that Denise will leave her couch again.

PRACTICE WITH THE ABC MODEL

The first step of learning optimism is to understand the ABC link. In the first part of this section are six scenarios presenting several adversities (A) and their consequences (C). Your job is to generate beliefs that would lead to the consequences described. There is no single correct answer. In order to judge whether the belief you come up with is correct, ask yourself whether, if you firmly held this belief, you would feel and act in the way specified in the consequence. The six examples are written for adults, as is the diary exercise that follows. Once you do the adult ABC exercises, you will use the child ABC exercises that follow to teach your child.

1. *A.* You plan a surprise weekend away for your spouse to celebrate his birthday. When you arrive at his office Friday afternoon to whisk him away he is annoyed and says he can't possibly go.
   B. You think _____
   C. You feel very embarrassed and do your best to avoid him.

2. *A.* You plan a surprise weekend away for your spouse to celebrate his birthday. When you arrive at his office Friday afternoon to whisk him away he is annoyed and says he can't possibly go.
   B. You think _____

    C. You feel disappointed, but decide to treat yourself to a fancy lunch and movie in town.

3. *A.* Your spouse has been distant and distracted lately.
   B. You think _____
   C. You become increasingly irritable with him and notice yourself picking fights.

4. *A.* Your spouse has been distant and distracted lately.
   B. You think _____
   C. You become sad and withdrawn.

5. *A.* You run into your teenage son and his friends at the mall and he pretends not to see you.
   B. You think _____
   C. You laugh to yourself and plan to tease him about it later.

6. *A.* You run into your teenage son and his friends at the mall and he pretends not to see you.
   B. You think _____
   C. You become furious and storm over to him and his friends, demanding not to be ignored.

Now, let's take a look at these situations and see what types of beliefs would lead to these consequences.

1 and 2. In the first example, a personal, permanent, and pervasive belief such as "I'm always screwing things up. He's got a busy schedule and I act like he should drop everything for me" would lead to embarrassment and withdrawal. If instead you believed that "It was a good idea gone awry" or "He must be having a really tough week at work" (both temporary, specific, and external), then you might feel disappointed, maybe frustrated, but you would not feel down about yourself.

3 and 4. In the third example, thoughts of trespass set off your anger and irritability: "He has no right to take his moods out on me" or "He's such a child. Whenever something is bothering him, he pouts." In contrast, if you interpret his distance as a sign that he is losing interest in you, then sadness may be the consequence.

5 and 6. In the fifth example, external, specific, and temporary interpretations, such as "Looks like my son is officially an adolescent

now," will enable you to keep your sense of humor. If, instead, you view his behavior as a sign of impudence and disrespect, then you will end up feeling angry.

Now I'd like you to practice catching your own beliefs. The best way to do this is to keep an ABC diary. For the next three days, whenever you find yourself confused or surprised by your reaction in a situation, record the adversity on a piece of paper. That evening, take five minutes to fill out your ABC diary for the day using those adversities. An "adversity" can be almost anything — a car that won't start, a phone call that goes unreturned, a toddler who won't nap. So, for example, you are working at the office over the weekend to put the finishing touches on a report and your coworker is ten minutes late. You find yourself furious. This would be an ABC entry for you to record. A particularly good time to use the ABC model is when you think that your emotional reaction is out of proportion. When this happens, it is a sign that you have some strong and illogical beliefs at work.

The ABC diary has three columns. In the first column, Adversity, describe the facts of the situation. It is important to make your entry as descriptive as possible. Record the "who," "what," "when," and "where." The "why" is part of your beliefs; do not enter it under Adversity. So, when your coworker shows up ten minutes late, record "Dana and I scheduled to meet at 4:00 on Sunday to finish our quarterly report. She did not arrive until 4:10." Do not record "Yet again Dana was late. She's always doing this kind of thing. She's so irresponsible. I hate working with her. I was furious." The goal in the Adversity column is to be specific and nonevaluative.

The second column is Beliefs. In this column you record how you interpreted the adversity. Make sure to distinguish between your thoughts and feelings: thoughts are recorded in the Beliefs column; feelings will be recorded in the Consequences column. "He thinks I'm immature" and "Things never work out for me" are beliefs. You can evaluate the accuracy of your belief by checking it against the available evidence. For example, "I feel guilty about it" is a feeling: in contrast to beliefs, feelings cannot be right or wrong, and you cannot check their accuracy. When you record your beliefs, make a note of how certainly you believed each interpretation you record. Use a scale of 0 to 100, with 0 meaning that you did not really believe the thought at all and 100 meaning total certainty in the belief. So if one of your interpretations about Dana's lateness was "She never keeps her word" and you very much believe this is true, then give it a high rating, an 80 or 90.

The third column is Consequences. In this column record each feeling you experienced after the adversity or anything you did in reaction to the adversity. For each feeling that you list, using a scale of 0 to 100, record the intensity of each feeling, with higher numbers meaning greater intensity.

MY ABC DIARY*

Adversity	Beliefs	Consequences
1._____	_____	_____
_____	_____	_____
2._____	_____	_____
_____	_____	_____
3._____	_____	_____
_____	_____	_____
4._____	_____	_____
_____	_____	_____
5._____	_____	_____
_____	_____	_____

*In the Adversity column, record only the who, what, when, and where. Be specific and nonevaluative. In the Beliefs column, record each belief you had about the adversity. Rate each belief from 0 to 100 according to how certain you were about each one. In the Consequences column, record each feeling you experienced and how you acted. Rate the intensity of each feeling from 0 to 100.

After you have filled out each column, look it over. Make sure that each feeling and action can be connected to a belief that makes sense of why you reacted as you did. You may not like how you reacted, but the first step in changing your reactions is to understand the beliefs that cause them. When I fill out ABC situations for myself, I often notice that there are one or two feelings or actions that still don't make sense given the beliefs I've noted down. When this happens, I spend a minute or two trying to identify what I was thinking when I was experiencing each of the feelings. I close my eyes and imagine the situation and that feeling in my mind. Then I can usually pinpoint the specific belief that triggered my emotion.

If after identifying your ABC sequence you still are confused by the intensity or type of your reaction, this is a clue that you have not fully identified your beliefs about the situation. You have succeeded at this exercise when you can almost always find a belief that makes sense of your feeling and action. Here are a few guiding examples.

Adversity: My fiancée and I had plans to spend a quiet night together because we had both been so busy lately. At about 7:30 she called me and asked whether I minded if she invited Lori to join us.

Beliefs: I knew it. I'm always the one who tries to make this relationship work (80). As far as she's concerned, she'd be happy if we saw each other once a month (85). I'm kidding myself if I think we'll ever get married (70).

Consequences: I felt a lot of different things. First I was feeling really angry at Deb and I just wanted to slam the phone down (90). I guess I was also feeling pretty down, sad (90). I told her I wasn't feeling so great, that she should just hang out with Lori and that I'd catch up with her tomorrow. I ended up moping around the house all night long.

Adversity: My husband and I were going for a walk around the neighborhood and he took his shirt off. I asked him to put it back on and he just glared at me and shook his head.

Beliefs: He's got to make a big deal out of everything (60). I just don't like it when he walks around like that, and he's turning this into another example of how I'm "always so uptight" (80).

Consequences: I shouted that he's always blowing things out of proportion and told him I wanted to walk by myself. I ended up not enjoying my walk at all because I felt so frustrated and misunderstood (80).

Adversity: Alex was supposed to rake up the leaves before he left for football practice, but when I went outside I saw that his father was raking the leaves instead.

Beliefs: Doesn't this just figure! James is always undermining me with the kids (75). I can't stand this anymore. I'm sick of always being the bad guy around here (90). Every time I give them a chore to do or punish them for something, James waltzes in and lets them off the hook (75).

Consequences: I just got really mad and marched over to him and started laying into him about how bad a parent he is (95). I didn't even stop to ask why he was raking the leaves instead of Alex. It took me almost forty minutes to feel totally calmed down.

TEACHING YOUR CHILD THE ABCs

Now I will show you how we teach the ABCs to the children in the Penn Prevention Program so that you can use these methods with your child. The optimum age for these exercises is eight to twelve, but by improvising more sophisticated language, you can use them for children up to fifteen. First, let me suggest the way to set the stage. It is important that your child find the exercises engaging, and so the program is designed to be interactive, creative, and fun. You will need to generate an atmosphere in which your child feels safe and supported, and able to laugh and joke. Do not be too rigid about the amount of time you spend on these activities. If your child sees this as "homework," or like cleaning out her bedroom closet, she will not engage.

Start off spending fifteen minutes on the activities (adjust the time upward for older children) and gradually increase the time to about thirty minutes. The general atmosphere you want to create is one of curiosity. Help your child to be curious about her feelings and thoughts by showing her that you are curious about your own. Throughout the day, when you find yourself feeling a strong emotion and your child is around, work through the ABC model aloud. This does not have to be done in any formal way (in fact, I suggest that you don't do it in a formal way — you don't want to set off your child's "my mom is so weird" detector). Rather, simply say what your belief was and the feeling it created. For example, if you're driving your child to school and a driver cuts you off, verbalize the link between your thoughts and feelings: "I wonder why I'm feeling so angry because that driver is driving slowly. I guess it's because I was saying to myself, 'Now I'm going to be late because the guy in front of me is going so darn slow. If he's going to drive like that he shouldn't drive during rush hour. How rude.'"

Introduce the Internal Dialogue. The first step is to explain the ABC model to your child. Begin by introducing the concept of an internal dialogue. Some children are aware of the things that they say to themselves when bad things happen, but other children are not. Here is roughly what to say:

> When problems happen, like getting into a fight with a friend or getting punished at home, we all talk to ourselves about what just happened. We think about it inside our head and since it is inside our head, no one else can hear the things we say to ourselves. Everybody does this, kids and adults, and it is totally normal. A lot of the time, we may not even really notice what we are thinking when a problem happens. It's just like a voice inside our head turns on automatically. Imagine that your teacher blamed you for something you didn't do. You might say to yourself, "Why is she picking on me? She's always blaming me for things I didn't do. She must really hate me." A little while ago I had trouble finding this book. I was thinking "Great. I wanted to do the ABCs with you and I've already lost my materials. Now I'm not going to be able to remember everything I wanted to tell you."

The most important point to make is that "talking to yourself" is completely normal, that everyone does it. Now talk through a couple of examples with your child. Here are a few you can use.

Sam is looking in the mirror after coming home from the barbershop. He is thinking to himself . . .

Sam: Man, I can't believe the haircut I just got. He practically scalped me! I'm almost bald! How can I go to school like this? All the kids are going to laugh at me and it's going to take months for my hair to look good again. I look like such a geek.

Susan is sitting down on the bench in gym class. She is thinking to herself . . .

Susan: I can't believe Julie didn't pick me to be on her team. When I'm captain I always pick her first. She picked Tammy, and Tammy isn't even her best friend. I'm supposed to be her best friend. She must not like me anymore.

Greg finds out that he didn't get invited to John's party. He is thinking to himself . . .

Greg: Why didn't John invite me to his party? He's in two of my classes and we have fun together. He must be mad at me, 'cause all the other kids got invited. Everybody's talking about it and I'm going to have to tell them I wasn't invited. I'll be so embarrassed. They'll all think I'm a loser. I guess they're probably right.

Patty goes to the coat closet at the end of the day and sees that her new jacket is missing. She is thinking to herself . . .

Patty: I can't believe someone took my jacket. Someone must have stolen it. What am I gonna tell Mom? She's going to kill me! That jacket was real expensive and I begged her to buy it for me. I told her I'd take care of it and now it's gone! She's never going to trust me again and she sure won't buy me any more nice clothes for school. I'm going to look like a dweeb in all my old stuff.

Once your child gets the idea that she has an internal dialogue too, ask her if she can think of a recent example when something went wrong. Now ask her what she was thinking when it happened. The goal of this is to help your child to start paying attention to the things she says to herself so that later you can work together to evaluate the accuracy of these statements. If your child is having a hard time coming up with examples from her life, you can use the probes provided in the next paragraph or make up some probes tailored to the kind of experiences your child is likely to have. Tell her to imagine that each situation was happening to her, and ask her to talk out loud about the things she might say to herself.

1. You are walking to school and you notice a group of kids whispering and pointing in your direction. You think to yourself _____

2. Your teacher calls on you in class and you realize that you have no idea what she asked you because you've been daydreaming. You think to yourself _____

3. You and your best friend planned to go into town to see a movie that you've been dying to see. A half an hour before he's supposed to come by your house, he calls to say that he can't go because he's going to another friend's house to play Nintendo. You think to yourself _____

4. Your brother has a bunch of his friends over, and no matter what you do, they make fun of you. You think to yourself _____

Introduce the ABC Model. After your child is tuned in to his internal dialogue, it is time to explain the ABC model to him. The key point is that how he feels doesn't just come out of the blue and isn't *determined* by the things that happen to him. Instead, it is what he says to himself when problems arise that makes him feel the way he does. When he suddenly feels mad or sad or afraid, there was a thought that triggered the feeling, and once he's able to uncover the thought, he can then change how he feels.

ABC CARTOONS: Use the cartoon strips to illustrate the link between thoughts and feelings.

Each cartoon strip has three frames. In the first frame is a simple adversity, such as a teacher yelling at a child or a boy asking a girl on a date and being told "No thank you." In the third frame, a feeling is shown. The character feels angry or sad or okay. The feeling is labeled beneath the drawing. Do each cartoon with your child. Ask him to describe what is happening in the first frame and how the character ends up feeling in the last frame. Then direct his attention to the middle frame. In the middle frame, the character is drawn with a

thought bubble above his head. Tell him that when something bad happens, it is the middle frame that is the most important step. Explain that the things that he says to himself determine how he feels.

After explaining the first cartoon strip, give him the series of cartoons that follow. Have him fill in the thought bubble so that the first frame and the third frame make sense together. The cartoon technique, because it is graphic, is particularly useful to help younger children visualize the connection between thoughts and feelings, and it does not require the use of words like *adversity, beliefs,* or *conse-*

quences. If your child is a teenager, you can use the ABC language, but make sure to explain each term very clearly.

ABC: Matching Thoughts to Feelings. Tell your child that her job is to draw a line connecting each thought with the feeling that goes with it. You can say, for example, "If you got into a fight with your best friend, you could have different thoughts about the fight. Each thought would make you feel a different way. I want you to imagine that you really did get into a fight and that you were thinking each of these thoughts. Then I want you to draw a line from each thought to how it would make you feel."

1. You get into a fight with your best friend.

Thoughts	*Feelings*
Now I don't have any friends.	Mad
My friend was being mean to me on purpose.	Okay
We'll make up and be friends again soon.	Sad

2. You get a low mark on your spelling test.

Thoughts	*Feelings*
I'm going to get in big trouble at home.	Okay
I've been goofing off too much instead of studying.	Scared
I can work hard and do better on the next test.	Guilty

3. Your older brother is allowed to stay up late to watch a movie and you aren't.

Thoughts	*Feelings*
I'm never allowed to do anything fun.	Mad
They love him more than me.	Okay
They took me to the amusement park and not him.	Sad

ABC Verbal Examples. Once your child gets the idea from the cartoons and matching exercise that thoughts, rather than adversity, directly cause feelings, work through each of the following verbal examples with him. After each example, have him explain it to you in his own words. Pay close attention to whether he describes the connection between beliefs and feelings. After he explains it in his own words, ask him the questions at the end of each example.

Adversity: Today was my birthday and I had a party for a lot of the kids in my class. Right after we ate the cake, a bunch of my friends started whispering and they wouldn't tell me what they were saying.

Beliefs: They're such jerks. It's my party and they're telling secrets about me. I wish I never invited them.

Consequences: I got really mad at them and asked my mom if I could tell them to leave.

Ask your child why the boy felt mad. Why did he want the kids to leave his party? If he thought that the kids were whispering because they had a birthday surprise for him, how do you think the boy would have felt? Would he have wanted his mother to make them leave?

Adversity: My favorite teacher, Mrs. O'Leary, left to have a baby, and I don't like our new teacher, Mr. Watts. Yesterday he asked me to come to the front of the class and solve a fraction problem. I got it wrong and he said, right in front of the whole class, that I needed to spend more time on my studies and less time on daydreaming.

Beliefs: Mr. Watts has it in for me. He's going to pick on me all year and now everybody thinks I'm a loser.

Consequences: I felt really stupid. I wanted to just get up and leave and never come back. My face turned all red and I couldn't stop it.

Why did this boy want to leave and never come back? Why did his face turn red? Did he want to leave because he got the fraction problem wrong? Why did he feel stupid? How do you think he would have felt if he believed that other kids in the class thought it was mean of Mr. Watts to scold him in front of the whole class?

Problem:

Thought

Thought

Thought

Adversity: Most of my friends are real skinny. Especially Barb and Megan. All the boys like them. No matter how little I eat, I can't get skinny. I even tried to just eat carrots and stuff for a week, but by nighttime I'd be so hungry that I'd end up eating dinner like I always do.

Beliefs: I'm such a pig. I don't have any willpower. I'm never going to have a boyfriend. I just better face it. No guy is ever going to want to go out with me. Fat pigs aren't popular.

Consequences: I felt so bad. Really, really bad. I would have started crying, but I was still at school and I didn't want anyone to see me cry. When I got home, I just ran up to my room and then I started to cry. My mom wanted to talk to me, but I told her to leave me alone. I didn't even want to look in the mirror anymore.

Why did this girl feel so bad? Was it because her friends were skinny and she wasn't? If you believed that no one would ever want to go out with you, how do you think you would feel? What might another person say to herself in this situation? How do you think this would make her feel?

Real-Life ABCs. When you start tomorrow, spend a few minutes reviewing the adversity-beliefs-consequences connection and review an example or two. Then, ask him for an example from his own life. It is important to stress that the example does not have to be a time in which something horrible happened. Rather, it could be any time in which he felt sad or mad or embarrassed or afraid or acted in a way he didn't like — was nasty to a friend or gave up easily — even if he didn't feel this way or act this way for long. Then help him identify his beliefs and the consequences of those beliefs. Try to work through at least three real-life examples this way. Use the blank cartoon work-sheets (*opposite*) and ask your child to first describe in words what happened and how he felt and acted. Then, together, illustrate it in the cartoon frames and record the beliefs in the thought bubble.

Once your child works his way through the real-life ABC sequence with little prompting from you, you can move on to changing your child's explanatory style in the next chapter.

11

Changing Your Child's Explanatory Style

ONCE YOUR CHILD SEES the connection between what he thinks and how he feels, you can focus on the most crucial aspect of his thinking, his explanatory style. Before you teach these skills to your child, have him fill out the CASQ in chapter 7, if he hasn't done so already. The CASQ will tell you how optimistic or pessimistic your child is. The skills in this section are a must for children who score below the 50th percentile in either their G − B score or their Total B score. Even if your child scores in the optimistic range, you may still find it helpful to teach him these skills, since no one will ever teach them to him in school and they will come in handy when he faces the challenges and setbacks of puberty.

Before you undertake to teach these skills to your child, practice the adult version of the skills first. A child's pessimism is partly learned from the adults he respects and spends the most time with — parents, teachers, and coaches. Your children are sponges, they soak up both what you say and how you say it. So one way to help your child is for you to acquire the skills that keep your own pessimism at bay.

YOUR OWN EXPLANATORY STYLE

You will remember that there are three critical dimensions of explanatory style: permanence, pervasiveness, and personalization. A pessimistic person believes that setbacks are unchangeable and will undermine many areas of her life. She believes that she — not circumstances, not chance, not others — is the sole cause of these setbacks. The most pessimistic people believe that they suffer from a characterological flaw that will doom them to a life of missed opportunities, failed relationships, mediocrity, and loss. And even when they recognize that a problem is not their own fault, they still see the situation as unchangeable and so do not struggle to change it.

You have already begun to acquire the skills of changing pessimism to optimism by recognizing the close link between what you think and how you feel. Now you are ready to refine your ability to detect and change your explanatory style. A series of events and explanations follows. For each example, label the explanation according to the three dimensions of explanatory style. Remember, each dimension is a continuum. An explanation falls on either the permanent or the temporary side of the continuum; on either the pervasive or the specific side of the continuum; and on either the personal or the impersonal side of the continuum. After each example, rate whether the explanation is more permanent or more temporary, more pervasive or more specific, and more personal or more impersonal. This is not a simple task, so take your time. Here are some brief definitions of each dimension to help you make the ratings.

> Permanent = the cause is something that will persist
> Temporary = the cause is changeable or transient
> Pervasive = the cause will affect many situations
> Specific = the cause will affect only a few situations
> Personal = I am the cause
> Impersonal = the cause is something about other
> people or circumstances

1. *Event:* My husband and I agreed that he would pick my mother up at the airport, since I had to work late that night and he didn't. Then, a couple of hours before her scheduled arrival, he

called me at work to tell me that he couldn't leave, and that I'd have to go in his place.

Explanation: He's always doing things like this. He can't be trusted for anything.

    a. Is this explanation more permanent or more temporary?
    b. Is this explanation more pervasive or more specific?
    c. Is this explanation more personal or more impersonal (for the woman making the explanation)?

2. *Event:* I recently found out that my son has been taking drugs for the past six months. I was informed by a guidance counselor at his school.

    Explanation: I've been so busy on this new project that I haven't made any time for Joey. He must be doing this because I've been so negligent lately.

    a. Is this explanation more permanent or more temporary?
    b. Is this explanation more pervasive or more specific?
    c. Is this explanation more personal or more impersonal?

3. *Event:* My girlfriend called me last night and told me that she wanted more space.

    Explanation: There she goes again. She's in one of her moods. It'll pass in a week. They always do.

    a. Is this explanation more permanent or more temporary?
    b. Is this explanation more pervasive or more specific?
    c. Is this explanation more personal or more impersonal (from the boy's point of view)?

In the first example, the explanation is fairly permanent ("He's *always* doing things like this"). It is on the pervasive side of the scale — if he can't be trusted for anything, his lack of trustworthiness will affect many situations. And it is his fault, not hers — impersonal.

In the second example, the explanation is more temporary. She has been caught up in a new project, but this explanation does not imply that the situation will never change. It is on the pervasive side of the scale. Being too busy at work affects many of the situations a person encounters. It did affect her relation with her son and her work life. And it is personal. She believes that her son's drug problem was caused by her negligence.

In the last example, the explanation is temporary (moods are fleeting), pervasive (moods affect many situations) and impersonal (it is her mood, not his).

Now work through two ABC examples from your life and label the beliefs according to the dimensions of explanatory style. In each case, if you identify a pessimistic belief, see if you can generate a more optimistic one as well.

EVENT 1:

Explanation:

permanent————————————————temporary
pervasive————————————————specific
personal————————————————impersonal

EVENT 2:

Explanation:

permanent————————————————temporary
pervasive————————————————specific
personal————————————————impersonal

TEACHING EXPLANATORY STYLE TO YOUR CHILD

Optimism. Begin by introducing the concepts of optimism and pessimism. Ask your child to define these terms his own way and to describe in as much detail as he can the characteristics of an optimist and a pessimist. How do an optimist and a pessimist look, think, and act? One seventh-grader described a pessimist this way: "Down, down, down. They look down. They think down. And they act down. They aren't too fun to be around." Make the point that just as people have a particular style of dressing, they also have a particular style of thinking about things. But if someone tends to see the downside and this makes them feel bad, they can learn to see the upside of situations as well.

Now read the following skits together. Gloomy Greg and Hopeful Holly are the characters that represent pessimism and optimism. Read both skits aloud and then discuss the differences between Greg and Holly.

Gloomy Greg Skips the Tryouts

Jeff: Hey Greg! Did you see the poster in the hall? Basketball tryouts are starting next week.

Greg: Yeah? Well, who cares anyway.

Jeff: I do. I mean, I thought we could try out. It would be really cool to be on a school team. You get uniforms and everything. What do you think?

Greg: About what?

Jeff: Well, do you think we're tall enough to play?

Greg: Nah. We're just about the shortest sixth-graders. Most of the other guys are at least twice our height!

Jeff: Well, there's always a chance we'd grow, right?

Greg: No way. And even if we did grow, all the other guys would grow too, so we'd still be the shortest. Anyway, even if we were tall enough to play, I never get picked for anything.

Jeff: Yeah. Well, maybe if we practiced this week it would help. I've got a hoop in my back yard.

Greg: Stop dreaming. We'd just be wasting our time. We'd have to practice for years for it to do us any good. And even then we probably wouldn't make it. Give it up.

Jeff: Oh, maybe you're right, Greg. Maybe we should wait for baseball this spring.

Greg: Are you kidding? We don't stand a chance. Baseball is even harder than basketball. And anyway, most of the kids who play basketball are on the baseball team. By spring they're in even better shape.

Hopeful Holly Goes for It

Jenny: Hey Holly! Did you see the poster in the hall? Basketball tryouts are starting next week.

Holly: Great! Do you want to try out?

Jenny: Yeah, I think it would be really cool to be on a school team. You get uniforms and everything. What do you think?

Holly: About what?

Jenny: Well, do you think we're good enough to play?

Holly: I think so. Some of the other girls are pretty big, but maybe we're faster.

Jenny: And we can work on dribbling and shooting at my house after school.

Holly: Sure! We might even hit a growth spurt this year and end up being the tallest on the team. That'd be pretty cool. Remember when Tanya grew about three inches over the summer? Let's hope that happens to us.

Jenny: Yeah. Well, maybe if we practiced this week it would help. I've got a hoop in my back yard.

Holly: That's a good idea. My brother plays for the high school team. Maybe I can ask him to come over and give us some pointers. I'll meet you at your locker after school, okay?

After you've read the skits with your child, ask her what she noticed about Gloomy Greg and Hopeful Holly. Highlight the fact that Gloomy Greg always sees the negative side of a situation, while Hopeful Holly sees the positive. Ask your child what it would feel like to be Greg and Holly and discuss which one they'd rather have for a friend. Be open with your child and tell her about a time when you felt pessimistic. Explain to her the effect your pessimism had on your mood and your perseverance. Then ask your child to share a time when she felt pessimistic, and contrast the consequences of pessimism with the consequences of optimism.

Accuracy of Beliefs. Once your child understands the distinction between optimism and pessimism, you can tackle accuracy.

There are two crucial issues involved. The first is personal responsibility. Some parents, when they first hear that I teach children how to be more optimistic, and that this entails helping them to judge whether or not they are responsible for the things that go wrong in their life, believe that I am teaching children to shirk responsibility. "I don't want my kid to go around blaming everybody else when things go wrong," these parents say. I agree. It is simple-minded and misguided to believe that teaching children to say "It's not my fault. I didn't do that" is going to help them live more successful lives. On the contrary, it is very helpful to teach children to see that there are many contributing causes to any problem and to take responsibility for what they have contributed to the problem, without blaming themselves for things out of their control.

The second issue is "empty optimism." Some parents, when they hear that our program is coming to their child's school, say, "I don't want my child to walk around the world saying 'Everything is wonderful,' 'The world is wonderful,' 'I am wonderful.' That won't do him any good at all. Everything isn't always wonderful and he's got to learn that." They are right. Repeating cheery thoughts over and over again is not going to enable you to live up to, or surpass, your potential. Hence much of what passes for "positive thinking" is indeed footless.

Positive thinking often involves trying to believe upbeat statements such as "Every day, in every way, I'm getting better and better" in the absence of evidence, or even in the face of contrary evidence. Many educated people, trained in skeptical thinking, cannot manage this kind of boosterism and do not want their children to acquire it. Again, I agree. Learned optimism, in contrast, is about accuracy.

We have found that merely repeating positive statements to yourself does not raise mood or achievement very much, if at all. We teach children to think accurately about real problems. Thinking accurately does not mean thinking pessimistically about real problems. There are high and specific costs of pessimism: children who believe that nothing they do matters, who believe that their problems are unchangeable and forever, will not search to find solutions. Negative beliefs such as these are usually inaccurate. Many children catastrophize and see the worst possible causes; from all the potential causes, they select the one with the direst implications. One of the most effective techniques in disputation is for your child to search for evidence pointing to the distortions in his catastrophic explanations. Most of the time he will have reality on his side. Learned optimism works not through an unjustifiable positivity about the world but through the power of "nonnegative" thinking.

Children who are prone to depression focus on the worst-case scenario, about their own troubles and about the problems of the world. They blame themselves for the uncontrollable; they gravitate to the most negative interpretation. It is difficult for them even to consider more-optimistic and more-accurate alternatives. Such children can learn to think about other factors that may have contributed to the problem, so that they can problem-solve by focusing their energy on the parts of the problem that are under their control. Tyhema, a seventh-grader in our program, describes it well.

> I learned to think of each problem like a pizza pie. My job was to make each slice equal one of the things that caused the problem to happen. Like when I get into a fight with my brother, instead of just thinking that it's all his fault or all my fault, I have to try to think up all the reasons we started fighting. It's like I have the pizza in my head, and I figure out how many slices to cut it into. It was really hard to do at first, 'cause I would just think up one reason and then that would be it. But now I can come up with lots and lots of reasons and that's good, because then I don't blame myself or my brother too much. Oh, and then I can figure out which slices I ought to change and which I can't do anything about. Like with my brother, I can stop teasing him 'cause that makes him mad. But I can't do anything about his getting into trouble with my mom. When that happens he gets in a real nasty mood, and if I'm around, he sometimes takes it out on me. Now I just stay out of his way when he's nasty.

PERMANENCE

Once your child understands the general issue of optimism versus pessimism and the importance of accurate explanations of what goes wrong, you can teach him to pay close attention to his explanatory style. The first dimension to introduce is permanence, the most important dimension for resilience.[1] Tell him that when something bad happens, we always try to explain to ourselves why it happened and we try to foresee the repercussions. Sometimes we may believe that the problem is going to last forever and that we can't do anything to make it better. Such "Permanent" thoughts make us feel down and ready to give up without even trying. In contrast, if we believe that the situation is temporary and changeable, then we will feel energized and strive to find a way to change it.

This is the most crucial dimension of explanatory style, and you should spend solid time working with your child on it until she has it down cold. There are three ways to practice this with your child: using the Hopeful Holly and Gloomy Greg skits, using cartoons, and using real-life explanations. Because permanence is so important to optimism, you should teach all three.

Using the Gloomy Greg and Hopeful Holly Skits. Read the "Gloomy Greg at the School Dance" skit aloud and then ask your child to say which of Greg's thoughts are Permanent and which are Temporary. Then read the "Hopeful Holly at the School Dance" skit and have your child contrast Greg's thoughts to Holly's. Link the thoughts to the consequences that follow so your child understands that pessimism and optimism change how he feels and acts.

Gloomy Greg at the School Dance

Greg: Hey Cindy, do you want to dance?

Cindy: No thanks. I'm tired.

Greg [*thinks to himself*]: Way to go! I'm such a loser. Why did I even bother to ask her to dance? I never have any fun at these things. I should have known she'd say no. She's popular and I'm a geek. No one's ever going to dance with me. I always get shot down. I'm just never going to be cool enough. I don't know why I even bothered coming to the dance. They're always really boring.

[*Greg sits down on a bench and looks very sad.*]

Here are the points to emphasize: When Greg thinks "I'm such a loser" and "No one's ever going to dance with me" and "[Dances are] always really boring," he is explaining his rejection by Cindy with Permanent thoughts. This causes Greg to feel sad, and he decides to throw in the towel and not ask anyone else to dance. Since Greg spends the rest of the night sitting on a bench, he is sure to feel bored and have an even worse time. Make it clear to your child that when someone truly believes that nothing's going to get any better, then it makes sense to give up and stop trying. But the problem is that there are often actions one can take to make things better. So if your thoughts are causing you to give up, it's much harder to make things better for yourself.

Hopeful Holly at the School Dance

Holly: Do you want to dance?

Joe: No thanks.

Holly [*thinks to herself*]: Ugh! That's embarrassing. I hate it when that happens. I guess Joe just isn't into dancing tonight. I'll try to ask someone else. [*speaks to Sammy*] Hey Sammy, how about a dance?

Sammy: No thanks, Holly.

Holly [*thinks to herself*]: Oh, man. Another no. I'm in a rut. Maybe I wasn't friendly enough. Okay, I'll give it another shot, but this time I'll smile nice and big and I'll be real friendly. [*speaks to Fred, with big, warm smile*] Hi, Fred. Are you having a good time?

Fred: Yeah. I can't believe that this is the smelly old gym. They really made it look cool.

Holly: Yeah. I heard that Mr. Rothera spent all week getting it to look like this. I really like that shirt. Is it new?

Fred: This one? Oh, thanks. Yeah, I just got it this weekend. I went to that new store that opened in the mall.

Holly: Oh, yeah, I heard about it, but I haven't gone there yet. Hey, I really like this song. Do you want to dance?

Fred: Oh, okay. Sure.

Holly understands her difficulty finding a dance partner differently than Greg does. She thinks, "Joe just isn't into dancing tonight" and "I wasn't friendly enough." These thoughts are about a temporary and changeable situation. Joe might not be in the mood to dance, but that doesn't mean other boys won't be. And if Holly believes that she wasn't friendly enough the second time, then she can be friendlier the third time. Unlike Greg, Holly keeps trying. Ask your child what enabled Holly to keep trying to find a dance partner when Greg gave up. If she attributes it to "facts" such as "I guess Holly is more

popular than Greg" or "Greg must be ugly," review the ABC connection with her. Do not dismiss the "facts"; certainly they matter, but help her understand that how a person interprets the facts matters just as much, if not more.

Using Cartoons. After your child has labeled the thoughts in the skits, use the cartoon on the previous page and those that follow to practice generating Temporary versus Permanent thoughts. In the first cartoon, a boy is being picked on by other children. They shout, "We

said, get out of here, wimp!" In the second frame, one of the thought bubbles is labeled Permanent Thoughts and the other Temporary Thoughts. Provided is one Permanent thought: "They are always picking on me." Ask your child for another Permanent thought that might explain why this boy is being excluded (for example, "I never have any friends," "No one likes me," "I never fit in"). Then, in the Temporary bubble, ask your child for two Temporary thoughts about the situation. Temporary thoughts include "They're being mean to

me today," "They're mad at me," "I've been nasty a lot lately." In the third frame are two faces. After your child has named a Permanent thought, ask him to complete the face to show how this thought would make the character feel, and ask him to describe what the character would do. So, in "They are always picking on me," the boy would feel very sad and lonely, and he would avoid these kids for a long time. Then, do the same for a Temporary thought about the problem. "They're being mean to me today" may make the boy feel a bit sad, but certainly not as sad as the Permanent thoughts. He might avoid these kids for the rest of the day, but later he will reapproach them.

Now use the two other cartoons, following the same approach as described in the previous example.

Using Real-Life ABCs. Now you are ready to use the ABC (adversity-belief-consequence) sheets included here to analyze examples from your child's life. This time the format is a little different. First, ask him to record a recent adversity. Remember, he should record only the who, what, when, and where. Ask him to tell you what his beliefs were. If it is a Permanent belief, record it in the space marked Permanent Belief. If it is a Temporary belief, record it in that space. Next, in the space provided, ask him to record the consequences this thought generated. Then, using the same situation, ask him to come up with an example of an opposite belief (Temporary, if his first belief was Permanent, or Permanent, if his first belief was Temporary). Record it on the sheet and talk about the consequences this thought would lead to.

Pay attention to whether the consequences follow from the beliefs your child generates. If he writes down "I'm always going to be an outcast" as his Permanent belief but says he would feel okay, stop and ask him about this. Say, "If you one hundred percent believed that you'd always be an outcast, never have any friends for the rest of your life, do you really think you'd feel okay? A child who firmly believed this would feel dejected and despairing." Use at least three examples from your child's life before moving on to the next section.

1. *Adversity:* _____
   _____

   Permanent Belief: _____

   Consequences: _____

   Temporary Belief: _____

   Consequences: _____

2. *Adversity:* _____
   _____

   Permanent Belief: _____

   Consequences: _____

   Temporary Belief: _____

   Consequences: _____

3. *Adversity:* _____
   _____

   Permanent Belief: _____

   Consequences: _____

   Temporary Belief: _____

   Consequences: _____

PERSONALIZATION

Children at risk for depression blame themselves whenever things go awry. Though most real problems are caused by a complex set of contributing factors, these children often think in black and white and shoulder the entire blame. They become overwhelmed with guilt and feelings of worthlessness, which causes them to withdraw from friends and family. This cycle further increases their risk for depression.

In this section you will help your child develop a sophisticated way of understanding how much blame he deserves. The first step is to teach him to recognize his style of blaming. There are two patterns you want to look for. Whenever problems arise, does your child always assume that he is to blame? Does he always say, "It's my fault"? Pay close attention to how he places blame for problems that arise in the family and among his friends. Second, does your child attribute the blame to his behavior or to his character? Behavior is changeable, character is not. Consider the following examples. In the first one, Jeremy, a seventh-grader in our program, describes how he understands the problems he is having with his older brother.

Richard and I fight a lot. A real lot. It seems like ever since he turned sixteen, he just doesn't want to have anything to do with me anymore. It gets really bad when his friends are around. Then he just acts like I don't even exist. When we are alone, at least, he talks to me, though most of the time it's to tell me that I'm a brat or something.

When Richard and I fight, I try to figure out why he is being so mean. My mom says that it's "adolescence" and that it may take a while for him to be back to his old self. I know what she means 'cause my friend Loren has an older brother too and I've seen him just get on Loren's case for every little thing. And stupid things, too, like not answering the phone right or not putting a CD back in the exact spot it was.

But sometimes I think it's partly my fault too. Like the other day I asked if I could wear his Steelers jacket and he said I could. I couldn't believe it 'cause he almost never takes that thing off. And the other time I asked if I could wear it he just laughed at me and told me to get a life. So I wore it over a friend's house and we were playing football and I got hot so I took it off. Anyway, I left it there by mistake and when I got home he asked me for it and I didn't have it and he went ballistic. I felt really bad. I think I probably do little things like that a lot. You know, forget things or not give his stuff back right away. I'm going to try real hard to be more careful. At least that way maybe things will go a little better.

In Jeremy's search to understand the source of conflict, he has come to believe that he has contributed to the problem and that his contribution is a particular behavior. This is called "behavioral self-blame." Since behaviors are changeable, behavioral self-blame leads to action to try to rectify the problem. Behavioral self-blame, because it is temporary, forestalls despair and hopelessness. Contrast Jeremy's interpretation to Talia's understanding of the difficulty she is having with her mother.

My mom and I fight more and more. My mom and my sister and I used to have a lot of fun together — like take canoes out on this river by my house, and once we rented Rollerblades and my mom kept pretending to fall down out of control. It was really funny. But we don't have fun like that anymore. Last Saturday we drove to that place where people who don't use electricity live, out in the country — I think they're called Hamish or something. It was horrible. It started out okay. But then I ruined everything. My mom was driving and Sarah and I were in the back. Sarah was whispering to her doll and I started to tease her, just a little though. My mom told me to stop, but I didn't. I kept on whispering to Sarah but real quiet so my mom couldn't hear me. Anyways, Sarah then started crying and my mom got really mad. She started yelling at me and said that if I didn't knock it off, she would turn the car around and we'd stay home.

I felt really bad. I always make my mom mad. It seems like there's just something about me that ruins everything. Like no matter what, I'm always going to make my mom mad. I must be just bad or something 'cause Sarah isn't like me. Can a kid just be bad?

Talia, like Jeremy, is blaming herself for the conflict. But Talia is entertaining the idea that she is "just bad." In contrast to Jeremy, Talia is not only blaming a specific behavior — teasing Sarah may indeed be the trigger for her mother's upset — but also indicting her whole character: "I must be just bad." "Characterological self-blame" is worse than behavioral self-blame. Behaviors are changeable, but character isn't. Jeremy can change the behavior that he believes is the source of the problem. Talia is stuck. Talia, then, believes not only that she is the cause of the turmoil, but also that there is nothing she can do about it — hopelessness and helplessness. As you work with your child, keep in mind that personal and unchangeable explanations for bad events, particularly regarding one's character, are highly pessimistic.

The same three activities that you used to teach your child the permanence dimension will be used for personalization. For younger children, we use two simple terms. "Because of Me" thoughts represent self-blame (internality). "Because of Someone or Something Else" thoughts represent externality. Keep the discussion of these terms value-free. Don't say "It's better to believe Something Else thoughts than Because of Me thoughts" or "If you have Because of Me thoughts then you're being like Gloomy Greg." You do not want to communicate to your child that it is better to ascribe blame to other people or to circumstances than it is to herself. And it would be equally unwise to communicate to your child that it is better to see oneself as the cause of all problems. In extremes, neither is accurate and neither is healthy. Together you and your child want to discover her pattern and assess the consequences of this pattern. Then you want to begin to evaluate the accuracy of your child's habitual style.

Using the *Gloomy Greg* and *Hopeful Holly* Skits. First, explain the personalization dimension. Keep it simple. Tell your child that when things go wrong, we may believe that we caused the bad thing or we may believe that it was caused by someone else or something else. Use this example to show the difference.

Jennifer comes home from school and says to her mother that she wants to have dinner at Holly's house. Her mom says angrily, "No, you certainly cannot. I've already made tonight's dinner. You can't just waltz in here and announce your plans for the evening and expect us all to accommodate you." Jennifer can think of a lot of things about why her mom got angry. If she thinks, "I didn't ask right; I should have asked more nicely," this is a Because of Me thought. Jennifer believes her mother is angry because she didn't ask to go to Holly's in the correct manner. Instead, if Jennifer thinks, "Uh-oh. Mom must have had one of those days. She's in that mood," this is a Because of Someone or Something Else thought. Jennifer believes that her mother is angry because she had a tough day.

Tell your child that you want to practice the two types of thoughts. Read the Gloomy Greg skit and then ask your child to circle the Because of Me thoughts.

Gloomy Greg Drops the Ball

Greg's flag football team loses to Clifton Heights. At dinner that night, his father asks about the game.

Dad: So, Mom tells me you had a tough loss today. Sorry to hear it, kiddo.
Greg: Yeah, we got smeared. We could've won, too. I blew it.
Dad: What do you mean? What happened?
Greg: Toby passed it to me and nobody was even around and I dropped it. I should have scored a touchdown, but instead I dropped the ball. We would have won, too.
Dad: That's too bad. That couldn't have been the only reason you lost, though. What was the score?
Greg: It was twenty-one to seven, I think. We would have won if it wasn't for me. I messed it up every time I got the ball. I stink

at football. I'm never going to be any good. I'm going to quit. Maybe then we'd win a game.

Greg takes the entire responsibility for the loss. Look at the thoughts your child circled. "I blew it," "I should have scored a touchdown, but instead I dropped the ball. We would have won, too," "We would have won if it wasn't for me," "I messed it up every time I got the ball," "I stink at football," and "I'm never going to be any good" are all Because of Me thoughts. Ask your child the following questions: Do you think Greg's beliefs about why the team lost are accurate? If the team lost 21 to 7, could one person on the team have made all of the mistakes? When a team loses a game, what might some of the other reasons be? Did Greg want to quit the team because his team lost or for some other reason? Does Greg think he can do anything to improve his skill? Why not? Tell your child that when someone takes *all* the blame for bad things, this can make the child feel very bad about himself and he may decide to give up.

Now read the Hopeful Holly skit and compare the thoughts Holly has to the ones Greg had. Ask your child to underline all the Because of Someone or Something Else thoughts and to circle all the Because of Me thoughts.

Hopeful Holly Drops the Ball

Holly's kickball team loses to the Primos' team. At dinner that night, her father asks about the game.

Dad: So, Mom tells me you had a tough loss today. Sorry to hear it, kiddo.

Holly: Yeah, we got smeared. We could've won, too. We really stunk today.

Dad: What do you mean? What happened?

Holly: Well, this girl kicked a pop-up and it was right at me and I dropped it. I couldn't believe it. It was right in my hands and I blew it. I was so embarrassed.

Dad: That's too bad. That couldn't have been the only reason you lost, though. What was the score?

Holly: It was ten to four, I think. We all played pretty bad. Ms.

Cross wasn't too happy. Sharon dropped the ball a couple of times. Dana didn't even get on base and she usually kicks homers, and Kimberly dropped a pop-up too. And they have this really big girl on their team and she killed the ball. She hit like three home runs. Ms. Cross says we need to concentrate more in the field.

Holly is more evenhanded than Greg in her assessment of the loss. She takes responsibility for her mistakes, but she is also able to blame the rest of the team. She recognizes a fact about the opposing team which contributed to their success. Look at the thoughts your child underlined. "We all played pretty bad," "Sharon dropped the ball a couple of times," "Dana didn't even get on base and she usually kicks homers, and Kimberly dropped a pop-up too," and "They have this really big girl on their team and she killed the ball" are all examples of Because of Someone Else thoughts. "I dropped it. I couldn't believe it. It was right in my hands and I blew it" is a Because of Me thought.

Ask your child the following questions: Do you think Greg or Holly is seeing the situation more realistically? Which one do you think enjoys playing on the team more? Do you think Holly will quit the kickball team? Why not? Which child are you more like? Tell your child that you want her to take responsibility for the things she does that contribute to a problem, but that you don't want her to blame herself for things that weren't her fault. Tell your child that children who can be like Hopeful Holly and can say "this part was my fault, these parts weren't my fault" feel good about themselves and work hard to figure out how to make sure they don't contribute to the problem again. Children who are more like Gloomy Greg and say "it's all my fault" feel bad about themselves and usually decide to give up without even trying to correct the problem.

If you are concerned that your child does not take enough responsibility for problems, or if your child is angry a lot, read the following skit together. After you have read the skit, discuss the questions in the previous paragraph, including Angry Adam as the main character — for example, Who sees the situation more realistically: Greg, Adam, or Holly? Who do you think has more fun on the team?

Angry Adam Misses the Shot

Adam's soccer team loses to the Tigers. At dinner that night, his father asks about the game.

Dad: So, Mom tells me you had a tough loss today. Sorry to hear it, kiddo.

Adam: Yeah, we got smeared. We could've won, too. Sam really blew it.

Dad: What do you mean? What happened?

Adam: Sam really can't play goalie. He let four shots go by. He didn't even stop the ones he dove for.

Dad: That's too bad. That couldn't have been the only reason you lost, though. What was the score?

Adam: Five to four. We would have won if it wasn't for Barry. He missed the penalty shot. He's such a spaz. I told him to let me make it but the coach said it was his turn. I took a penalty shot earlier — but I missed it because Frank kept telling me what to do and I couldn't concentrate. I'm on the worst team ever.

Using Cartoons. Next, use the cartoon worksheets to practice both kinds of beliefs. These worksheets are similar to the ones you used for the permanence dimension, except the thought bubbles are labeled "Because of Me" and "Because of Someone or Something Else." In the first example, the girl finds out that her friend just got an invitation to Mike's party and she did not. The Because of Me thought is "I'm a geek and no one likes to hang out with geeks." Ask your child to write down one other Because of Me thought and then to fill in the face to show how this would make the girl feel. Then ask your child to come up with two Because of Someone or Something Else thoughts and to record them in the space provided. Then have him draw a face in the circle to show how this thought would make the character feel, and ask him to describe what the character would do.

Now ask your child to respond to the other two cartoons in the same way. Remember to make sure the consequences follow logically from the thoughts generated.

Using Real-Life ABCs. Now your child is ready to use the ABC format. Ask him to provide an adversity of his own and his initial beliefs about the situation. Ask him whether his belief is a Because of Me thought or a Because of Someone or Something Else thought. Have him record it in the appropriate space, along with the consequences this thought generated. If the initial thoughts were Because of Me, ask him to think of some Because of Someone or Something Else thoughts and record them on the sheet. Then ask him how he would feel and act if he believed these thoughts instead. Record the consequences on the sheet as well. If the initial thoughts were external, go through the situation again, focusing on internal thoughts instead.

1. *Adversity:* _____

_____

Because of Me Belief: _____

Consequences: _____

Because of Someone or Something Else Belief: _____

Consequences: _____

2. *Adversity:* _____

_____

Because of Me Belief: _____

Consequences: _____

Because of Someone or Something Else Belief: _____

Consequences: _____

3. *Adversity:* _____

_____

Because of Me Belief: _____

Consequences: _____

Because of Someone or Something Else Belief: _____

Consequences: _____

The Pie Game. The final activity to use with your child is called the pie game. This game is particularly useful for children who tend to see their contribution to problems as black or white and are having difficulty allocating partial blame.

Below is a picture of a pie. Your child's job is to slice the pie so that each slice represents one of the causes that contributed to the problem. He should write each cause on a slice. Go over the first example with him.

> Melanie, a sixth-grader in our program, was given the "silent treatment" by some of her friends. Initially she could think of only one reason: "They don't like me anymore and they're dropping me." She had a hard time thinking of any other reasons, partly because she was feeling so sad about having no friends.
>
> When we gave Melanie a picture of a pie like the one below, she was able to slice the pie into five pieces. She labeled each one with a possible cause: "They're getting back at me 'cause I told Scott that Tyeshia likes him," "Tyeshia turned them against me," "They're mad because Carolyn invited me to the shore and not them," "I was calling Julie 'ski-slope nose' and they're sticking up for her," and "They're immature."

Initially, you will have to help your child consider a range of possibilities. We did this with Melanie by asking questions that guided her thinking: Did anything happen before they gave you the silent treatment? Were you in a fight? Do they act like this all the time?

Go over Melanie's example with your child. Explain that at first Melanie could think of only one explanation of her getting the silent treatment. But then, when she thought about it more, she could come up with five different causes, each of which may have partly led her friends to ignore her. Tell your child that this helped Melanie decide what she wanted to do about the problem.

Ask your child how Melanie probably felt when she believed they would never be her friends again. What did she probably do? Then ask your child if he thinks she felt differently after she sliced the pie. Make sure your child understands that once Melanie thought of the many contributing factors, she was in a better position to problem-solve. She can apologize to Tyeshia for telling her secret to Scott. She can talk to her friends about her trip to the shore with Carolyn. She can find out if Julie's feelings were hurt when she teased her.

Now work through two examples from your child's life. First, ask your child to describe the adversity and record it in the space provided. Then ask him to come up with as many possible causes as he can. Sometimes children believe the goal of this activity is to make as many slices as possible, so they generate many unreasonable causes. To avoid this misunderstanding, tell your child that the goal is to divide

the pie into as many realistic slices as possible. Every time he mentions a possible cause, have him draw a slice and write the cause inside it. For children who tend to see problems as all their fault or never their fault, you will have to help them consider a more diverse array of causes. You can do so by asking leading questions like the ones we just described. Once he has sliced the pie, number each of the slices. Ask him to label each slice along the permanence and personalization dimensions. There is a space to record this at the bottom of the worksheet. If your child suggests mainly Permanent and Because of Me thoughts, point this out to him and ask him to try to think of some Temporary and Because of Someone or Something Else thoughts.

1. The adversity was _____

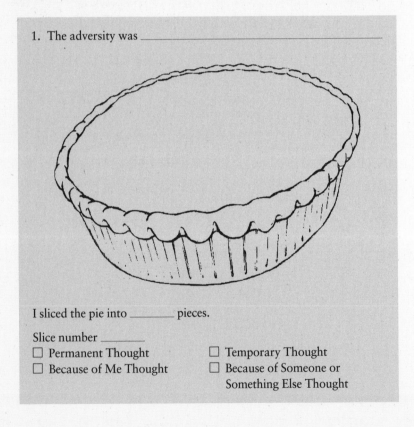

I sliced the pie into _____ pieces.

Slice number _____
☐ Permanent Thought   ☐ Temporary Thought
☐ Because of Me Thought   ☐ Because of Someone or
                                   Something Else Thought

Slice number _____
☐ Permanent Thought
☐ Because of Me Thought

☐ Temporary Thought
☐ Because of Someone or
   Something Else Thought

Slice number _____
☐ Permanent Thought
☐ Because of Me Thought

☐ Temporary Thought
☐ Because of Someone or
   Something Else Thought

Slice number _____
☐ Permanent Thought
☐ Because of Me Thought

☐ Temporary Thought
☐ Because of Someone or
   Something Else Thought

Slice number _____
☐ Permanent Thought
☐ Because of Me Thought

☐ Temporary Thought
☐ Because of Someone or
   Something Else Thought

Slice number _____
☐ Permanent Thought
☐ Because of Me Thought

☐ Temporary Thought
☐ Because of Someone or
   Something Else Thought

Slice number _____
☐ Permanent Thought
☐ Because of Me Thought

☐ Temporary Thought
☐ Because of Someone or
   Something Else Thought

Slice number _____
☐ Permanent Thought
☐ Because of Me Thought

☐ Temporary Thought
☐ Because of Someone or
   Something Else Thought

2. The adversity was _____

I sliced the pie into _____ pieces.

Slice number _____
☐ Permanent Thought   ☐ Temporary Thought
☐ Because of Me Thought   ☐ Because of Someone or
                                     Something Else Thought

Slice number _____
☐ Permanent Thought   ☐ Temporary Thought
☐ Because of Me Thought   ☐ Because of Someone or
                                     Something Else Thought

Slice number _____
☐ Permanent Thought   ☐ Temporary Thought
☐ Because of Me Thought   ☐ Because of Someone or
                                     Something Else Thought

Slice number _____
☐ Permanent Thought   ☐ Temporary Thought
☐ Because of Me Thought   ☐ Because of Someone or
                                     Something Else Thought

Slice number _____
- ☐ Permanent Thought
- ☐ Because of Me Thought

- ☐ Temporary Thought
- ☐ Because of Someone or
  Something Else Thought

Slice number _____
- ☐ Permanent Thought
- ☐ Because of Me Thought

- ☐ Temporary Thought
- ☐ Because of Someone or
  Something Else Thought

Slice number _____
- ☐ Permanent Thought
- ☐ Because of Me Thought

- ☐ Temporary Thought
- ☐ Because of Someone or
  Something Else Thought

Slice number _____
- ☐ Permanent Thought
- ☐ Because of Me Thought

- ☐ Temporary Thought
- ☐ Because of Someone or
  Something Else Thought

SUMMARY

At this point your child understands that the things he says to himself directly change how he feels and acts. When something bad happens, he can "catch" his internal dialogue and predict its consequences. He may still require prompting from you ("When you got your grade back, what did you say to yourself?"), but once prompted, he can work his way through the ABCs. He can also differentiate between permanent and temporary beliefs and personal and impersonal beliefs. Finally, he has begun to consider the accuracy of his beliefs. It is the disputing of inaccurate beliefs that is the central skill of the next chapter.

12

Disputing and
Decatastrophizing

ALTHOUGH MOST ADULTS and children are naturally skilled disputers when accused by someone else, we are poor disputers when we are our own accusers. We know that others' opinions of us can be biased and wrong, yet we treat our own opinions of ourselves as indisputable. Self-disputing is a lasting and effective way to challenge the validity of your unrealistic interpretations. You expose the inaccuracy of your beliefs and you prove to yourself that your beliefs are exaggerated or even plainly false. The invalid beliefs then occur less and less frequently. This cognitive method involves treating your beliefs as hypotheses that can be tested and then changed if they prove to be inaccurate. Once you master the adult versions of disputing and decatastrophizing, you can begin to teach these skills to your child.

To beat pessimism, your own opinion of yourself needs to become the target of skepticism. Don't blindly accept your own insults. Take a step back and consider them with an open mind. If they turn out to be true, fine. Then you need to work on changing the aspects of yourself or your world that bring discontent. You may find that your beliefs about yourself aren't true, that they tend to be catastrophizations — interpretations of bad events in extremely permanent and pervasive terms. If this is so, you need to correct them.

Successful disputation requires a lot of practice. What follow are two examples of an adult's attempt to dispute her pessimistic beliefs.

Elana is the mother of a child in the Penn Prevention Program. As I got to know her, she expressed interest in using the skills we were teaching her daughter for herself. So I taught her the ABC model. The first ABC record that follows contains one of Elana's early attempts at disputing after just a few instructions on how to dispute her own pessimistic beliefs. The second shows how she handles her pessimism after practice.

I now add two elements to the ABC model, *D* and *E*. *D* stands for the disputation, the argument you make to counter your beliefs (B). *E* stands for the energization, the emotional and behavioral consequences of your disputation. The numbers in parentheses after specific beliefs and disputations are ratings (on a 1–100 scale) of how certain you are that the belief is true. The numbers in parentheses after specific consequences and energization indicate the intensity of your feelings (on a 1–100 scale). The best way to see how well a dispute works is to look at "Energization." Does the intensity of negative feelings go down?

Adversity: I'd been working on an ad campaign for several weeks. It was a big client and I knew that if my boss liked it, I had a chance of getting promoted. I submitted it to my boss but didn't hear anything for a while. One morning I get in and the proposal is sitting on my desk with a memo attached to it. All it said was "Okay. Needs work. More punch."

Beliefs: Oh, lovely. There goes the promotion (100). I killed myself on this one and all I get is "more punch." I can't be punchier (100). I might as well forget it. That was the best I can do, so I might as well quit (90). I'm not cut out for this (90).

Consequences: I was real upset. I'd describe it as half angry (80) and half really depressed (100). I didn't even look at that account again for a couple of weeks. Every time I'd start to work on it, I'd get knots in my stomach, so I'd put it aside. But I couldn't concentrate on my other stuff either. It's like the job went flat for me.

Disputation: Come on, hang in there. You'll get the promotion (20). You're the best (10). You've gotta just keep at it!

Energization: I still felt really miserable, mainly depressed still (90). My dispute didn't seem to work at all. Maybe I felt a little more into my work for a day or two, but not really. I kept thinking that I ought to quit and find another line of work.

Elana's attempts at disputing were feeble, and her mood did not improve because she did not believe her disputations. She felt as though she had given herself a facile pep talk: "Go, Elana, go!" Elana's disputations failed for the same reason most pep talks fail — they are empty positive thinking, a form of sheer boosterism. Hollow slogans are not going to change your mood, not for longer than a short period. Effective disputation requires substance. You must convince yourself that your judgments are inaccurate. Compare Elana's early attempt with this more recent one.

Adversity: Ted and I had our twenty-first wedding anniversary last week. We take turns planning something special each year, and it was Ted's turn this year. He took me to a bed-and-breakfast in town and got tickets for a play. Instead of having a good time, we ended up fighting most of the weekend. First it was about whether Mimi could start dating. Then we fought about whether we should use some of our retirement money to build a deck off the back bedroom. It seemed like we were going to spend our anniversary screaming at each other.

Beliefs: This figures. We hardly ever get any time alone together and when we do, we fight the whole time. He's just so rigid about everything (80). As far as he's concerned, once a decision is made, it's made for life. It's like he's never heard of rethinking things. He's so selfish (90). He's never willing to negotiate (80). He's always got to have his way (90). I'm sick of it!

Consequences: I was simply furious (100). I couldn't calm down. I wasn't even able to listen to him. He wanted to put the conversations on hold until after the weekend, but I couldn't let them go. I just kept getting more and more angry (100).

Disputation: Hold on there. I'm really upset. I wonder if I'm blowing things out of proportion. Okay, Ted doesn't seem ready to budge on the dating issue and is very reluctant to spend any of our retirement money. He definitely is less easygoing than me, but he certainly isn't rigid. There have been lots of times when he's given up what he's wanted to accommodate me or the kids (95).

Like last summer when we had decided to go to the shore. He was willing to go to the Berkshires instead. And he had already spent a lot of time looking into places in Cape May. And I can hardly call him selfish. He even relocated so that I could go back to school. He made a lot of sacrifices to do that (100). Maybe he's just anxious about Mimi growing up (80). It is pretty frightening to imagine her dating some of the jerks she knows. And the deck would take a substantial chunk out of our savings. I could see that making him feel uneasy (90).

Energization: I calmed down a lot. I still felt a bit angry, but nothing like I did before (20). I was able to put the dating issue and the renovations aside, so that I could enjoy what was left of the weekend.

Elana is no longer giving herself hollow pep talks. Disputing reduced the intensity of her anger from 100 to 20, and she was able to relax and enjoy the rest of her anniversary. What made these disputations so effective? Let's look at a few in detail. First, Elana told herself to slow down. This is important. Her negative thoughts were racing faster than she could dispute them, so she needed to put on the brakes. By telling herself to slow down, Elana was beginning to distance herself from her beliefs. This is a crucial first step. Then Elana acknowledges the grain of truth in her automatic thoughts. Yes, her husband is less easygoing than she is, but less easygoing is not the same as being rigid. If there is some truth in your belief, don't dismiss it. But it is crucial to separate the kernel of truth from the chaff of catastrophizing.

Next Elana cites specific examples of times when Ted compromised or was willing to negotiate a change of plans. Elana marshaled evidence against her belief. Finally, Elana considered alternative hypotheses for Ted's behavior. Perhaps he was feeling anxious about Mimi's entering puberty. Perhaps he was uneasy about their financial security. Gaining distance on your thoughts, separating fact from catastrophization, considering the available evidence, and generating alternatives make disputations solid. Your mood gets better and your energy returns because your pessimism has been deflated.

Effective disputation rests on four pillars. The first is *evidence gathering.* When you identify pessimistic beliefs, ask yourself, What is the evidence for this belief? Be careful. You've been a pessimist for a long time, so you have developed methods for maintaining your pessimism. When you first begin to look for evidence, you will probably find lots of it that supports your pessimism and little that refutes it. This is the confirmation bias. We see more readily the facts that support our beliefs than the facts that contradict them. To fight the confirmation bias, do not simply scan your life for any evidence that impinges on your belief. Instead, break the task into two separate components. First, set out to find all the evidence that supports your belief. Then ask yourself, *What evidence counts against this belief?* By forcing yourself to consider both sides, you weaken your confirmation bias. Of course, your disputation is only as good as the evidence you collect. So be specific and concrete and list each piece of evidence individually.

The second tactic is generating *alternatives.* Ask yourself, What are other ways of viewing this adversity? Perspective taking is difficult when you are a pessimist. You may be completely convinced that your interpretation is the only valid one. Humor yourself. Set out to list as many other interpretations as you can. If you still believe there are no other reasonable interpretations, then ask yourself, How would my best friend understand what has happened? My father? How would an impartial observer understand it? Once you've generated other interpretations, use evidence to evaluate their truth. Remember, events are almost never caused by one factor; the world's complexity gives you the freedom to find and focus on any of several explanations. So don't oversimplify with one monolithic, pessimistic explanation. Look at the whole range of contributing causes to problems.

The third tactic of disputation is decatastrophizing, or accurately evaluating the *implications,* the "what ifs," of the adversity. When things go wrong, do you immediately fantasize about a cascade of horrible things that will ensue? If you get a "needs work" message from your boss, are you overwhelmed by ruminations about the demise of your career? Pessimists are "what-if-ers." They catastrophize. The boss is mildly disappointed and the pessimist launches into his "what ifs": What if he decides to fire me? What if I can't find another job? What if I have to switch fields? On and on it goes. The best way to deal with the "what ifs" is to take yourself seriously and explore the question. "What if" questions are scary because they are vague and ominous. Some horrible "undertoad" is lurking in your future waiting to seize you.

When you start to "what if," ask yourself three questions. Each one helps you decatastrophize. First, What is the worst possible thing that could happen, no matter how remote it may be? Be detailed. Don't be vague. Give the monster a face and a name. Then ask yourself, How likely is this? If it were to happen, what could you do to improve the situation? Next ask yourself, What is the best possible thing that could happen? Again, be specific. After you've defined the best and worst boundaries, ask yourself what the most likely outcome will actually be. In all probability, the worst consequence won't happen and neither will the best. The implications will fall somewhere in between.

Once you've specified the three consequences, you can plan for them. Developing a *plan of attack* is the fourth strategy of disputation. Spend most of your energy developing a plan of attack for the most likely case. Don't neglect planning for the best case or the worst case. Is there anything you can do to facilitate the best case coming about? At rare times the worst case is accurate. Awful things do happen. Relationships end irretrievably and people get fired. We make mistakes. We treat people harshly. Our character is flawed. This does not mean you are helpless, however. What specific actions can you take to improve the situation? How can you correct the mistake? Or soften the parts of your character that create problems for you? Or control the damage that has occurred? By forming a plan of attack, you can stave off helplessness and maintain your ability to persevere through dire circumstances.

Elana identified herself as a "what-if-er." Here is an example of how she has learned to decatastrophize.

Adversity: Ted and I had a horrible fight. We both said some pretty hurtful things. It was so bad that he stormed out. He called a couple hours later and said he was going to sleep at his brother's house.

Beliefs: This is bad. We've never fought like this before. I've never seen him so mad. What if he doesn't calm down? What if we don't resolve this? What's going to happen?

Decatastrophizing: Slow down, Elana. The worst possible outcome is that he refuses to ever come home again: he gathers his things while I'm at work and then he leaves for good [*worst case*]. But even if this happened, I could get by. It would be the hardest thing that I could imagine going through, but I could ask my family to help me through it [*plan of attack*]. And anyway, be reasonable. That's not going to happen. We've been married too long, he cares too much for our kids to just disappear like that [*evidence*]. I guess the best-case scenario is that he comes home in a few hours, with a box of roses, and tells me that it was all his fault. Fat chance. Ted hasn't bought me roses in twenty years. Okay, so what's the most likely outcome? Well, I guess he'll stay the night at Henry's and come home in the morning [*most likely*]. It'll be a little cold between us at first. We both said some pretty nasty things, so I imagine it'll take a little time for us to feel real warm about each other, but we'll work through it. Maybe I'll drop the kids at Mom's so that we can have some space to sort this out [*plan of attack*].

Once Elana named the worst case and thought through how she could handle it, she saw that it was improbable and she was able to calm those fears. She knew that her best-case scenario was equally unlikely, but she was then able to focus on the most realistic consequences of the fight. Now that she was thinking realistically, she was able to plan for them, further increasing the likelihood that things will work out.

PRACTICE WITH DISPUTATION FOR ADULTS

Before you teach your child how to dispute his pessimistic beliefs, practice the skills yourself. Here are two examples to get you started.

Adversity: One of my closest friends separated from her husband. While I've known Janice much longer, Steven and I have become close over the years. After Janice moved out, I continued to speak to Steven once in a while and he came for dinner twice. When Janice found out, she was furious. She said I was disloyal.

Beliefs: She's right. What was I thinking? Janice needs my support. Spending time with Steven is going to hurt her. I really blew this one. She's going to pull back, I know it. So much for the friendship.

Consequences: I felt pretty guilty about it. Steven left a couple of messages but I didn't return his calls. Then I felt guilty about that too. It was a real mess.

Disputation: Yes, I met Janice first. And I want to be supportive of her decision. But that doesn't mean I have to turn my back on Steven. It's a complicated situation. The best I can do is to make it clear that I care about both of them. Spending time with Steven doesn't mean I'm disloyal to Janice. I care about him too [*alternative*]. I've spoken to her almost every day on the phone since they've split [*evidence*]. And I've gone out of my way to include her in plans so that she doesn't feel isolated [*evidence*]. Janice may be mad now, but she'll calm down soon [*decatastrophizing*]. I'll give her some space. Maybe I'll send her a note explaining how I feel [*plan of attack*].

Energization: Instead of feeling guilty, I started to feel good about myself. I saw that I was managing a tough situation pretty well. I decided to call Janice and explain how I was seeing things.

Adversity: This is my first year teaching. I spent a long time arranging to take my eighth-grade class to a farm to learn about agriculture. Some of the veteran teachers told me I shouldn't do it, but I wanted to do something special for the kids. When we got there, they started misbehaving. They tried to feed a cow chewing gum. I caught two girls smoking cigarettes behind a haystack; they nearly burnt the place down with the matches. And a bunch of the boys tried to steal eggs from the hens.

Beliefs: What a fiasco! I should have known better! What is wrong with me?! I'm so damn naive. All these teachers warned me not to do this, but do I listen — no! I'm such a fool. The principal is going to find out about what happened and she's going to be pissed. I'll be lucky if I can keep this job a year. From now on, it's by the book. No more of this "classroom without walls" stuff.

Consequences: I felt so embarrassed. I simply did not want to show up on Monday. I couldn't stop replaying each catastrophe in my mind. I would have called in sick on Monday, but I was too embarrassed to do it in front of my husband.

Disputation: This is silly. I'm exaggerating. Yes, some of the kids got out of control. But most of the kids were just great and really enjoyed the trip and learned a lot. It wasn't naive of me to plan the trip. It was creative [*alternative*]. Sure, some of the teachers told me it was crazy, but that's because they're jaded. It wasn't foolish to try it. It's young teachers like me who are willing to try new things that are going to make a difference [*alternative*]. And why should Martha be mad? I caught everything before any big problems happened [*evidence*]. She might tell me to bring more chaperones next time, that's all [*decatastrophizing*]. Maybe I'll even write up a brief memo about it and tell her what changes I'd make for next time [*plan of attack*].

Energization: I felt a lot better. I didn't dread going to school and talking about the trip. Sure, I was still disappointed that it didn't go more smoothly, but I wasn't scared off from doing innovative things.

Now it's time for you to practice with examples from your life. Pay close attention to any setbacks and problems that arise in the next few days. Listen to your internal dialogue and then practice the disputation strategies. Here is a summary of the questions to ask yourself:

1. What is the evidence that this belief is true? What is the evidence that it is not true?
2. What is an alternative way to view this situation?
3. What's the worst that could happen? Is it likely?
4. What's the best that could happen? Is it likely?
5. What's the most likely outcome?
6. What is my plan of attack, particularly for the most likely outcome?

You do not have to ask yourself each question in each situation. Practice with all of them and find the ones that work best for you. Don't forget to rate your initial beliefs and the disputations on the 1–100 scale. Rate the intensity of your feelings as well, so you can monitor how well you disputed. Record your ABCDEs in the spaces that follow.

1. *Adversity:* _____

   Beliefs: _____

   Consequences: _____

   Disputation: _____

   Energization: _____

2. *Adversity:* _____

   Beliefs: _____

   Consequences: _____

   Disputation: _____

   Energization: _____

3. *Adversity:* _____

   Beliefs: _____

   Consequences: _____

   Disputation: _____

   Energization: _____

RAPID-FIRE DISPUTING FOR ADULTS

There is one more adult activity to practice before you teach disputing skills to your child. Systematically working through the ABCDE on a piece of a paper is a good beginning for disputing your pessimism. As you become more skilled, you won't need to rely on a worksheet. Just as your initial pessimistic beliefs have been an automatic response, your disputations will also become automatic. The goal is to practice fighting back against your pessimistic beliefs as quickly as they pop into your head.

The goal of rapid-fire disputing is for you to dispel pessimistic beliefs on the spot. Here's how it works. Ask a trusted friend or your spouse to help you. Make sure you select someone with whom you feel comfortable sharing your self-critical thoughts and feelings. Your partner's job is to criticize you in the way that you typically criticize yourself. You need to spend five minutes explaining to your partner the types of situations that typically trigger your pessimism and what you usually say to yourself. Your partner might feel uncomfortable at first. Explain that you will not take the criticisms personally, or rather, that you *will* take them personally, but you will not attribute the criticisms to your partner. These are your own accusations. Once your partner understands the purpose of the activity, she will relax. It is your job to convince her that she needs to be tough on you, not to let you off the hook without a fight.

Your job is to dispute the criticisms aloud. Marshal evidence. Decatastrophize the implications. Argue a more reasonable alternative. Then describe how you will handle the situation, particularly if the criticism is on target. Before you begin, read the following examples aloud with your partner.

> *Situation:* Danielle gets a call late at night from the police. They tell her that her seventeen-year-old daughter was involved in a car accident. Faith is fine, but the car was heavily damaged. Faith had been drinking.
>
> *Accusations [by partner]:* Drinking and driving! You're lucky she's not dead. How could she be so stupid! You obviously haven't

raised her very well. If you had done your job right, she'd never even consider getting near a car if she'd been drinking. Not to mention the fact that she shouldn't be drinking at all. You didn't even know she drinks. Where have you been?

Disputation: I *am* lucky she's not dead. Drinking and driving is about as stupid as you can get. It's true that I wasn't aware that she was drinking. That's not a good sign. But it doesn't mean that I haven't raised her well. I take being a mother very seriously [*alternative*]. And I have talked to her on several occasions about the perils of alcohol [*evidence*]. I even took her and her brother to a talk about alcohol and drugs at the community center [*evidence*]. Despite that, she has decided to drink. I can't control every decision she makes [*alternative*]. I can only give her the facts and my opinion.

Partner interrupts: Yeah, well that's all well and good, but the fact is your daughter totaled the car and nearly killed herself. She's heading for big trouble. If she's already drinking, then who knows where she'll end up. It starts with alcohol and then builds to worse drugs.

Disputation: There's no denying it. This is very scary. But there's no point in imagining the worst. Just because she's drinking at seventeen, doesn't mean she's going to end up a crack addict [*decatastrophizing*]. I need to understand what's been going on with her and I need to get her help if she needs it. If we handle this well now, Faith will be fine [*alternative*]. I'm just glad it came to my attention before something worse happened.

Situation: Christopher and Georgia have been married for five years. Adam is Georgia's law partner. He throws a party that Georgia and Christopher attend. Georgia spends the evening talking and laughing with Adam. Christopher begins to suspect that there is more to their relationship than he knew. On the ride home, he confronts his wife. Georgia admits that she is attracted to Adam, but says she would never act on her feelings for him.

Accusations [*by partner*]: This is the beginning of the end. Sure, she says she'd never act on her feelings, but get real, this is how it all starts. First she spends more and more time with him at the office, then they start going to lunches and dinners together. Hell, she works late so many nights, for all you know she's already having an affair. And if she hasn't yet, she sure as hell will, soon enough. The way they were flirting — it's just a matter of time.

Disputation: Hold on. Hold on. That's blowing things way out of proportion [*decatastrophizing*]. Yes, they were flirting. Yes, Georgia is attracted to him. But that's a long way from having an affair [*decatastrophizing*]. I've been attracted to other women since we've been married, but I haven't acted on it [*evidence*]. How could we not be attracted to other people? We're both flirts, always have been [*alternatives*]. But we also love each other very much and wouldn't want to jeopardize that.

Partner interrupts: Sure. Keep on telling yourself that, but the writing is on the wall. The rate of extramarital affairs has gone through the roof. What makes you think you're so different? And anyway, the way she flirted with him right in front of you, it was disgraceful. What an embarrassment. Everybody must have been wondering what's going on with you two. It sure didn't look very good.

Disputation: Look, I know we both love each other. If one of us makes a mistake and has an affair, we'll get through it if we want to [*decatastrophizing*]. I'm not saying it wouldn't be hard, but it doesn't have to mean the end of our marriage. I did feel a little left out. I wish she had spent more time with me and less with Adam, but no one else noticed. Everyone was caught up in their own thing [*evidence*]; they weren't worrying about me and Georgia [*alternative*]. And even if they did notice, I'm sure they just thought we were real secure with each other and didn't need to be attached at the hip [*alternative*]. The good thing is that Georgia was honest about how she feels [*alternative*]. That means she trusts me, and as long as we keep talking about things, we can handle whatever comes our way [*decatastrophizing*].

Situation: Arnie and Claudia are brother and sister. They have a long history of competitiveness. As adults, they have been working hard to overcome their rivalry. They are closer now than ever before. Arnie is the manager of a local restaurant. Claudia is an administrative assistant at the college in town. She recently decided to take advantage of her tuition benefits and enrolled in a history course and a psychology course. She excitedly calls her brother about it. He says, "History?! You hated history in school. And you certainly never did well in it. That's just going to be a waste of your time. And I've got to say, I don't see how you're going to have the time for this. You don't get to spend enough time with your family as it is."

Accusations [by partner]: He's right, you know. You really were pretty horrible in history. You never could remember any of the names or dates. You'd confuse the wars. And you already are working a full-time job. When are you going to spend time with the kids? It's not fair to them if you're now out two nights a week. They need a mother, not some wannabe scholar.

Disputation: First of all, history might not have been my best subject, but I wasn't that horrible either. I got mostly C's [*evidence*]. And anyway, I wasn't interested in it then, so I never really paid much attention to my work [*alternative*]. Now it fascinates me, so I'll put more effort into it [*alternative*]. It will mean less time with the kids, but they're not little children anymore. They're not even home until late a couple nights a week [*alternative*]. Megan has field hockey practice every day after school and Joey is late with band practice [*evidence*]. Maybe I can try to take one class that meets during my lunch hour instead of two after work [*plan of attack*].

Partner interrupts: Okay, okay. But what a creep of a brother. Here you go and do something exciting for yourself and he can't find anything supportive to say. He's always been like that. He never gives you any credit and he never shows you any respect.

Disputation: It's true that Arnie and I have been pretty cool to each other over the years, but that's changing. We've really worked hard on getting closer [*alternative*]. Yes, he wasn't actually my champion when I told him about this, but this must be hard on him. He's feeling really stuck in his job, so he might feel envious that I'm making some changes in my life [*alternative*].

And he's been real supportive of me lately at other times. Like when I was fighting with Glenn, he spent a lot of time with me on the phone. He helped me sort it all out [*evidence*]. I'll give him a day or two to adjust, and then I'll talk to him about it again [*plan of attack*].

Now it's your turn. Work through at least five situations with your partner. If you start to feel confused or stymied during the middle of the activity, call time-out. Remember, this is hard. It requires you to come up with persuasive decatastrophizing in the heat of the moment. So if you begin to feel overwhelmed, take a moment to clear your head and try to work out an effective disputation more slowly. Then, when you are ready, have your partner start again. Make sure she uses the same accusation that threw you, so you have a chance to conquer it. As with all the skills, don't try to do too much in one sitting. Rapid-fire disputing takes a lot of practice. If you spend fifteen minutes a couple of times a week on the skill, you will soon be able to challenge your pessimistic beliefs on your feet and with force. If you find your disputing skill waning over the months, this is the exercise to revitalize it.

TEACHING DISPUTATION TO YOUR CHILD

You are now ready to teach your child to dispute and decatastrophize. This is the marrow of the Penn Prevention Program. Once learned, these skills maintain themselves and your child will be armored against failure and rejection for the rest of his life. Bad things will continue to happen. He will do poorly on tests. He will be cut from teams. He will not get hired for his dream job. Women will reject him. But you will have taught him how to persevere in the face of these setbacks. He will not collapse helplessly and he will be much more likely to find his way out. This will be your legacy to him.

The overriding principle for teaching your child disputation is accuracy: The disputations must be based on fact. They must carry the weight of proof. If your child's disputations are vague or just cheery positive thinking, they will not dent his pessimism. When this happens, help him to develop a more concrete disputation. Make sure to model effective disputation even when you aren't formally teaching him the skill. The more he hears you challenge your own pessimism, the faster he will learn to challenge his own.

Accurate Disputation: Hemlock versus Sherlock. Tell your child that you want to teach her how to challenge pessimistic beliefs. Explain that the goal is to help her view herself as accurately as possible, so that she feels good about herself and can solve her problems.

Start by reading the story about Sherlock Holmes and Hemlock Jones in chapter 9 (pp. 120–22). Ask your child which detective she would want if it was her bike that was stolen. Ask her to describe why Sherlock was the better detective. If she answers because Sherlock solved the crime and Hemlock didn't, ask her to explain what Sherlock did that helped him solve the crime. Explain that Sherlock did two important things that Hemlock didn't do. First, he made a list of the possible suspects. Then, he looked for evidence to help him decide which person was the thief. Hemlock, in contrast, just assumed it was the person whose name popped into his head first. Tell your child that we all act like Hemlock from time to time. When something bad happens, we often believe the first thought that pops into our head, without taking the time to figure out if it is true or not. Explain that you want to help her be like Sherlock Holmes. When problems happen, you want her to look for evidence so that she can figure out whether her beliefs about the problem are accurate. Remind her that not only do pessimistic beliefs make her feel bad and cause her to give up easily but they also often aren't even accurate. Tell her that you want her to think about the problem from different angles, instead of believing the first thoughts that come to her mind.

Next read this skit with your child to show her how generating alternatives and looking for evidence works.

Russell and Mom

Russell: Hey, Mom, a bunch of kids from school are going to Wildwood for the weekend. It's going to be a blast. Can I go?

Mom: Well, Russell, I don't know. I have to think about it. Who's going and who's driving?

Russell: Rob Reckless is going and his dad, Mr. Reckless, is driving.

Mom: Who else is going with you? I don't want you hanging out with that Turner girl. She's a bad influence.

Russell: Jeez, Mom, lighten up. Lisa's not that bad. She just got in trouble that one time. Other kids will be there too.

Mom: Is there a telephone number where I can reach you?

Russell: Sheesh, Mom, relax. I'm not a little kid anymore. I can take care of myself. I doubt there's a phone. The place we're staying at is right on the beach. And anyway, none of the other kids' parents are making such a big deal about this. Why are you always getting on my case?!

Mom: I don't like the sound of this. I'll tell you what: Dad and I will take you to the beach next weekend.

Russell: Oh hey, great! Won't that be fun. Me and my parents hanging out at Wildwood. I can hardly wait! Why not just ground me instead?

Mom: Russell, I've made up my mind. You're not going. That's final.

[*Russell goes to his room.*]

Russell [*thinking to himself*]: I really hate her. She's such a witch. She always does this to me. She never lets me do anything fun. She makes me look like such a loser in front of my friends.

Wait a minute. I'm pulling a Hemlock. Sherlock wouldn't let himself get all upset over the first thought that pops into his head. He'd look for evidence. Let's see . . . Does my mom ever let me do fun things? Well, last week she *did* let me go to Great Adventure, and she lets me go alone to the movies all the time [*evidence*]. And, oh yeah, she usually lets me invite friends over to play Nintendo [*evidence*]. I guess she does let me do some fun stuff. Maybe she's just worried about Mr. Reckless [*alternative*]. He does have a bad driving record. And maybe she doesn't really like me to be around Lisa [*alternative*]. After all, she did get into a lot of trouble for stealing from the girls locker room. Maybe she's worried about there not being a phone because she likes to be able to get in touch with me in case something goes wrong, like when I broke my ankle playing soccer last year [*alternative*].

I'm still mad that I can't go. But I guess I don't hate Mom. I feel a little bit better knowing that at least she had some good reasons for saying no. Maybe she'll let me bring Andrew to the shore with us. That would be a lot better than just me and them. I think I'll ask.

After reading the skit, discuss it with your child. Here are questions to use in the discussion. What was Russell's first explanation about why his mom wouldn't let him go to the shore? If Russell was like Hemlock, what would he have done? How did Russell act more like Sherlock instead? What evidence did he find? Did Russell come up with any other ways of understanding why his mother said no? If Russell hadn't looked for evidence about whether his mother never lets him have any fun, how do you think he would have felt? What do you think he would have done? How do you think he felt after he looked for evidence and thought of other reasons why his mom wouldn't let him go? What do you think he does next?

ABCDE Examples. Next, read the following ABCDE examples with your child. Ask him to point out each time the child used evidence to help challenge his or her pessimism and when more realistic and optimistic alternatives were offered.

Adversity: I went to a party at my friend Meredith's house. Her parents took us all to a movie. They said they'd pick us up at ten. Once it got dark, Lauren took out a squeeze bottle from her backpack. She said she filled it with stuff from her parents' liquor cabinet. Beth and Steph and Tammy were psyched about it and they all started taking turns drinking it. They started giggling like it was so funny. The people around us kept telling us to be quiet. Lauren told me to take some but I didn't want to. Then they started telling me that I was a wimp and no fun and stuff. They kept on hassling me about it.

Beliefs: I'm such a wuss. They're all doing it. I should too. I'm always such a baby. Everybody I know drinks. It's not a big deal. Anytime we do something fun or wild I get scared and back out. I'm such a baby.

Consequences: I felt stupid — really, really stupid. I pretended like I didn't care — I just kept staring at the movie — but I really felt like crying. It's like I felt embarrassed and scared and sad all at once. I hated it.

Disputation: Just because I didn't drink doesn't make me a wuss. I mean, it's not brave to just do what everybody else is doing. That can be wussy too. Sometimes it's even harder not to do what all your friends are doing. It's like what Mr. Riley called being a majority of one. I guess that's what I am. And anyway, not everyone drinks. I know Sari and Lisa Eckles don't drink. And I do a lot of wild things. Like I was the one that played the practical joke on Miss Harmony. And it was my idea to wrap the toilet paper around Ms. Gretchen's house after the championship. That was pretty fun.

Energization: I started to feel a little better. I still couldn't wait to get out of there 'cause I was scared they'd get caught, but I didn't feel so sad or embarrassed. I just watched the rest of the movie and ignored them.

What evidence did this girl use to challenge her pessimistic thoughts? She disputes her belief that she is a wuss by listing the wild things she has done — playing practical jokes, toilet-papering the coach's house. What alternatives does she come up with? Her abstinence becomes a sign of courage rather than cowardice. Going along with the pull of a crowd is seen as the truly cowardly behavior.

Now read the others, and after each one ask your child to point out the evidence that is used and the alternatives suggested.

Adversity: My brother is five years older than me. He's sixteen. But he can't drive. He's got Down's. So he looks different. He isn't as smart as most kids his age. But he tries real hard at stuff. I love him but sometimes I get mad at him. Like the other day. We walked over to Suburban Square. We were going to buy a birthday present for our dad. We went in this store called Sharper Image — they have all these neat machines and stuff. Anyway, a couple kids from my school came in. They're okay guys. I started talking to them and then Stevie starts calling me. I told him to hold on a minute, but he just kept on calling me, all excited like. The guys I was with started laughing, so I turned around. Stevie was lying down on this bed that has these rollers that move up and down. It like gives you a massage. Stevie was clapping his hands and acting real goofy. He kept on calling me and laughing real loud. Everybody started staring. I got really mad and pulled him off it. I yelled at him pretty bad. I told him he can't ever hang out with me ever again.

Beliefs: I hate Stevie. How come I got stuck with a brother like him. He's always doing stupid stuff to embarrass me. Everyone at school thinks I'm a weirdo 'cause of him. They're always calling me names and stuff. He's such a loser. I wish he wasn't ever born.

Consequences: I was feeling really mad. I wanted to punch him real hard. I guess I was also embarrassed. I wanted to get out of there as fast as I could. And I didn't even want to look at Stevie. Like I wanted to pretend I didn't know him.

Disputation: Sometimes it's really hard to be with him. He does do goofy things at times. But it's not like he does it on purpose. He just can't help it. It's like he's a little kid in a big body. When I'm mad I sometimes think it would be better if he weren't around, but we have a lot of fun together too. He makes me laugh a lot and he cheers me up when I'm in a bad mood. I'd miss him if he weren't my brother. Sometimes I do get called "retardo" at school, but not so much. And it's really only by Alex. He's mean to everyone. Last time he started getting on me, Kathy and Billy told him to knock it off, so I guess they don't think I'm weird.

Energization: I started to feel less mad at him. I was still feeling embarrassed, but not so much as before.

Adversity: My mom and dad split up a couple years back. Now she's dating this new guy named Lamar. He's starting to come around a lot. My mom acts so different when he's around. Like the other night, Lamar came over for dinner. She made me and my sister clean the whole entire house. We even had to move all the furniture and clean behind it. We never do that. Then she cooked this really fancy meal and she made me polish the silverware. I hate the smell of that stuff. It makes me sick. Then she got all dressed up and put on all this goopy makeup and put her hair up all fancy. She never does that either. She never wears makeup. I don't even think she combs her hair. When he came over he tried to be so nice and polite and funny. It was pathetic. Whenever I started talking, my mom barely listened. She'd just grunt something in my direction. But when Lamar opened his mouth — she was so into it. He started talking about that movie where the lady doesn't talk and wants to play the piano all the time. He was saying how great he thought it was and she acted like she liked it too, but it was a total lie. Me and Becky saw it with her. We were bored out of our minds and she said she didn't think it was so good either. She said it was overrated.

Beliefs: She's so two-faced. She acts all different for Lamar. And she never pays us any attention anymore. I bet she wishes we weren't around so she could spend all her time with her new boyfriend. All she cares about is him. She doesn't care what happens to me anymore. I don't think she loves me so much anymore.

Consequences: I was really sad and mad too. I didn't want to say anything else all night. I just wanted to sit there real quiet and wait to be excused. I just kept staring at my plate and hoped real hard that Lamar would choke on his food. I tried to turn my body so that I could only see Mom and Becky. I pretended Lamar wasn't there.

Disputation: Well, she does act different when he's around. I mean, our house is cleaner than it's ever been. But I guess she's just trying to make a good impression. I do that too sometimes. Like when I liked Timmy. I tried to look real nice and say things that were cool. I guess grown-ups do that too. She definitely spends a lot of time with Lamar, but that doesn't mean that she doesn't love me or doesn't want to be with me too. Like last week, he wanted to come over and take us all to this museum — *oooh,* fun — but she said that we couldn't 'cause we were going to the park. I think he wanted to come, but she said it was girls' day out. And next week, me and her are going to lunch and to a movie, just the two of us. I hope she ends up not liking him. That'd be great. I can't take all this cleaning.

Energization: I started to feel okay again. Becky started talking about our school and I said some things too. I even looked at Lamar a couple times.

Real-Life ABCDEs. After you've discussed these two examples with your child, use the worksheet that follows to help him dispute his own pessimistic beliefs. First, ask your child to write down some adversity from his life, his beliefs, and the consequences. Then have him write down evidence that supports his belief in the space labeled "Evidence For," and evidence that refutes the belief in the space labeled "Evidence Against." Ask him to write down two more-optimistic beliefs about the situation in the space labeled "Other Ways of Seeing It." Finally, in the "Energization" space, have him record how the optimistic beliefs make him feel and act. Work through at least three situations in this manner, and when a new situation arises, be sure to use the worksheet.

1. *Adversity:* _____

   Beliefs: _____

   Consequences: _____

   Evidence For: _____

   Evidence Against: _____

   Other Ways of Seeing It: _____

   Energization: _____

2. Adversity: _____

Beliefs: _____

Consequences: _____

Evidence For: _____

Evidence Against: _____

Other Ways of Seeing It: _____

Energization: _____

3. Adversity: _____

Beliefs: _____

Consequences: _____

Evidence For: _____

Evidence Against: _____

Other Ways of Seeing It: _____

Energization: _____

Decatastrophizing. Now you are ready to teach your child how to decatastrophize. Tell him that so far you have been talking about alternative thoughts about *why* a problem happened. For example, if he failed a test at school, he might think about why he failed. He might think, "I didn't study enough" or "I'm stupid" or "The test wasn't fair." Tell him that there is another kind of thought that people have when problems happen: *what will happen next*. If he failed a test, he might think about what will happen next, like "I'll be grounded for life" or "Now I'll never get a good grade in this course." Explain that these thoughts are about how the problem is going to affect the future.

Read the Gloomy Greg and Hopeful Holly skits that follow. Gloomy Greg illustrates catastrophizing and Hopeful Holly illustrates how to handle these "what will happen next" thoughts.

Gloomy Greg and the C+

Henry: Hi Greg! How's it going?

Greg: Horrible. I just got my test back from English class. I got a C-plus on it.

Henry: Well, that's not great, but it's not so bad. You'll do better on the next one.

Greg: Are you kidding? What do you mean it's not so bad! A C-plus. Don't you know what that means?

Henry: No. What?

Greg: It means I'll never get an A in English, and if I don't get an A that means I won't make the honor roll, and if I don't make the honor roll then I'll never get into the Honor Society, and if I don't get into the Honor Society then I might as well forget about ever getting into Princeton, and I've got to get into Princeton.

Henry: What are you talking about?! It's one C-plus. You can still get an A in English if you nail the rest of her tests. Gosh, relax, Greg. Why are you even thinking about college now — you're thirteen!

Greg: Aw, forget it. You don't understand. I'm finished. There goes my future.

Tell your child that people often "catastrophize." When something bad happens, they immediately think of the absolutely worst thing that might happen as a result. And usually, these things are very unlikely to happen. This way of thinking makes something bad into an utter catastrophe. Ask your child to describe how Greg turned his C+ into a catastrophe. Ask your child whether he thinks that the horrible things Greg imagines are really going to happen.

Now read the Hopeful Holly skit.

Hopeful Holly and the C+

Hannah: Hi Holly! How's it going?

Holly: Horrible. I just got my test back from English class. I got a C-plus on it.

Hannah: Well, that's not great, but it's not so bad. You'll do better on the next one.

Holly: Are you kidding? What do you mean it's not so bad! A C-plus. Don't you know what that means?

Hannah: No. What?

Holly: It means I'll never get an A in English, and if I don't get an A that means I won't make the honor roll, and if I don't make the honor roll then I'll never get into the Honor Society, and if I don't get into the Honor Society I might as well forget about ever getting into Princeton, and I've got to get into Princeton.

Hannah: What are you talking about?! It's one C-plus. You can still get an A in English if you nail the rest of her tests. Gosh, relax, Holly. Why are you even thinking about college now — you're thirteen!

Holly: Yeah, I guess you're right. I was overreacting a little, huh? I guess one C-plus doesn't mean that the rest of my life is ruined. Maybe I've been exaggerating a bit. But it's going to be hard to get an A now. I'll have to work a lot harder. If I study really hard for the rest of the marking period I can get my grade up to a B-plus, maybe even an A-minus. I'm doing pretty well in the rest of my classes, so I can still be on the honor roll if I work real hard. Thanks, Hannah.

Holly caught herself catastrophizing and slowed down. Unlike Greg, she was able to see that the likelihood of being denied the college of her dreams because of one C+ was minute. She was able to focus on more-realistic outcomes and develop a plan of attack. Holly decided that she'd have to work harder in order to get a high grade in the course. Ask your child whether Holly or Greg is more likely to give up and not work hard in English class. Tell him that when we make problems into catastrophes, it leads us to feel dejected and often we decide there's no point in trying, so we give up.

Tell your child that when something bad happens and he catastrophizes, you want him to think of three things. First, he should ask himself, "What is the worst that could happen?" Then, he should ask himself, "What is the best that could happen?" Then, he should be like Sherlock Holmes and ask himself, "What is the most likely thing that will happen?" Then, after he has mapped out these three possibilities, he can make a plan of attack for each. Ask him to tell you one thing he can do to lessen the chances that the worst will happen, one thing he can do to increase the chances that the best will happen, and all the things he can to do handle the most likely consequences.

"What Will Happen Next" Examples. Here is an example from a sixth-grade girl in the Penn Prevention Program.

Situation: Carly is my best friend and she lent me this really cool sweater she has. It's got all different colors in it and pieces of leather and stuff too. I wore it to the party and Molly and Marcus even said it was nice. But somehow, I don't know how, I got icing all over the front and the sleeve. It was bad. Like the chocolate smushed into the sweater. I couldn't brush it off or anything. My mom says I ought to just dress in plastic 'cause I'm always spilling things on my clothes. She says that way she could just hose me down at the end of the day. Anyways, I was really scared to tell Carly. I knew she was gonna be way mad.

What is the worst thing that might happen? The very worst is that Carly will get so mad that she'll tell me she doesn't want to be best friends anymore. She'll tell Joanie and Heather, too, and they will be mad at me.

What is one thing you can do to help stop the worst thing from happening? I can use my allowance money to buy Carly another sweater that looks just like it.

What is the best thing that might happen? She'll tell me that she isn't mad at all.

What is one thing you can do to help make the best thing happen? I can say I'm really sorry. And I can give her one of my favorite sweaters.

What is the most likely thing that will happen? I think she'll be kind of mad at me. She won't talk to me for a little bit.

What can you do to handle the most likely thing if it happens? I can tell her I'm sorry. I can be super nice. I can play with Lisa more.

Use the decatastrophizing worksheets that follow to help your child practice this skill on the events I give you.

Situation: Sandra's mom told her that she expected Sandra to clean the bathroom by the time she got home from work. When Sandra's mom gets home, she sees the bathroom is a mess and Sandra is outside playing.

What is the worst thing that might happen? _____

_____

What is one thing Sandra can do to help stop the worst thing from happening? _____

_____

What is the best thing that might happen? _____

_____

What is one thing Sandra can do to help make the best thing happen?

_____

_____

What is the most likely thing that will happen? _____

_____

What can Sandra do to handle the most likely thing if it happens? ____

_____

Situation: Joey is fifteen and likes a girl named Maggie. His friends convince him to ask her out. He manages to get up the guts, and when he asks her, she says no.

What is the worst thing that might happen? _____

_____

What is one thing Joey can do to help stop the worst thing from happening? _____

_____

What is the best thing that might happen? _____

What is one thing Joey can do to help make the best thing happen? ___

_____

What is the most likely thing that will happen? _____

_____

What can Joey do to handle the most likely thing if it happens?

_____

_____

Situation: Jackie's parents are fighting a lot. She lies in bed at night and listens to them yell at each other. It seems as if they are fighting more each day.

What is the worst thing that might happen? _____

_____

What is one thing Jackie can do to help stop the worst thing from happening? _____

_____

What is the best thing that might happen? _____

What is one thing Jackie can do to help make the best thing happen?

_____

_____

What is the most likely thing that will happen? _____

_____

What can Jackie do to handle the most likely thing if it happens?

_____

_____

Real-Life "What Will Happen Next" Now use the following blank worksheets to practice this skill with situations from your child's life. After each situation, ask your child to think about how he feels when he imagines the worst compared to how he feels when he imagines the most likely outcome. Ask him how imagining the worst affects his behavior, and compare imagining the most likely outcome instead.

Situation: _____

What is the worst thing that might happen? _____

What is one thing you can do to stop the worst thing from happening? _____

What is the best thing that might happen? _____

What is one thing you can do to help make the best thing happen? ____

What is the most likely thing that will happen? _____

What can you do to handle the most likely thing if it happens? _____
_____

Situation: _____

What is the worst thing that might happen? _____

What is one thing you can do to stop the worst thing from happening? _____

What is the best thing that might happen? _____

What is one thing you can do to help make the best thing happen? ____

What is the most likely thing that will happen? _____

What can you do to handle the most likely thing if it happens? _____
_____

Situation: _____
_____

What is the worst thing that might happen? _____

What is one thing you can do to stop the worst thing from
happening? _____

What is the best thing that might happen? _____

What is one thing you can do to help make the best thing happen? ____

What is the most likely thing that will happen? _____

What can you do to handle the most likely thing if it happens? _____

Situation: _____

What is the worst thing that might happen? _____

What is one thing you can do to stop the worst thing from
happening? _____

What is the best thing that might happen? _____

What is one thing you can do to help make the best thing happen? ____

What is the most likely thing that will happen? _____

What can you do to handle the most likely thing if it happens? _____

Complete the ABCDEs. Now you are ready to practice the full ABCDE with your child. Remind your child of the disputation techniques. If his beliefs are "why" thoughts, he should look for contrary evidence and he should generate alternatives. If his beliefs are "what will happen next" thoughts, he should decatastrophize, using the strategy of worst, best, and most likely. After school, have him work through several examples with you as setbacks happen over the next week. Here are the questions to help your child focus his disputation.

1. Be like Sherlock Holmes: What is the evidence for my belief?
2. Be like Sherlock Holmes: What is the evidence against my belief?
3. What are some other ways of seeing this situation?
4. What's the worst that could happen?
5. What can I do to help stop it from happening?
6. What's the best that could happen?
7. What can I do to help make it happen?
8. What's the most likely outcome?
9. What is my plan of action if that happens?

Adversity: _____

_____

Beliefs: _____

_____

Consequences: _____

_____

Disputation: _____

_____

Energization: _____

_____

Adversity: _____

_____

Beliefs: _____

_____

Consequences: _____

_____

Disputation: _____

Energization: _____

Adversity: _____

Beliefs: _____

Consequences: _____

Disputation: _____

Energization: _____

Adversity: _____

Beliefs: _____

Consequences: _____

Disputation: _____

Energization: _____

Adversity: _____

Beliefs: _____

Consequences: _____

Disputation: _____

Energization: _____

The Brain Game. Once your child can effectively dispute her pessimistic thoughts from real-life setbacks, you are ready to teach your child the brain game. Rapid-fire disputing is the ultimate disputing exercise. Don't rush this. If your child is having difficulty working up effective disputations, keep at that. Remember, you are teaching your child skills that will last a lifetime. She did not learn to walk in a week. She did not move from addition and subtraction to long division and fractions without a lot of practice. The brain game adds speed to already effective disputations. If your child's disputations aren't yet effective, adding speed will be of no benefit. So be patient with the disputation skills. Set aside twenty minutes, two or three times a week, to practice disputation with your child, and once you are satisfied with her progress, start the brain game.

The brain game is the children's favorite activity in the Penn Prevention Program. Tell your child that you want to play a game with him that helps him to fight back against his pessimistic thoughts just as fast as they occur. Explain that he won't always have time to whip out a worksheet and make lists of all the evidence for and against each thought he has. For example, if he's standing at the plate in gym class and he catches himself thinking, "I stink at softball. I know I'm going to strike out. I always do!" he has to challenge this thought right there on the spot so he can maximize his chances of hitting the next pitch.

Ask your child to think of other situations when he might want to fight pessimistic thoughts right on the spot — taking a test, performing in the school play, presenting a report in front of the class, asking someone out on a date, and so on. It's good to challenge your thoughts on the spot anytime your thoughts are about to get in your way of doing what you want to do.

Tell your child that you want to teach him a game called the brain game. Explain that in this game, you pretend to be the part of your child's brain that hits him with pessimistic thoughts. You will give him a problem and then you will tell him the pessimistic thought that his brain comes up with. His job is to fight off the thought by coming up with one piece of evidence that shows why the thought isn't true or by coming up with a more optimistic way of looking at this situation.

Before you begin, read the following examples with your child to show him how it works. You play the part of the brain and let your child read the script of the main character.

Adversity: Molly is in the seventh grade. She likes her school a lot, but recently Debbie, a girl in the eighth grade, has started picking on her. One day after school, Molly is walking with some of her friends when Debbie and some of her friends start making fun of her. They stand in her path and say, "Hey, look at little Miss Blubber here. You're so fat, if you won the Miss America contest they'd sing 'Here she is, North America.' It's a day trip just to walk around you. You don't just eat like a cow, you are a cow. *Moooo. Mooooo.*" Molly turns bright red. She's ashamed of how she looks. She tries to ignore them but she can't. She bursts into tears and runs away.

Molly's brain: I'm such a baby. I can't even stick up for myself. They're right. I'm a fat cow. Nobody's ever gonna want to hang out with me.

Disputation: I am heavier than some of the other girls, and I wish I were skinny like Susie, but I'm not a fat cow. I exercise and dress real nice. I look pretty good. And I have lots of friends. They don't care that I weigh more than them. Susie and Jessica and Dana like me a lot and we have fun together.

Adversity: Carl just moved to Tenafly this summer. He likes his new house but he misses his friends a lot and he's nervous about starting the sixth grade. The first day of school is very hard for Carl. He doesn't know anyone. He sits by himself at lunch, and during recess no one plays with him.

Carl's brain: Already everybody hates me. I'm going to hate it here. I'm going to spend the rest of the year sitting alone at lunch. I'll never fit in.

Disputation: All right. So I didn't exactly make a million friends today. It was my first day. No one knows me yet. That doesn't mean I'll never have friends. I had lots of friends at Birchtree. Mom said it would take time. She's right. Maybe tomorrow I'll say hi to the boy who sits next to me in math. He looked nice.

After you've read through these examples with your child, practice rapid-fire disputing with the following examples. Tell your child that you are going to read him a situation and then you will throw five pessimistic thoughts at him one at a time. After each thought, his job is to combat it rapidly. Tell him you will be reading the thoughts in the first person, so that he can imagine that they are thoughts his brain is saying to himself. As you do this with your child, listen very closely to his disputations. If they are weak, stop him and help him find a more powerful dispute. Here are five situations, and five pessimistic thoughts for each situation.

1. You're supposed to take care of your neighbors' plants while they are away, but you lose the keys to their house and the plants die.
   A. I can't be trusted.
   B. My neighbor will never forgive me.
   C. I botch everything up.
   D. My parents are going to think I don't take responsibility seriously.
   E. I can't even do a simple thing like water a person's plants. I'll never be able to make it in life.

2. Your mother has been yelling at you a lot lately.
   A. She's the worst mother in the world.
   B. Whatever I do around the house is wrong.
   C. She must not love me as much as she used to.
   D. We're never going to get along again.
   E. All my friends have great relationships with their mothers. I'm the only one who gets in fights with my mother.

3. Someone copies your math homework and the teacher accuses you of cheating.
   A. The teacher is going to hate me from now on.
   B. My parents are going to be really angry at me.
   C. I am a bad person.
   D. My friends are going to look down on me now.
   E. No one is going to trust me.

4. You tease your brother all day and he starts to cry and screams, "You're the worst brother [or sister] in the whole world."
   A. He's right. I am the worst.
   B. I'm such a mean person.
   C. Now my brother is going to hate me forever.
   D. I never can control my temper.
   E. My parents are going to think I'm a rotten child.

5. It's the first week of seventh grade and you don't feel like anybody likes you.
   A. I'll never have any friends.
   B. Nobody likes me because I'm too boring.
   C. I'm going to be lonely for the rest of the year.
   D. If I were better looking, people would like me.
   E. If I had a better sense of humor, I'd have friends.

Once you've practiced using these situations, use a few of the situations from your child's ABCDE worksheets. Practice this skill three times a week for fifteen minutes at a time. Your child will soon learn how to respond to his own pessimism with force and speed. This is the skill to boost every few months to keep your child's disputing and decatastrophizing techniques sharp.

SUMMARY

"She has my eyes." "He has my athletic ability." "She has her mother's brains." Parents say these things with pride. Just think how proud you will feel when you say "She has my optimism" or "He has my perseverance." And that is what you have done. You are well on your way to immunizing your child against depression, underachievement, and helplessness. The skills you have taught yourself, and then taught your child, will become part of the arsenal of skills that you both will use throughout the rest of your lives. You have taught your child to maintain a "seize the day" attitude no matter what obstacles appear. All parents want to teach their children to value hard work, dedication, and drive. These values are important. But values and talent without optimism often come to nothing. You have done more than teach your child good values. You have developed your child's ability to struggle against life's challenges, fight to achieve her goals, and strive to surpass her potential.

In the next chapter I will teach you social and problem-solving skills that build on the cognitive skills you have just imparted. Together, these chapters will provide your child with the fundamental skills of optimism and mastery.

13

Boosting Your Child's Social Skills

IN CHAPTERS 10, 11, AND 12, you learned how to help your child challenge pessimistic beliefs and search for a more accurate understanding of the causes of setbacks. This crucial first step will help prevent your child from becoming depressed and giving up in the face of adversity. But one step is not enough. Once your child is able to interpret problems accurately, she will often find that there is a real problem that needs to be solved. Optimism will not make the problem disappear. On the contrary, it allows your child to get to the root of the problem so that she can focus on correcting the situation. Your child now needs to learn skills that allow her to handle the real problems she faces.

Late childhood marks the beginning of the lifelong task of developing and maintaining relationships outside of the family, as children turn to their friends, not just their parents and siblings, to meet their social needs. As your child's social sphere widens, you have ever-diminishing control over what happens away from home. This fact often makes parents feel helpless as they watch their child face dangers and setbacks at school or with friends. But there are skills you can teach your child, skills that he won't learn in any school, that will prepare him for dealing with such problems on his own.

Children with good social and problem-solving skills make new friends. They are comfortable in new situations. They say hello to children they have not met before and join in novel activities. They also know how to maintain friendships. They cooperate. They compromise. They trust others, and others develop trust in them. Children with good social and problem-solving skills handle conflicts well. They respect differences. They state their wishes clearly and assertively. They apologize when they are wrong, but they stick to their guns when they are right. Many children, especially children at risk for depression, do not have these skills. For these children, their new social life feeds feelings of depression and worthlessness. Take Christine, for example.

Christine is entering the seventh grade. Her parents have noticed changes in her behavior and in her grades and they are worried. Last year Christine was usually pretty cheerful. She had her moods, but they didn't last. She got A's and B's in most subjects, and she'd throw herself into new projects with a lot of enthusiasm. After school, she would hang out with a few girlfriends, and then run to call them as soon as she got home. This year is different. Christine sulks and stays in her room. When she isn't alone, she prefers to play with her younger sister instead of her friends. Her first report card showed two C's and only one A.

On back-to-school night, Christine's parents are surprised to hear that Christine isn't getting along with her friends and has been slow in finishing her work. Christine is angry and irritable at home, and when her parents ask her why, she refuses to talk about how she is feeling. But one day she comes into the house and bursts into tears:

Christine: They all hate me now! I don't know what I did, but they don't like me anymore.
Mom: Who's so mean? What happened?
Christine: My ex-friends. They were passing notes in the library today. I knew they were about me. I told them they should cut it out. Then I started to cry. I didn't want to, but I couldn't help it. They started laughing. They wanted me to cry. I just ran out of the library. Laurie tried to talk to me but I told her to leave me alone. She tried to show me the notes they were writing. I told her she was a traitor and that I hated her. The rest of the day was awful . . . they kept looking at me, and I tried to ignore them, but I couldn't stop crying.

Christine is having problems that are common for children at risk for depression. Let's look more closely. First Christine jumps to conclusions when she sees her friends passing notes. She assumes that the notes say bad things about her. Then she reacts to this assumption as if it were true, and she begins to cry. She's going on automatic, without much planning or thought about how her friends might react to this. When Laurie tries to talk with her, she rejects the help she is offered. In addition, she refuses to look at the notes, so she remains sure that the notes were about her. The rest of the day she keeps to herself and gets no support and no disconfirmation of her belief that her friends now hate her. If Christine continues to accuse her friends of being cruel and then withdraws, regardless of the accuracy of her accusations, her friends will retreat.

The relationship between depression and problematic friendships creates a vicious circle.[1] Problems with friends may contribute to Christine's feelings of depression. Once depressed, Christine will have a more difficult time dealing with conflict, which will worsen her friendships further. Now even if Christine starts to feel better, she will have lost friends and recovery will be harder. Together, lost friendships and weak social skills predispose Christine to another episode of depression.

Depression can affect boys and girls differently. Like Christine, girls tend to withdraw. They feel sad and cry. Boys, on the other hand, often get into physical fights. Let's look at Tony.

Tony is a fifth-grader, big for his age. He spends most of his time building models of cars and rockets. He loves to read books about race cars and plans on designing and racing cars when he is older. Usually an easygoing boy, Tony has been more irritable lately. When his parents ask him to do his chores or remind him about homework, Tony mopes and tells them to leave him alone. Initially, Tony's parents attribute his change in mood to "a stage" and back off. Their concern increases when they hear from a school guidance counselor that Tony has started to hang around a boy named Harvey, the class bully. Harvey is always picking fights and has been suspected of vandalizing the school.

One day on the bus, a kid in the fourth grade bumps into Tony as the bus rounds a corner. It isn't clear whether the kid did it on purpose or accidentally. Tony is sure that it was deliberate. He stands up and pushes the kid back into his seat. The boy looks scared and Tony starts to laugh at him. "Ahhhh, don't cry, little boy. Do you want your mommy? Here, maybe you better suck your thumb, that'll make you feel better." Tony grabs the boy's hand and tries to force it into his mouth. The boy starts to cry. Harvey laughs and claps Tony on the back. "You sure showed him, Tony!" Tony smiles, happy to be accepted by his new friend.

The next day there is another incident. Tony walks into the bathroom and sees four sixth-grade boys that he sometimes hangs out with. He plays basketball on the weekends with Scott, and Jared lives down the block. Jared was on the bus and saw Tony pick on the fourth-grader.

Jared: Well, if it isn't tough boy. You're real good at picking on puny fourth-graders. How are you with kids your own age?

Tony [*getting mad*]: What's it to you? Mind your own business.

Scott: Take it easy, Tony. He just means that you shouldn't pick on kids that much smaller than you.

Tony: Shut up, Scott. I didn't know you were such a baby. You guys are a bunch of wusses. Grow up.

It doesn't take long for a fight to erupt. Tony bangs his head on the sink basin and Jared gets a bruise on his arm. Tony's reputation flourishes. Tony gets in three more fights that year and is suspended twice from school. He stops playing basketball with Scott, and he and Jared ignore each other. His only friend, Harvey, is mainly interested in causing trouble. Together they start to steal things and spray graffiti on the school at night.

Tony is angry, but is he depressed? If someone asked him, Tony would say he's been feeling down lately, that he's not interested in things anymore, and that he's not as confident at school or with friends. He feels better when he wins a fight, but this feeling is short-lived. When he gets home after his latest fight, his parents are disappointed in him and he doesn't feel good. Tony would tell you that he's extremely frustrated because he knows how he should be acting but can't get himself to act that way.

Many parents don't ask kids like Tony how they are feeling because outwardly they don't look depressed. Instead of crying or moping around, Tony is getting in fights and misbehaving. Most parents will remain focused on his misconduct and will handle the situation by punishing him more and more.

In spite of the different outward signs, Tony was having some of the same problems as Christine. He misinterpreted other kids' intentions and reacted quickly and uncritically. The difference between Tony and Christine has to do with the interpretations they make. Christine automatically blames herself. She feels sad and withdraws because she believes she has done something to make her friends stop liking her. Tony, in contrast, automatically blames others. His basic view of the world is "People are out to get me."

The "people are out to get me" worldview is common in depression. These "hot" thoughts — fast and biased, instead of cool and critical — lead to impulsive and aggressive behavior.[2] Tony believes others want to harm him, so he retaliates. Tony needs to learn to control his anger and slow down his decision-making process, so he can sort through options and perhaps avoid another fight.

For Tony, it will be even harder to get back on track than it will be for Christine, even if he gets less depressed. Tony now has a reputation with the other kids. His peers expect him to be more aggressive, and challenge him or pick fights with him. Tony is headed down a very different path than he was a few months before. If he continues on this path, he is more likely to end up in a detention center than in college.

TEACHING PROBLEM-SOLVING AND SOCIAL SKILLS

Christine and Tony are caught in cycles that are difficult to break once they take hold. They can, however, be prevented. Children with a firm sense of competence and a bedrock of social and problem-solving skills will be less likely to get trapped in either of these cycles.

The social skills taught in the Penn Prevention Program are useful for all children, but they are essential if your child is beginning to show some signs of depression or problems with friends and at school. The first step, then, is to assess your child's current social skills and problem-solving abilities. Complete this questionnaire about your child's behavior.

Rate Your Child's Problem Solving and Social Skills

Rate each statement as follows:

1 = Rarely
2 = Sometimes, when under stress or in a bad mood
3 = Many times

PROBLEM-SOLVING SKILLS

A. Stop and Think: Interpretations about Problems

_____ Tends to jump to conclusions; gets angry easily.
_____ Is easily hurt by others at school.
_____ Is easily hurt by siblings or parents at home.
_____ Reports that others "don't like me."
_____ Reports that others are mean.

B. Perspective Taking

_____ Has difficulty understanding reasons for rules or limits.
_____ Has difficulty understanding other children's motives.
_____ Sees problems from own perspective only.
_____ Shows little concern for others' feelings.

C. Setting Goals and Generating Alternative Solutions

_____ Acts impulsively, without thinking.
_____ Shows poor planning.
_____ Is easily bored unless there is a planned activity at home.
_____ Gets stuck easily; asks for help at all times.

D. Pluses and Minuses: Choosing a Course of Action

_____ Has difficulty predicting consequences of actions.
_____ Gets locked into one way of handling problems, even if it doesn't work very well.

_____ Has difficulty making own decisions; constantly asks for assistance.

E. Trying Again When a Solution Fails
_____ Gets frustrated easily when goals are not met.
_____ Acts dissatisfied even when something works out well.
_____ When something doesn't work, gives up or gets angry.

SOCIAL SKILLS

F. Assertiveness
_____ Needs help to address a problem with a teacher or friend.
_____ Pouts or whines when unhappy with rules at home.
_____ Is overly aggressive with peers; has reputation as bully or bossy.
_____ Is overly passive with peers; lets himself/herself be taken advantage of.

G. Negotiation
_____ Has difficulty working out compromises with friends.
_____ Pouts when doesn't get his/her way.
_____ Sees all solutions as losses or wins; sees no shades of gray.

Scoring: Review each category. If you answered 2 or 3 for any statement, there is some difficulty in that area. If you answered 3 on two or more statements in any category, there is serious difficulty in that area.

Before you learn the problem-solving and social skills for children outlined later, bear in mind three rules of thumb. First, don't solve every problem for your child. Parents, especially those of depressed children, often feel that they need to "fix" their child's problems. They want their child to be happy, so they try to make her problems disappear. Unfortunately, this is harmful, not helpful. By intervening, parents prevent their child from learning the skills they need and they send the message "You can't handle things on your own." Not surprisingly, such children rely on their parents and, as they get older, on others to solve their problems. Rather than solve your child's problems, remain supportive and interested, but let your child think through the situation on his own. If he gets stuck, provide guidance but not answers.

Janice, the mother of one of the children in the program, describes how she used to deal with her son's problems:

> Eric is such a sweet kid. Ever since he was little, he's always had such a good heart and is real tuned in to feelings. Even when he was a toddler he'd ask me things like, "Mommy, are you sad today?" or "Do I make Craig happy when I show him books?" I remember when he was about two and his younger brother was less than a year; I was still breast-feeding Craig, so I was holding him a lot and giving him lots of attention. I remember I had just gotten Craig down for his nap and Eric walked over to me and asked "Mommy, do you miss me?" I was surprised, because I stay home with the kids so we're together all day long. The night before, my husband took Eric shopping, so I thought that's what he meant. So I asked if he meant did I miss him when he and Daddy did things alone. He got very serious, like he was really considering it, and then he said, "Ummm, no, not shopping. I mean . . . do you miss me when you hold Craig?" That really had a big effect on me. I kept thinking about that for a long time. I mean, some kids would feel real jealous about all the attention their sibling was getting, and maybe Eric did too, but he expressed it in such a sweet way. I remember thinking that he has such a gentle spirit.
>
> Anyway, ever since he was little, maybe I felt that he was so sensitive that he could get really hurt. So, I'd do whatever I could to protect him from things. I think all moms are like this to some extent, but now I think I may have protected him too much. Especially since I was probably more protective of him than his brother. I guess it really struck me just a few months ago. I was at the park with the boys and they were playing with some other kids. I was sitting with some other parents, just talking, you know. All of a sudden, this boy named Jesse started teasing Eric. I

couldn't hear what about, but I could tell Eric was getting upset. My immediate reaction was to jump up and put a stop to it. But for some reason I didn't. I decided to let him handle it. The problem is, Eric didn't handle it. He stood there for a minute just kind of listening to Jesse and then Craig walked over and told Jesse to knock it off. Craig was really great. He didn't tease the kid back or make things worse, he just told him in a really strong way to stop it, and Jesse listened.

Anyway, this really got me thinking. I started to pay more attention to what happens when Eric is struggling with something and I noticed that we all tend to get involved real quick. For all sorts of things, like figuring out his homework, or dealing with his friends, or even things like figuring out the best route for his paper route. And I started noticing the difference between the boys. Craig dives into his problems, he takes the lead. If he's really stuck, he'll seek us out, but usually he manages to figure things out on his own. Eric does the opposite. He'll come to us first. Instead of wrestling with it, he'll ask us for help. I used to feel good about it, like Eric knew how to get help when he needed it, but now I'm wondering if we've made him doubt himself too much. I worry that we took the struggle out of him.

The second rule of thumb is that once you give your child space to solve his own problems, you must not be overly critical of his attempts. He will surely make some bad starts and handle some situations poorly. But if you come down too hard, he will stop trying. As your child begins to learn these skills, keep your eye on the process rather than on the outcome. If he approaches the problem well but things don't work out as planned, compliment him on the steps he took and then help him evaluate where things went awry. Stewart, a father of a sixth-grade girl in our program, describes his struggles with this.

I'll tell you, it is hard to watch your child screw up. The thing is, I know she's trying and the skills she learned in the project make a difference, but every time I see her tackle a problem in a way that I think isn't the best, I want to tell her how to do it better. I guess it's okay to do that sometimes, but I want to do it every time. And I've got to be careful because I've got a fierce tongue. So even when I don't mean to be harsh, it sometimes sounds that way anyway. Like the other day, she got into a fight with some of her girlfriends. Seems they wanted her to make some nasty calls to some girl they don't like and Tori didn't want to do it. Says she felt bad for the girl. So I asked her what she did and she said she just lied and told them that she needed to get home to babysit her little sister. Now when I heard this, I wanted to tell Tori that I didn't think that was a good way to handle it. I want her to stand up to girls like that and tell them she's not going to be involved in their immature games. My wife thinks I'm crazy. She says it was real good of Tori to leave and that if lying helped her do it, then that is okay. Anyway, I ended up telling Tori that she took the easy way out, and she got real upset and my wife got upset too. It wasn't good. I felt pretty bad afterward. I'm working on it. I really am. My wife says I should help Tori think about her decision instead of telling her what's right and what's wrong. She's a lot better at it than me. But, hey, I'm trying.

The third rule of thumb is to model a flexible problem-solving strategy yourself. Let's look at two different ways you might handle the same situation:

Helen is getting her roof fixed. The roofer gives her an estimate based on repairing a section of asphalt tile, a gutter, and one downspout. He asks for half of the payment upfront. Helen pays him and then leaves to pick up her child at school. When she returns, the workmen are gone. The asphalt tile is finished, but there's no gutter or downspout.

Helen shouts: "Where are they? Don't tell me they're gone! Those bastards! They didn't do the gutter! I should have known this would happen. They're trying to rip me off, but I'm not going to stand for it. Mitchell, get out of the car . . . I've got to go call them and give them a piece of my mind!"

Sound familiar? We all overreact at times. But if this is the main style of problem solving that Mitchell witnesses at home, he'll learn to jump to conclusions, fly off the handle, and act impulsively. Let's look at another way to handle the same situation.

Helen says: "Where are they? They're not finished yet. The gutter's not done. I wonder if they are taking a break? Or getting supplies? I hope they didn't forget the gutter! It's going to be a real problem if they don't finish today, because I can't stay home again tomorrow. Maybe I'll wait a few minutes and see if they come back. Better yet, maybe I'll give the supervisor a call and find out what the deal is."

By thinking it through out loud, Helen is modeling a slower, more thoughtful response style. In the second example, she listed several possible interpretations or ways to handle the situation, rather than jumping to conclusions. She ultimately chose the one that allowed her to gather more information so that she could make an informed decision about how to react.

PROBLEM SOLVING: THE FIVE STEPS[3]

Step 1: Slowing Down. There are five steps your child needs to follow in order to solve problems effectively. The first is to teach your child to *slow down*. Your child needs to stop himself from acting impulsively. Start by reading the following situation to your child and then have him complete the worksheet that follows.

You are standing in line at the drinking fountain. There are five kids behind you, waiting their turn. Two kids at the back of the line are playing around and they bump into the person in front of them. That boy falls into Tommy, who is standing behind you. Tommy bumps into you while you are drinking from the fountain, and you get your face pushed into the water. Now, you didn't see all this happen, because you were drinking the water. All you know for sure is that Tommy bumped into you and your face is all wet.

As you go over this worksheet with your child, point out to him that how he handles the situation depends on what he thinks. Tell him that the first step in being an ace problem solver is to "stop and

YOU'RE ALL WET . . .

Be like Sherlock Holmes and make a list of all the reasons that might explain why your face got wet.

1. One reason is . . . _____

_____

2. Another reason is . . . _____

_____

3. Another reason is . . . _____

_____

4. Another reason is . . . _____

_____

5. Another reason is . . . _____

_____

think" for a minute before he does anything. Ask him what he would do if he believed each reason he listed in the worksheet. Stopping also gives him a chance to find out what really happened.

One way to help your child slow down is to teach him to replace his "hot thoughts" with "cool thoughts." Tell your child that hot thoughts are the thoughts that come to mind the second a problem happens. They are "people are out to get me" thoughts. Children who have a lot of hot thoughts believe that whenever a problem happens between them and someone else, the other person caused the problem on purpose. The problem with hot thoughts is that they lead us to react without first understanding what happened or how best to handle the situation. If we follow our hot thoughts, we'll often regret it because we can end up making problems even worse.

Cool thoughts are thoughts that help us figure out more about what has happened so that we can consider all the available information before we decide how to respond. Cool thoughts help us to slow down and think rather than speed up and act.

William was a seventh-grader in our program. He describes a typical problem that hot thoughts cause for him.

My dad always used to say I act first and think later. He says that's not too good. I used to just think he was getting on my case 'cause he does that a lot, but now I sort of see what he means. Like last year I got into this killer fight with Lenny, a kid in my school. He's tough, pretty mean. We were at lunch and Lenny was sitting at the table behind me. I wasn't paying him any attention, you know, I was just eating my lunch. I get up to drop off my tray and *slam!* Lenny wallops into me. My tray spilled all over me. It was so gross. I had disgusting school spaghetti hanging off my shirt. Everybody was laughing. All day long kids were calling me "Sp'ged head" and stuff. I was really mad. Anyways, I figured Lenny had done it on purpose, you know, trying to make a fool of me, so I just popped Lenny right in the face. I didn't say anything, I just hit him. And hard, too. That was it. Lenny just started pounding me big time. I gotta say, I was scared. Finally, Mr. Harlin comes over and pulls him off me. But I was hurting. I had this purple-and-yellowish bruise on my cheek for the longest time. And it hurt a lot. So, we get dragged to Mrs. Lyman's office and Lenny says he didn't even do it on purpose. She believed him, and I guess I did too a little, but I didn't say that. He got in trouble for pounding me, but I got in bigger trouble for picking the fight. It was bad.

My parents were really mad at me. The program I was in taught me what to do when things like that happen. They called it thinking cool, not hot. They said that the problem with thinking hot is that a lot of times you end up just sort of doing things before you get a chance to figure stuff out. Just like what my dad says. So, this year I'm trying not to hot-think so much. Sometimes I still do, but at least not all the time anymore. My dad says I've gotten a lot better about it.

Read the following situations and thoughts with your child. Ask him to tell you which are the hot thoughts and which are the cool thoughts and where each thought would probably lead.

After you've practiced identifying hot and cool thoughts, you are

BE COOL . . .

1. Tony is playing dodge ball at recess and someone throws the ball and it hits him real hard right in the face. He thinks:
   A. What happened? Was that an accident or is he trying to start something?
   B. He did that on purpose! I'm gonna get him. He's gonna wish he never messed with me.

2. Tara leaves three messages for her friend to call her back as soon as she gets in. Tara's friend doesn't call all night. Tara thinks:
   A. Why isn't she calling me? I wonder if she's mad at me? Or maybe she forgot to listen to the answering machine. Or maybe her brother played the messages and didn't tell her I called.
   B. She's being mean. She's just acting like she doesn't know I called.

3. Jonah's supposed to meet his friend at the mall at 3:30. He waits for half an hour, but his friend doesn't show up. Jonah thinks:
   A. Figures. George is such a creep. He's supposed to be my best friend but he's always jerking me around like this. I'm not gonna take this anymore!
   B. What's the deal? This really sucks. If he just decided not to come, I'm gonna be really pissed. Maybe he got in trouble or something. I'll call him later to find out what happened.

ready to have your child practice coming up with cool thoughts on his own. This game, called the hot seat, is just like the brain game in the last chapter. This time your child is faced with situations and a hot thought, and he has to supply a more rational or thoughtful alternative, a cool thought. Here are the instructions.

Sit down with your child and explain that you are going to play a game called the hot seat: "I'm going to tell you about a problem that might happen to someone your age. Then I'll read you a hot thought that a kid could have in the situation. Remember, hot thoughts make you act without first thinking through the problem. After I tell you the hot thought, I want you to come up with a cool thought. A cool thought is one that helps you slow down so that you don't jump to conclusions and act without first thinking things through. Cool thoughts help you to take a step back and look at the problem in lots of different ways so that you can understand what is going on before you act."

1. You arrive at the corner where you are supposed to meet your friends to walk to school. None of them are there. You wait five more minutes, but they still don't come.
   Your hot thought: They ditched me!

2. You are waiting in line in a store. The store clerk waits on the man standing behind you before he rings up your order.
   Your hot thought: He hates kids.

3. You want to play on the soccer team. When you go into the locker room on the first day, you hear all the other kids laugh.
   Your hot thought: They are making fun of me.

4. You get to the front of the line at the water fountain and, as you begin to drink, you get pushed from behind and your face gets all wet.
   Your hot thought: Someone pushed me on purpose.

5. You let your brother borrow a tape that you borrowed from your friend. You tell him that you need it back by 3:00 because you promised to bring it by your friend's house. It's 3:15 and your brother and the tape are nowhere to be found.
   Your hot thought: He's trying to get me in trouble.

There are many right answers for each of these examples. Remember, the goal is to help your child develop a more thoughtful style. In the first situation listed above, if your child says any of the following, he is heading in the right direction:

Maybe they are late.
I wonder where they are. Is there a late start today?
Maybe I'm late and they went ahead.
Maybe they got a ride.

Could they all be sick or something?
I better go to school and find out what happened later.

On the other hand, if your child gives a response such as those that follow, he is supplying an equally hot thought:

They must have planned this to get back at me.
I bet they are all hiding from me.
They don't like me. This always happens.

If your child replaces one hot thought with another, ask him how he would act if he believed the new thought. After he describes his actions, ask him if he thinks this would be the best way to handle the situation. Then help him construct a cool thought that allows him to keep an open mind about the problem he is faced with.

Step 2: Perspective Taking. After your child is able to slow himself down by replacing hot thoughts with cool thoughts, he is ready to learn the second step of problem solving: perspective taking. Explain perspective taking like this: Before we can decide how to handle a problem we are having with another person, we first need to understand what the other person was thinking or why she acted the way that she did. For example, in the water fountain situation, why did Tommy bump into you? Most people would handle the situation differently if Tommy did it on purpose or if it was an accident. Tell your child that the best way to understand why someone acted the way he did is to stand in the other person's shoes and look at the situation from his perspective. Then you can be like Sherlock Holmes and look for evidence and clues. Ask your child what are some kinds of clues she could look for to help her figure out why Tommy bumped into her.

One way to find out what other people are thinking and feeling is to look at their faces. If Tommy looked embarrassed or afraid, why might you think you got pushed? If he looked embarrassed, then it was probably an accident. If Tommy looked mad, what might be the reason? If he looked angry, then it's possible that he did it on purpose.

Tell your child that another way to get clues is to ask the person a question. Ask your child what she could ask Tommy to help her figure out why he bumped into her. She could ask, "Why did you do that?"

or "What happened?" Asking a question helps you get more evidence about what happened.

Now you can help your child practice stepping into other people's shoes using the following worksheets. Each worksheet tells a story involving three different people. Read each story aloud and ask your child to try to figure out what the three people are thinking.

LOOK FOR CLUES, STAND IN ANOTHER'S SHOES

The Problem: Kelly is just about to start the sixth grade. She and her friend Jody decide to get short haircuts. Just as they are walking out of the hair salon, they run into their friend Eric. Eric tells Jody that he likes her haircut. All Eric says to Kelly is "How are you doing?" Kelly gets annoyed and doesn't say anything back to Eric. Jody tells Kelly that she thinks her haircut looks great, but Kelly doesn't say a word for the whole walk home. Jody is supposed to call Kelly later that night, but she doesn't.

Why did Kelly get mad? What was she thinking? _____

_____

_____

_____

Why did Eric say he liked Jody's haircut but didn't say anything about Kelly's? What was he thinking? _____

_____

_____

_____

_____

Why didn't Jody call Kelly? What was she thinking? _____

_____

_____

_____

The Problem: Ellen, Lynn, and Carol all went to Roslyn Elementary School. They used to sit at the same table during lunch. Today is their first day of junior high. Ellen walks into the cafeteria and doesn't see anyone she knows. Finally she spots Lynn and Carol sitting at a table with a big group of kids. Seeing them makes her feel better, because she was beginning to feel really dumb just holding her tray and not knowing where to sit. She walks by the table and says hello to Lynn and Carol. Lynn says hi to her and Carol whispers something to the girl sitting next to her. Neither of them invites Ellen to eat at their table. Ellen feels really sad and sits with some kids she doesn't know at the other end of the cafeteria. Lynn looks mad and Carol surprised.

Why did Ellen feel sad? What was she thinking? _____

_____

_____

_____

Why did Lynn look mad? What was she thinking? _____

_____

_____

_____

Why did Carol look surprised? What was she thinking? _____

_____

_____

_____

The Problem: Betsy, Robert, and Denise live in the same neighborhood. Betsy is a couple of years younger than Robert and Denise, but they all hang out together after school. One night there is a big snowstorm, and the next day in the park a lot of the older kids start throwing snowballs and tackling the younger kids. A couple of Robert's friends start picking on Betsy. Betsy sees Robert and Denise laughing and she gets really mad. Later that day Robert and Denise come to Betsy's door to see if she wants to go sledding with them. Betsy says no and slams the door in their faces. Robert looks really sad and Denise seems angry.

Why did Betsy slam the door? What was she thinking? _____
_____
_____
_____

Why did Robert laugh with Denise? What was he thinking? _____
_____
_____
_____

Why did Denise get angry? What was she thinking? _____
_____
_____
_____

Another way to practice perspective taking is to use conflicts that arise between the two of you. When you have a disagreement with your child about rules or chores, try switching roles for a minute so that you can each understand why the other is acting that way. Look for an occasion that parallels the example of Cory, who wants to postpone his chore of washing dishes. Here's how you can use such an opportunity to teach perspective taking.

Mom: Cory Sand, this is the third time I've had to ask you to do the dishes. I don't want to ask you again.

Cory: Ah, Mom. Come on. I'll do them later. They're not going anywhere. What's the big deal?

Mom: All right, Cory, let's hang on a minute. We're obviously having trouble working this out. Let's try something different. I'll stand in your shoes and you stand in mine.

Cory: Huh? What are you talking about?

Mom: Come on, come on. Let's switch places. Really, you come and stand here and I'll sit on the couch. [*Mom flops on the couch and hands Cory the potholder she is holding.*] I'll try to see if I understand your position first. Okay . . . I'm Cory. I don't want to do the dishes now because my favorite shoot-em-up show is on. And I spent all afternoon doing my homework, which is now finished, so that I could watch a lot of people on my favorite show get shot but not seem to bleed much or be in much pain. Even though it is my night for the dishes, I think I should be able to do them later on, after the show. Is that right, Cory? Did I miss anything?

Cory [*rolling his eyes and laughing*]: Well, that's pretty good. But you missed that I helped Dad with that crazy project he's working on and that took almost an hour and it wasn't even part of my chores.

Mom: Okay, and the other thing is that I also spent an hour this morning helping Dad out with his ingenious project and I didn't even have to do that. Okay, now it's your turn. You stand in my shoes and describe my position.

Cory: Okay. [*speaking in a high-pitched voice*] Well, now, each of you kids has your chores around the house and there are lots of times when you don't get them done when you are supposed to. Especially that pesky Benjamin. Then I end up having to nag, nag, nag and I don't like doing that. How's that?

Mom: Good. I also get mad because sometimes I end up doing the chore myself.

Cory: Okay. And sometimes, when you kids don't do your work, I end up doing it myself. That really bugs me.

By role-playing the other person, Cory and his mom were able to break the tension and understand each other's behavior. Guided by this information, they were able to negotiate that on Thursday nights Cory would do the dishes at nine o'clock, after the show, and on Tuesdays he would do them right after dinner. They both felt understood and felt good about the plan.

You can also play the "perspective-taking game." The next time you are watching a video with your child and the scene has focused on one of the main characters for a few minutes, stop the tape. Ask everyone in the room to guess what one of the more minor characters is thinking or feeling, based on what you've seen in the video. Then watch the rest of the tape and see whose idea was closest to the truth for that character. Give points for creativity if it also matches what you've seen in the movie. This game will help to teach kids to look for cues in someone's behavior to tip them off about that person's perspective.

Step 3: Goal Setting. The third step in problem solving is to decide what you would like to have happen, to set a goal, and then to list the things you could do to help you reach the goal. Tell your child that a goal is something that you want to happen, so you do all you can to make sure it comes true. For example, if you had an ugly fight with your friend and your goal was to stay friends, you might apologize, do something special for her, and agree to change the things that you do that annoy her.

Tell your child that people could have all sorts of different goals if they got bumped into by Tommy at the water fountain. One person might want to make sure that Tommy doesn't ever bump into him again, and another person might want to make sure Tommy stays his friend. Tell your child that before she figures out how to solve a problem, she first needs to decide what her goal is. And before she sets a goal, she first needs to try to understand the situation from the other person's point of view by standing in his shoes.

After your child picks a goal, she should list as many ways as possible to reach it. Many children get locked into one path, only to get stuck when it is a dead end. Your child should list all the paths that occur to her or that she could imagine someone else having. The best atmosphere for "unlocking" solutions is one in which there is no penalty for outlandish ideas. Later, some will be tossed out because they are impractical, others because they could cause a different sort of problem, and still others because your child just doesn't want to do it that way.

To help your child practice thinking about goals and solutions, complete the following worksheet.

GOING FOR THE GOAL

Here are three problems and the beliefs the child has about the cause of each problem. Ask your child to come up with a goal that follows from the beliefs and as many things as he can think of that will help him reach his goal.

The Problem: Bobby gets his math test back and sees that he has gotten a B. As he looks it over, he notices that the teacher has added up the score wrong and that he should have gotten an A.

If Bobby thinks: "My teacher did that on purpose. She doesn't want me to get an A."

His goal might be: _____

_____

Bobby could reach this goal by:

1. _____
2. _____
3. _____
4. _____

If Bobby thinks: "She must have made a mistake."

His goal might be: _____

_____

Bobby could reach this goal by:

1. _____
2. _____
3. _____
4. _____

The Problem: While Courtney is waiting in the cafeteria line for lunch, someone butts in front of her.

If Courtney thinks: "Maybe her friend was saving her place while she went to the bathroom or something."

Her goal might be: _____
_____

Courtney could reach this goal by: _____
_____

1. _____
2. _____
3. _____
4. _____

If Courtney thinks: "She's a bully. She thinks she can do whatever she wants."

Her goal might be: _____
_____

Courtney could reach this goal by:

1. _____
2. _____
3. _____
4. _____

The Problem: Billy, Karen, and Pat were playing a game. Billy won the game, but Pat started yelling and told Billy that he cheated.

If Billy thinks: "Pat's just mad that she lost. She doesn't mean it."

His goal might be: _____
_____

Billy can reach this goal by:

1. _____
2. _____
3. _____
4. _____

If Billy thinks: "Pat's a lousy liar and she's trying to make me look bad."

His goal might be: _____

_____

Billy could reach this goal by:

1. _____

2. _____

3. _____

4. _____

Now ask your child to describe two recent problems she has had with another person and to complete the worksheet for those problems.

The Problem: _____

_____

If I thought: _____

_____

Then my goal might be: _____

_____

I could reach this goal by:

1. _____

2. _____

3. _____

4. _____

If I thought: _____

_____

Then my goal might be: _____

_____

I could reach this goal by:

1. _____
2. _____
3. _____
4. _____

The Problem: _____

_____

If I thought: _____

_____

Then my goal might be: _____

_____

I could reach this goal by:

1. _____
2. _____
3. _____
4. _____

If I thought: _____

_____

Then my goal might be: _____

_____

I could reach this goal by:

1. _____
2. _____
3. _____
4. _____

Step 4: Choosing a Path. The fourth step in problem solving is to choose a course of action. Tell your child that once he sets a goal and lists all the paths he can follow to reach this goal, then it is time to decide which path offers the best solution to the problem. Part of the decision process is to compare the pros and cons of each course of action. Explain to your child that the pros are any good consequences that might result from a particular course and that the cons are any bad consequences. A consequence is any action or feeling stemming from a choice. When listing the pluses and minuses, think about the immediate consequences as well as the long-term consequences. How will you feel about your decision in three days? What will happen a week later because of the decision you made? Considering the pluses and minuses is particularly important if someone has two competing goals for the same situation. For example, if after Pat accuses Billy of cheating, Billy has both the goal of staying friends with Pat and the competing goal of making it clear that she is lying, then it is crucial that he compare the pluses and minuses of each, staying friends versus exposing her lie. Of course, the best solution to choose is the one that has a lot of pluses and not many minuses.

The next exercise asks your child to list two paths to a goal, then to list the pluses and minuses for each path and decide which path is best. First, here is an example of the plus-and-minus approach from a seventh-grader in our program for you to read to your child. Before she listed the pluses and minuses on paper, our seventh-grader had a hard time thinking through the consequences. Once they were down on paper, however, she was able to decide that the minuses of solution 2 were not as bad, nor as likely, as the minuses of solution 1. She then decided how to handle the conflict.

PLUSES AND MINUSES

1. Your parents go out to visit some friends. They won't return until late. Your mom says you can have one friend over. Your friend wants to have a party.

   Your goal is: You want your friend to like you, but you don't want your parents to be mad at you.

Solution 1: I invite a couple other kids from school over, but I tell them that they have to leave by ten o'clock so I can clean up the house before my parents get back so that they'll never know.

Pluses	Minuses
1. My friends think I'm cool.	1. I get caught and get in big trouble.
2. I have a lot of fun.	2. I feel guilty later and feel bad for breaking the rules.
3. The others like me better and want to hang out more. I become more popular.	3. I can't get everyone out by ten and they think I'm a loser for making them leave so early.
4. I don't feel like a goody-goody.	4. I'm so worried about getting caught that I don't have a good time anyway.

Solution 2: I tell my friend that I can't have a party, but I call my parents and ask if I can have a party another night. My friend and I spend the night talking about who to invite and planning what the party will be like.

Pluses	Minuses
1. I don't get into big trouble with my parents.	1. My parents say no and then I don't get to have a party and I could have had one if I sneaked.
2. My friend and I get to have fun planning the party together.	2. My friend doesn't want to come over unless we have a party, so I spend the night by myself.
3. I feel good about handling things in the right way.	3. My friend tells other kids at the school that I was a baby.

4. I get to have a party and don't have to worry about being caught.

4. My friend comes over but we have a boring time.

Now have your child do the first problem:

1. It's your friend's birthday and you go to the mall to buy her a present. At the mall you see a tape that you really want. You don't have enough money for both the tape and the present.
   Your goal is: You want to buy the tape.

Solution 1: _____

_____

Pluses	Minuses
1. _____	1. _____
2. _____	2. _____
3. _____	3. _____
4. _____	4. _____

Solution 2: _____

Pluses	Minuses
1. _____	1. _____
2. _____	2. _____
3. _____	3. _____
4. _____	4. _____

Solution _____ is the better decision.

Now ask your child to practice this with two problems of his own.

2. **Problem:** _____

_____

_____

Your goal is: _____

_____

Solution 1: _____
_____
_____

Pluses	Minuses
1. _____	1. _____
2. _____	2. _____
3. _____	3. _____
4. _____	4. _____

Solution 2: _____
_____
_____

Pluses	Minuses
1. _____	1. _____
2. _____	2. _____
3. _____	3. _____
4. _____	4. _____

Solution _____ is the better decision.

3. Problem: _____
_____
_____

Your goal is: _____
_____

Solution 1: _____
_____
_____

Pluses	Minuses
1. _____	1. _____
2. _____	2. _____
3. _____	3. _____
4. _____	4. _____

Solution 2: _____

_____

_____

Pluses   Minuses
1. _____   1. _____
2. _____   2. _____
3. _____   3. _____
4. _____   4. _____

Solution _____ is the better decision.

Step 5: How Did It Go? The last step of good problem solving is to check if it worked. Often, even with the forethought and planning of steps 1–4, solutions don't work the way we hope. Tell your child not to give up at this point. If his first plan of action didn't work, if the consequences were not what he intended, then he can pick another solution from his list and give that one a shot.

PRACTICE PROBLEM SOLVING: STEPS 1 TO 5

After you have practiced each of the five steps with your child, use the following scenarios to practice working through the entire problem-solving process aloud. Here are the key points to follow. You should prompt your child with each step if he does not remember them.

> Step 1 — Slow Down: Stop and Think. Use cool thoughts, not hot thoughts.
>
> Step 2 — Take the Other Person's Perspective: Stand in another's shoes.
>
> Step 3 — Go for the Goal: Choose a goal and make a list of possible paths.
>
> Step 4 — Plan of Action: What are the pluses and minuses of each path?
>
> Step 5 — How Did It Go?: If the solution didn't work, try another.

1. Randy's mother comes into his room one night and tells him, "Your dad wants you and your brother to spend the holidays with him. But I think you should stay here. I told him no, but he really wants you guys, so we decided that you will go to see your dad and that your brother will stay here and spend the holidays with me. I just wanted to tell you what we decided."

2. Some kids from Laura's class pick on Laura every day on the way to school. One day they grab her homework assignment and run away with it, laughing. Laura is afraid to tell her teacher because the other kids might hear about it and pick on her even more. During class, the teacher yells at Laura for not having the assignment and says she will have to call Laura's mother to discuss it with her.

3. Rick is getting ready to present his science project to his entire class. His project is about the development of turtles. As he begins his speech, he realizes that the baby turtle and its mother are not in the box. He glances around the room and does not see them anywhere. His teacher says from across the room, "Rick, we don't have all day."

4. Katrina is walking home from school when she sees two really cool kids from her class in an alley. She says hello, and sees that they are smoking cigarettes. She's not sure what to do. She wants them to like her, but she doesn't think it's good to smoke. They say, "Hi, Katrina. Want a puff? I like your new jacket. Where did you get it?"

5. Malcolm's teacher calls him in after class and tells him that his grades are getting worse in English. The teacher thinks he's spending too much time playing basketball after school and thinks he should quit the school basketball team. He tells Malcolm that he'll get the coach to cut him if Malcolm doesn't quit.

SOCIAL SKILLS

Assertiveness. Children who are at risk for depression find it difficult to state what they want in a clear, forceful manner. This is especially true if they are feeling depressed and withdrawn from other people, or irritable and angry. Instead of being assertive, they can be overly passive or overly hostile. No matter how well your child works through the five problem-solving steps, if he is too passive or too aggressive when it comes time to put his solution into practice, his solution won't work well. Assertiveness is the useful midpoint between passivity and aggression, and it is the strategy that usually works best.

Carla was a sixth-grader in our program. She describes how well she used assertiveness.

I was in a huge fight with my friend. See, Darlene was supposed to come with my family on a rafting trip. We were going to camp out overnight and raft down this really wild river. Everything was all planned. My mom even went food shopping and bought things that Darlene liked. Then the day before we were going to leave, Darlene calls and says she can't go 'cause she's sick. I was pretty upset 'cause it would have been a lot more fun with her there. But that's not why we had a fight. The fight was 'cause when I got back Gina told me that she saw Darlene at Franny's party. She said she was dancing and messing around and that she didn't look sick at all. I was *so* mad. I wanted to just let her have it.

But I remembered all that stuff we learned in the Penn Project, so I told myself to be calm and slow down. Lisa taught us how to say things assertively. So instead of letting Darlene have it, I tried to be calm. I stopped and thought and I called her on the phone. I told her that I was mad about something and that I wanted to talk to her about it. Then I told her that I was really upset when she couldn't come with us but that I wasn't mad because she said she was sick and she couldn't help that. Then I told her what Gina told me and I said that I got mad when I heard it. I said that I was really excited about her going with us and that my parents went out of their way to make sure she would have a good time. Then I told her I was hurt and asked her why she said she was sick if she wasn't. That was really hard for me because I just wanted to level her, but I didn't. It went okay, I guess. She got real quiet and then started apologizing. She said she didn't want to lie but that she felt too stupid to tell me the real reason. She said that she started to get really scared about going. She's never rafted before and she was scared that she'd fall out and smack into a rock or something. I can sort of understand that, especially since my brother is always telling her how wild and dangerous it is. I really felt a lot better after I talked to her, and I told her that I wouldn't have gotten as mad if she had told me the truth. She said she would tell me the truth next time.

Here is a simple four-step approach to assertion.[4] First, tell your child that you want to role-play a couple of skits with him. Each of these three skits deals with the same situation: The child has plans to go to the mall with his friend. The friend backs out at the last minute. The child is upset. But in each skit, the child handles being upset in a very different way. Read each skit aloud.

Bully Brenda Skit (Aggressiveness)

Situation: Bully Brenda had plans to go to the mall after school with her friend Joe. Many times before when they have made plans, Joe has changed his mind at the last minute.

Brenda: So, are you ready to catch the bus to the mall?

Joe: Oh, I'm sorry, but Tony called me a couple of days ago and I made plans to go over to his house. We're going to play Nintendo. Sorry, but I have to go.

Brenda: Sure you did. You always do this to me. I can't count on you for anything. See if I ask you to go next time. Next time, I'll make plans with someone who can keep them! You're a lousy person and a lousy friend. You can't get away with this. I'll get you back sometime, you'll see.

Joe: Go ahead. See if I care.

After reading the skit, ask your child what she thinks about the way Brenda handled her disappointment. Point out that she started to fight with Joe. Ask your child if she thinks this will make the situation better or worse.

Now read the skit about Pushover Pete.

Pushover Pete Skit (Passivity)

Same situation: Pushover Pete had plans to go to the mall after school with his friend Joe. Many times before when they have had plans, Joe has changed his mind at the last minute.

Pete: So, are you ready to catch the bus to the mall?
Joe: Oh, I'm sorry, but Tony called me a couple days ago and I made plans to go over to his house. We're going to play Nintendo. Sorry, but I have to run.
Pete: Oh.
Joe: Have fun at the mall!
Pete: Yeah . . . okay.

Ask your child what she thinks about this skit. What did Pushover Pete do when Joe told him he had other plans? Do you think just saying OK will make the situation better? What do you think will happen the next time they make plans? Joe will probably be just as insensitive and make an alternate plan.

Ask your child what she thinks she could do instead of acting like Bully Brenda or Pushover Pete. Then tell her that there is one more skit to role-play.

Say-It-Straight Samantha Skit (Assertiveness)

Same situation: Samantha had plans to go to the mall after school with her friend Joe. Many times before when they have had plans, Joe has changed his mind at the last minute.

Samantha: So, are you ready to catch the bus to the mall?
Joe: Oh, I'm sorry, but Tony called me a couple days ago and I made plans to go over to his house. We're going to play Nintendo. Sorry, but I have to run.
Samantha: Joe, I'm really frustrated. You've been changing your plans a lot lately. It hurts my feelings because I think it means that you don't want to spend time with me.
Joe: Sorry, I guess I just didn't think about it.
Samantha: Next time, it would make me feel a lot better if you could stick to our plans.

Joe: Okay, I'll try not to let it happen again. How about going to the mall this weekend instead?

Samantha: Sounds good.

Ask your child what she thinks of the Say-It-Straight Samantha approach. What did Samantha do when Joe told her he had other plans? Who do you think will feel the best, Bully Brenda, Pushover Pete, or Say-It-Straight Samantha? Which child do you think handled the situation the best?

There are four things that Samantha did that constitute assertiveness, and it is important that you teach each step to your child. First, *Samantha described the situation* that was upsetting her. She said to Joe that she thought he had backed out of a lot of their plans lately. Notice how she did this. She didn't yell or scream and she didn't cry. She also didn't blame Joe. All she did is say, as clearly as possible, what the situation was. This is just like how your child learned to describe an activating event in the ABCs. She should describe only the facts of the situation, without letting her beliefs about why it happened or how she felt slip in.

Next, *Samantha told him how she felt.* Samantha said that the situation made her feel frustrated. Again, she didn't blame Joe for making her feel frustrated. Instead, she just described how she felt as clearly as she could. Blaming Joe right away would just have put him on the defensive.

Then, *Samantha told him what she wants him to change.* She told him she wanted him to stick to their plans or let her know earlier next time. Again, she is very specific, so Joe should know exactly what she wants him to do.

Finally, *Samantha told him how the change would make her feel.* She said she would feel better if Joe did as she asked. If Joe wants her to feel better, he knows what to do.

Assertiveness Situations. Now you are ready to practice these four steps with your child. Tell your child that you have some more skits, but this time there aren't any lines written out for her. Tell her that what you're going to do is read the situation and then you want her to act like Say-It-Straight Samantha and go through the four steps.

Remember the four steps:

Step 1: Describe the situation: just the facts.

Step 2: Say how you feel. Don't blame the other person for your feelings.

Step 3: Ask for a specific and small change.

Step 4: Say how this change will make you feel.

1. Your dad sometimes calls you "Squirt" and other nicknames in front of your friends and it bothers you.
2. Your mom has been yelling at you a lot lately for little things you've done wrong. You feel sad when she yells at you and you wish she could tell you what was wrong without yelling at you.
3. It's Friday night and you and your friend Jon have plans to go to a movie. Jon wants to see a movie you already saw, and he usually gets his way by saying he won't go out unless you do what he wants. You think you should take turns.
4. You are about to take a test in social studies and one of the kids in your class asks to copy from your exam. You don't want her to copy your test. You've studied a lot for the exam and are afraid you will get a bad grade because the teacher will think you copied.
5. A kid from the high school asks if you want to try some pot. He calls you "chicken." You don't want to try the pot and you're annoyed that he's asking you.
6. Your teacher gave you a D on a test. You think the test was unfair because it asked questions about material she said would not be covered. You want to tell her how you feel.
7. There's a kid at school who teases you every day at lunch. You want him to stop teasing you.
8. A boy took your homework and handed it in as his. Confront the student.
9. You are watching television when your dad comes in and changes the channel without asking you if you mind.

Few children (and few adults) are able to do all four steps well right away. Consistent practice over the course of several weeks greatly improves a child's ability to assert himself.

If your child is either very shy or very impulsive, you may want to build in some role-playing. Use whatever situation your child is actually facing, and ask him to practice what he would say with you. For instance, take the situation Carl is facing.

Carl, who has been an A and B student in the fourth grade, comes home one day very frustrated with his teacher. He's a smart but quiet boy, on the shy side. He tells his grandmother the following story:

Carl: Ms. Reider isn't being fair. She lets Jill do all the fun stuff in class now, like decorating the bulletin boards and making murals. Jill barely has to do any work anymore! I used to do those things, but Ms. Reider doesn't let me anymore, ever since I got a C on my spelling test. I hate school!

Grandma: You hate all of school? Slow down, Carl. I can see you're upset, so it sounds like you need to talk with Ms. Reider. Can you talk with her tomorrow?

Carl: I don't want to. . . . I don't think she'll have the time.

Grandma: Well, just in case she does have time, let's practice what you could say to her. I'll be Ms. Reider, and you tell me what's wrong.

Carl: Okay. Ms. Reider, I want to work on the murals more.

Grandma [as Ms. Reider]: Sorry, Carl. Jill's already doing them. Maybe next time.

Carl: See? That's what she'll say. Never mind.

Grandma: No, Carl, don't give up yet. You haven't told her what's bothering you yet. Can you do that? Just tell her what you told me when you walked in here this afternoon.

Carl: Okay. Ms. Reider, how come I don't get to paint the murals anymore? You always ask Jill, and it doesn't seem fair.

Grandma [as Ms. Reider]: Well, Carl, I thought you might need more time in class, since you've been having trouble with spelling.

Carl: But that was because I was sick last week. I'm not having trouble with spelling.

Grandma [as Ms. Reider]: Hmmm. I'm not sure. Let's make a deal, Carl. If you get an eighty-five or better on the next two quizzes, then I'll let you help out with the painting and the bulletin boards more. That way I'll be sure you don't need the extra time with your spelling.

Carl: "Okay. But Grandma, what if she doesn't say that?

Grandma: She won't say exactly that, Carl, but you explained yourself really well. Why don't you try it with her and see what happens?

If you are brave, you can encourage assertiveness by asking your child to think of one thing he would want to change at home and then to ask you. Warn him that you won't necessarily change things but that you will listen to what he says without getting mad. Outline the preceding steps first, and then have him practice on you directly.

Negotiation. So far you've taught your child how to express her views in an assertive but inoffensive manner. But what if the person she's talking to doesn't think your child's ideas are right? Or what if the other person has a different goal in mind? For example, let's say your child and her friend are spending the day together. What if your child wants to go to the movies but her friend wants to go to the mall? In those cases, your child has to be able to work something out that feels okay to both people. She has to be able to compromise. Tell your child that you want to read a skit that demonstrates how two people can reach a compromise.

Jeffrey's Curfew

Jeffrey: Mom, Danny just called and he wants to know if I can go over to his house to watch *Ninja Turtles* and *Total Recall*. Can I go?

Mom: Sure, sweetheart. Just make sure you call me by eight o'clock so I can pick you up. We have to meet Grandma tomorrow morning for breakfast, so it'll have to be an early night.

Jeffrey: Eight o'clock?! Nobody my age has to be home by eight! We won't be able to watch both movies by eight, and Danny's going to think I'm the biggest baby! Gosh, Mom . . . you never let me have any fun.

[Jeffrey runs off to his room.]

Mom [looking frustrated, slowly goes to Jeffrey's room, and knocks on the door]: Jeffrey, I think we should talk about this.

Jeffrey: There's nothing to talk about. You're the meanest mother in the whole world.

Mom: Jeffrey Scott! If that's the attitude you want to take, then fine. You can sit here all night and miss out on both movies. Or you can open this door and we can work this out . . . we can negotiate.

[Jeffrey opens the door.]

Mom: Now . . . How long do you think it will take to watch the movies?

Jeffrey: Well, each movie is probably two hours long, and then if we pop popcorn, it will take until at least midnight.

Mom: Midnight?! You've got to be kidding. If you stay out that late you'll be grumpy with Grandma tomorrow and you won't have a good time at breakfast. That's not very fair to Grandma or me, now is it? What about ten? And if you don't finish both movies, you can go over to Danny's house tomorrow to finish them.

Jeffrey: I guess that would be okay. Danny never gets to stay up until midnight anyway.

Tell your child that the process of compromising is called negotiation. Explain that the first thing he has to do is *figure out what he wants, as long as it is reasonable.* Since nobody ever gets everything he or she wants, explain that he will have to figure out what is within his reach. For instance, Jeffrey in the skit wanted to stay over at his friend's house until midnight, but he had to get up very early the next day. And since his friend doesn't usually get to stay up that late, Jeffrey probably would not have been able to get exactly what he wanted anyway. Ask your child what a more reasonable request would have been for Jeffrey.

Tell your child that after he figures out what he wants, he needs to *ask for it.* Remind him that he is an expert at that now, since he has been practicing assertiveness.

The next step is to *listen to what the other person wants.* Tell your child that he has to listen carefully. Even if he doesn't agree with everything the other person says, he might agree with something. If there is something he agrees with, he should tell the other person what it is. Ask him to describe what Mom agreed with in Jeffrey's request. Explain that Jeffrey's mother agreed that he should be able to watch both movies, but didn't agree that he could stay up so late. She listened to what he said and told him which part she agreed with.

Explain that after both parties describe what they want, you are ready to *compromise*. To compromise, you have to ask yourself: What am I willing to give so that I can reach a solution and get something that makes me feel good? Ask your child to describe the compromise that Jeffrey's mother suggested.

Tell your child that when he tells the other person what his compromise is, a good way to say it is this: "I'd be willing to _____ if you would _____." This makes it clear that he is offering a compromise. Then it is time to listen again. The other person might agree right away, or she might say "no way," or she might offer a different compromise. Ask your child to describe what happened in the skit.

Tell your child that if he can't reach agreement right away, he can *make another offer*. Encourage your child to think hard about other offers that might work. It is important to point out, however, that sometimes, especially with parents and teachers, they might not be able to find any compromise that the other person accepts. When this happens, your child can at least feel good that the other person knows that he is willing to speak up for what he wants and that he is willing to try to work things out.

Be Wise: Compromise! Practice negotiation with your child using the situations described next. Read the situation aloud, then ask your child to initiate the negotiation. After each scenario, give your child feedback. Was he too aggressive? Too passive? Were his suggestions unreasonable? Did he listen well?

The key points of negotiation are these:

> Step 1: Figure out what you want that is within reach.
> Step 2: Ask for it.
> Step 3: Listen to what the other person wants.
> Step 4: Be wise: compromise. Make an offer.

Step 5: Continue to look for a fair deal so that both people feel good about the compromise.

1. Bill and Kim are boyfriend and girlfriend. Bill wants to go to a party tonight where some of his friends will be. Kim doesn't want to go because she doesn't know anyone there and she doesn't want to hang out with a group of guys.
2. Sandra starts watching the movie-of-the-week on television. Her older sister brings a friend home and explains that they rented a movie and want to watch it now.
3. Scott's parents tell him that they want him to babysit for his little sister tonight because they are going out to dinner. Scott was already invited to spend the night at a friend's house.
4. Darlene's mother takes her shopping for school clothes. When they get to the store, Darlene finds an outfit she really likes. Her mother says she won't buy it because the skirt is too short and wouldn't be good to wear to school.
5. Sally wants to borrow her brother Ted's football so she can play outside with her friends. Ted doesn't want to lend it to her, because last time she used it she left it out in the rain.
6. Darion has to do five chores every week, and his parents pay him two dollars in allowance for doing them. It snowed four times this winter, and Darion shoveled the driveway by himself every time, even though it was not one of his chores. Darion wants to buy a new CD, but his parents say he has to wait until he saves enough money.
7. Josie has been at rehearsals for the school play every night for a week. On Saturday she wants to go to the mall with a friend, but her father says no because he's afraid Josie is catching a cold and has been up late all week finishing her homework.

CONFLICT BETWEEN PARENTS

I have focused so far on how children can solve problems, speak up for themselves, and negotiate. Even with these skills, conflicts will continue. Parents fight. Siblings fight. Such conflicts are unavoidable, so I want to close this chapter with advice just for parents.

While some experience with conflict is a necessary part of learning how to handle it, too much conflict, or very destructive conflict, is bad for your child.[5] Research has shown that even very young children are strongly hurt by conflict between their parents. Preschoolers show adverse physiological, behavioral, and emotional responses to anger between parents. Even videotapes of two adults disagreeing nonverbally upset young children. But avoiding conflict is not the answer. People, even best friends and people who love each other very much, disagree. Disagreement is a routine part of life, and children need to grow up with models of how to handle conflict when it arises. Research also suggests ways you can lessen the harmful effects of fighting.[6] Here are some guidelines you should follow.

- Don't use physical aggression in front of your child. This includes throwing things or slamming doors. Such actions are extremely scary for children.
- Don't criticize your spouse in front of your child with permanent and pervasive labels (for example, "Your father will always be good for nothing." "Your mother is a selfish witch.")
- Don't give your spouse the "silent treatment" and think your child won't notice. Your child will be almost as aware of this as he would be of a screaming match.
- Don't ask your child to choose sides.
- Don't begin a fight in front of your child unless you plan to finish it in that conversation.

- Express your feelings with words as much as possible. Use assertiveness rather than aggression.
- Model anger control. Slow things down and take time to cool down.
- Resolve conflicts and make up in front of your child. This teaches your child that conflict is a natural part of love and that it can be resolved.
- If you criticize your partner in front of your child, use language that criticizes specific behaviors rather than global personality (for example, "Your father is so grouchy when he is working

too hard." "I get so mad at your mother when she takes this long.")

- Leave your child out of some topics. Make an agreement with your spouse that you will protect your children from certain topics and find privacy when you are in the midst of one of those fights.

PART FIVE

The Children of the Twenty-first Century

14

The Pyramid of Optimism: Babies, Toddlers, and Preschoolers

O N   A   S C O R C H I N G   S A T U R D A Y   in Philadelphia, when the temperature in our back yard neared 100, I dragged out the hose and turned on the sprinkler. Soon my wife, Mandy, and our three small children came out. Lara, age five, and Nikki, age three, doffed their dresses and raced, shrieking with delight, through the arcs of cold water. Darryl, just eleven months, crawled in the direction of all this fun and sat in his diaper at the outer edge of the water's reach.

When the first arc of water spattered him, he looked startled. Twenty seconds later, when the next arc arrived, he looked bewildered. The third arc brought a whimper, and with the fourth he began to cry. Darryl, it must be said, is sturdy and curious, so his distress galvanized Mandy into action. First she turned the water pressure down several notches.

"WhoooOOOSSSHHH" sang Mandy into his ear as she crouched behind him, her volume locked to the approach of the next arc. Darryl stopped crying. "WhoooOOOSSSHHH" she sang in time with the next arc. After a few more, Darryl smiled. With Darryl's customary buoyant mood restored, Mandy stood him up, and *whooshing* all the while, held his fingers out to brush the outer edge of the spray. At the next *whoosh*, Darryl tentatively reached his own hand out, and when the water spattered his hand, he smiled. At the next *whoosh*, he grabbed at the spray with both hands, laughing at his handfuls of water. Next he toddled right into the path of the spray and, within a minute, had joined his big sisters in screams of romping, sopping joy that ended with Darryl exultantly waving the whirling sprinkler high in the air.

Mandy was laying the foundations of lifelong optimism in Darryl. Doing so in babies, toddlers, and preschoolers differs markedly from the techniques used in the Penn Prevention Program. The reason is obvious: very young children do not yet have the cognitive skills to recognize and dispute their own thoughts. But there are three crucial principles for grounding very young children in optimism, principles that come from basic research on learned helplessness: mastery, positivity, and explanatory style.

A caveat first: This book differs from most other books on child rearing. In a word, it is sounder. All thirteen chapters of the advice I have given you so far are based on carefully done, large-sample studies of children. Although I have presented lots of anecdotes to illustrate my basic points, these points are all firmly rooted in studies using control groups, long-term follow-ups, prospective, longitudinal designs, and stringent statistical methods. I have tough standards of evidence, and what passes for popular "expert" advice about how to rear your child does not usually meet them. The basis of popular advice is clinical and parental observation, politically congenial ideology, and sentimental anecdote. I have opted for a more responsible style because in the area of optimism for school children, large numbers of studies that meet my standards do exist.

As I turn to very young children, however, I do not find a body of evidence with control groups, prospective studies, and long-term follow-ups. So what I have to say in this chapter will be more speculative, more theory-driven, and more schematic than what has gone before. The proportion of parental "wisdom" and clinical "hunch" will rise accordingly, and most of the illustrations come from my own family. A compelling story can be told, nevertheless, and it begins with the central idea of mastery.

MASTERY

Nikki was ten months old when she was given a particularly fascinating octagonal box. On each side was a different animal, and when she turned one side faceup — say, the one with the picture of the dog —

and pressed it, a speaker boomed, "You found the dog!" This ability to control the announcement delighted Nikki. How could she tell that her pushing the dog picture controlled the announcement? She used two pieces of information: First, the likelihood of the announcement each time she presses the dog picture (which is high, but not certain, since the toy is temperamental and requires just the right touch). The second piece of information is crucial but easily overlooked: What would have happened if Nikki had not pressed the dog picture? Nothing. When the likelihood of "You found the dog!" is greater if Nikki presses than if she does not, Nikki *controls* the announcement. But if "You found the dog!" boomed out just as often if Nikki had not pressed the dog, Nikki would have concluded that she had no control over the announcement.

This insight was brought home to me when the toy went on the fritz and periodically boomed in the middle of the night, "You found the dog!" waking us all up. From then on, it was just as likely to sound off when Nikki had done nothing as when she pressed the dog panel. The announcement had become *uncontrollable,* not contingent on anything Nikki did or didn't do, and Nikki lost interest in the box.

Noncontingency or uncontrollability results in passivity and depression. The thrust of the hundreds of learned-helplessness experiments is that animals and people who experience noncontingency learn to give up. Contingency or controllability, in contrast, produces activity and fights depression. These two likelihoods — the probability of an outcome to a specific action, contrasted to the probability of the outcome if one does nothing — are the defining features of mastery and helplessness. Helplessness results from noncontingency, a situation in which the probability of an outcome is the same whether or not a response is made. When a rat gets inescapable shock, nothing the rat does matters: shock goes on and off whether or not he does anything. When the octagonal box became uncontrollable, Nikki was helpless: no action she took changed the likelihood of hearing "You found the dog!" Mastery, on the other hand, results from a contingency between action and outcome. In rat experiments in which pressing a bar turns off the shock, the rat has control, or mastery, over shock. When pressing the dog picture resulted in "You found the dog!" Nikki had control and experienced mastery.

Children, long before they can talk, are exquisitely sensitive to contingency and noncontingency. When a baby has mastery over an object, when there is a contingency between her action and the outcome, there are two results: the baby enjoys the object and she becomes more active. When a baby is helpless, when there is noncontingency between her actions and an outcome, she becomes sad or anxious and she becomes passive. It is not the noise of the rattle that makes a baby laugh, it is the fact that *she* rattles the rattle.

A classic experiment with mobiles twenty-five years ago demonstrated this fact. John Watson, a developmental psychologist at the University of California at Berkeley, gave three groups of eight-week-old infants a very special pillow for ten minutes a day. For the mastery group, every time the baby pressed the pillow with his head, a mobile over the crib spun. For the helpless group, the mobile spun just as much, but its spinning was not contingent on anything the baby did. Pressing the pillow had no effect. The third group saw a stabile. The mastery babies markedly increased their activity and smiled and cooed when the mobile spun. The helpless babies remained passive and did not show positive emotion when the mobile spun.[1] These experiments have been repeated with toys, with talking to an infant, and with strangers with parallel results: when the child controls the object, enjoyment and activity increase, while helplessness produces negative emotion and passivity.

When my daughter Amanda was eight months old, I took her, along with seven of my undergraduates, to a tavern for pizza and beer. She slept through most of the meal in her highchair but woke up over dessert. I was discoursing on the importance of contingency when she interrupted me by banging the table with her hands. To illustrate my point, I banged my cup in response. Her face lit up and she banged the table again. My students responded by banging their utensils. Amanda banged back. We all banged in response. This continued for ten minutes. The other customers must have been astonished at the sight of one baby, in gales of laughter, controlling the actions of eight adults.

When Mandy increased Darryl's exposure to the sprinkler by degrees, she was enabling Darryl to exert some control over being sprinkled. Mandy's making the approach of the arc predictable by *"whooshing"* removed his helplessness and allowed Darryl to exert control by approaching or withdrawing from the oncoming water. There are similar opportunities for parents to enhance mastery and prevent helplessness that arise several times a day with young children. When they do, there are two overarching strategies to use: grading and choice.

When a child faces a new task, it often seems very daunting. Use *small, achievable steps* to grade the challenges whenever possible — starting with a level she can easily control: start the sprinkler on a small stream and, when she's comfortable, turn the water pressure up a bit. Grading should, of course, be age appropriate. When putting an eight-month-old in a wading pool for the first time, don't just plunge her in. Let her play in one inch of water first, then in two inches. When teaching a three-year-old to dive underwater, start with a shiny coin at the depth of one foot, so all she has to do is put her face in the water, open her eyes, and reach to the bottom. Then put the coin at a depth of two feet, so she has to leave her feet to grab the coin. When she is comfortable with spending this much time underwater, lower the coin to three feet. Now she actually has to leave her feet and then propel herself to the bottom.

Maximize the amount of *choice* you give your child. As soon as he is old enough to indicate "yes" or "no," build choice in whenever possible. Don't, for example, just ram food at him. Dangle it and wait until he shows he wants it. Ask him if he wants this (or that) and be prepared to take no for an answer.

Opportunities for a parent to enhance mastery abound in every realm of your child's life.

Exploration and Play. Exploration starts at birth and continues all through childhood. It is the aspect of play with the most potential mastery because it contains a natural positive-feedback loop. (It is also the aspect of play with the most potential for physical danger.) When your child is successful and controls a new object or skill, he then tries out new actions and seeks to expand his control. This can lead to more success, a greater sense of mastery, and even more exploration. Exploration also has a potential negative-feedback loop: when your child fails and finds himself helpless, he may not try as hard next time. This diminishes his sense of control and leads to even less exploration, and so on. So don't leave him strapped helplessly in his stroller or his highchair for long periods. Stop and take him out of his car seat for play breaks on long drives. And don't swaddle him, since swaddling is the very antithesis of mastery. Your job is to help him get into the positive-feedback loop.

Your child has an exploration "space" that starts as a crib and expands to a playpen. Keep enlarging the safe "playpen" area; let him explore more of the house, more of the yard, and more objects and he will acquire more mastery. Don't obstruct or interrupt exploration until it becomes unsafe, and then with little fuss, switch to a safe alternative. Get her a walker once she can sit up unaided (but observe the stringent safety rules). Walkers vastly increase the domain under her control. Create lots of safe climbing areas indoors with pillows and bolsters. Outdoors, use the natural hillocks and swales around your neighborhood to grade the challenges of walking and climbing. Get a sandbox and a wading shell. For the older child, get tricycles, wagons, and sleds, then bicycles, ice skates, and roller skates. Observe the safety instructions scrupulously.

Toys are vehicles of exploration, and your choice of toys can be guided by mastery. Toys that operate only in response to your child's actions promote mastery: Toys that move when the baby hits them or pushes buttons do just this. Building blocks, boxes, baby gyms, books that sound when the characters are pressed, trucks, dress-up dolls, musical instruments, and peg people are all mastery-oriented toys. Drawing with chubby crayons, washable markers, dull pencils — even with ketchup and chocolate pudding for younger kids — are all masterful activities. Toys that make elaborate sounds but are not contingent on your child's actions do not promote mastery. Stuffed animals, soft toys, mobiles kept out of reach, wall decorations, radio, and TV are not loaded with mastery.

The computer is a revolutionary development, surely for the amount and speed of information, but even more for mastery. It is a truism that computers are educational; but in contrast to TV, radio, and movies, computers and video games, because they are interactive, provide mastery at the same time. For the increasing number of families that can afford computers, the investment is a fine one — as good an investment as college tuition. The quality of some children's software for producing an optimistic child is excellent. Nikki, almost three, likes "Mickey's Colors and Shapes." A rubber overlay on the keyboard allows her to type shapes and colors that dictate what Mickey will juggle. Using the mouse itself is an exercise in mastery for a two- to three-year-old. The "Even More Incredible Machine" appeals to Lara, age five. It is superbly graded, starting with mechanical puzzles she can solve quite easily, and imbuing her with mechanical intuition as it builds up to harder and harder puzzles. There is even "Baby Smash" for Darryl: he can club any key and make shapes appear and sounds blare. (Use a second, cheap keyboard.) The online service Prodigy has an interactive version of Sesame Street that both Lara and Nikki love. The storybook in Sesame Street gives them choices: they can buy Ernie a present at either the pet store or the music store. I cannot overstate the importance that kids' software can have in the development of mastery. So explosive are improvements in software that by the time you read this, there will be even better, and more affordable, products. For the latest advice from knowledgeable parents, I read the newsgroup "misc.kids.computers" on the Internet once a week.

Feeding and Mealtimes. Feed your baby on demand, not on a preset schedule. Offer him simple choices as soon as he is old enough to indicate yes or no, but don't overwhelm him with a bewildering array. Give him eating utensils as early as possible, and lots of finger food. The mess and waste are less important than the added sense of control.

Meals provide increasing sources of mastery for children as they grow. Rudimentary cooking lessons can start early. A one-year-old can stir the pancake batter, and a two-year-old can make shapes out of dough. When we make fritters on Sunday morning, we form an assembly line. Lara makes the batter, measuring out spoonfuls of flour and sugar. Darryl stirs the batter. Nikki coats the fruit. And Mandy then drops it into the fryer. Daddy eats the fritters.[2]

Children as young as two can grow food with you in a garden plot and later pick it. You'll be surprised what comes up if you just bury old scraps from the bottom of the vegetable crisper. When you go out to eat, pick a buffet or cafeteria (fast-food places suffice) rather than a restaurant with waiters. The kids can choose what they want, pick up their food, pay, and get the right utensils and condiments. For the urban family, shopping for food allows lots of mastery. We have a favorite supermarket that lets Lara and Nikki roll their miniature trolleys down the aisles. Each child gets to pick three items. Nikki picks blueberries, strawberries, and apple juice. Lara picks string cheese, dog biscuits, and bread. At the checkout counter, Daddy goes first and then Lara and Nikki empty their trolleys. Lara and Nikki each pay, and they both put their little sacks into the car.

Parental limits on choices are inevitable, and these limits are an important aspect of choice. I am not an advocate of what used to be called "permissiveness." Insouciant choice is a recipe for both "spoiling" and acquiring an impoverished sense of the real world. I am an advocate of giving children choice and control, but this does not mean that if you have to go off to work and your three-year-old is throwing a tantrum about the color of her socks, you should give in and be late for work. Choice within a clear structure is the beginning of learning to make the best of the very limited options the world allows us.

Diapering and Dressing. When diapering, stand her up. It makes for somewhat more awkward diapering (you'll soon get the hang of it, though) but for much less helplessness. Don't toilet-train until your child is ready. Those hours on the potty with rebukes and no results are grueling exercises in learned helplessness. Let your child pick out the clothes she will wear today. You may not be thrilled by the color combinations, but the extra mastery she will gain is worth it.

Socialization and Attention. The most significant area in which a child can feel helpless or masterful is interplay with other people. Build in social contingency from the first. Do not let your infant cry and cry when he's hungry or wet. Pick him up as soon as you can. One of the most fundamental building blocks is his learning that crying works to bring relief. Try not to talk to your infant only when *you* feel like it. Rather, vocalize *in response to* her vocalizing and take turns. When a stranger enters your infant's presence, let your infant's interest guide you in bringing the stranger closer. A better social relation will form with a stranger who is controllable than with one who intrudes. When reading to your child, encourage pointing and talk about what he points to.

From age two on, facilitate your child's ability to play at adult roles. Toy kitchens and workbenches, dramatic play, and arts and crafts provide excellent opportunities for social mastery. Playing Mommy or Daddy or Doctor provides surrogate control, particularly when the child acts out a conflict. I often overhear Lara or Nikki playing with their dolls and saying, "Now be quiet and go to sleep. If you're not asleep in five minutes I'm going to be very cross!" or "Really, child, it's not going to hurt!" Enlist the aid of the older child in caring for the younger child. Opportunities for mastery by bringing the ointment during diapering or finding the Barney tape for Granny are legion.

POSITIVITY

Mastery forms the base of the pyramid of optimism, and positivity forms the next layer. Mastery is behavioral — your child's having control over outcomes. Positivity is about her feelings — growing up in a sunny and warm emotional atmosphere. Wanting children to feel good has always been a strong motivation for parents, and in the current feel-good epoch, this motivation has reached new heights. I have an unfashionable view of feeling good, which was hinted at in my reservations about self-esteem in chapter 4. Just as I view self-esteem as a means toward good commerce with the world and not an end in itself, I view positive feeling only as a means toward the more important end of mastery.

For a generation, parents have been told that they should give their children "unconditional positive regard." This notion began as tactical advice for therapists from Carl Rogers, the leading humanistic psychologist of the 1950s. Rogers theorized that "unconditional positive regard" and "empathetic understanding" were the rock-bottom active ingredients in all successful psychotherapy.[3] In the 1950s, this was welcome and demystifying advice. Indeed, the sheer universality of Rogers's ingredients led to the successful search for more-specific psychotherapies that worked for specific disorders. Back in the '50s, Rogers's advice caught on and was soon extended to child rearing. At the same time, B. F. Skinner advised parents that punishment had been shown to be ineffective. As America moved into the present feeling-good era and moved away from doing well, these two pieces of advice were highly congenial. "No punishment" and "unconditional positive regard" soon became entrenched principles of humane American child rearing.

What is right and what is wrong about these maxims? What is right is straightforward. The more your child explores, the more mastery he experiences. When a child is afraid or insecure, he becomes constricted. He falls back on his safe but limited repertoire. He does not take chances. He does not explore, and he does not experience mastery. This lack of mastery heightens his dysphoria, which freezes him further. Conversely, when a child is happy and secure, he takes chances and explores. This makes him feel good, which in turn generates more exploration and more mastery. He becomes a veritable mastery machine.

Positive regard facilitates mastery because it dispels fear and allows more exploration. Punishment gets in the way of mastery because it can make your child fearful and constricted. So I, too, endorse positive regard, and I endorse refraining from punishment, but only *in as far as these tactics facilitate mastery.* Unfortunately, there are also ways these tactics can undermine your child's sense of mastery.

Unconditional positive regard is just that — unconditional, that is, not contingent on anything your child does. Mastery, in stark contrast, is conditional, defined as an outcome strictly contingent on what your child does. This distinction cannot be glossed over. Learned helplessness develops not only when bad events are uncontrollable but also, unfortunately, when *good events are uncontrollable.* When a person or an animal receives good events noncontingently — nickels that fall out of slot machines regardless of what the person does, food that is delivered regardless of what the animal does, praise that rains down regardless of whether a child actually succeeded — learned helplessness develops. This is called "appetitive" learned helplessness, in contrast to the helplessness that develops when bad events, like shock and loud noise, occur noncontingently (called "aversive" learned helplessness). Recipients of noncontingent good events do not become depressed like recipients of noncontingent bad events; but they do become passive and lethargic. Even worse, they have trouble learning that they are effective, seeing later on that their actions work, once they regain mastery. A rat, for example, that first learns it can get food regardless of what side of a maze it goes to has inordinate trouble later on learning to go to the correct side when food becomes available only on one side.[4]

This problem can be called "the parent who cried wolf." When a parent rewards a child, say with praise, regardless of what the child does, two dangers loom. First, the child may become passive, having learned that praise will come regardless of what he does. This is the first symptom of appetitive learned helplessness. Second, the child may have trouble appreciating that he has actually succeeded later on when he really does succeed and Mom praises him sincerely. He may fail to learn from his successes because of a steady diet of well-meaning, unconditional positive regard.

So unconditional positive regard puts parents on the horns of a dilemma: On the one hand, unconditional positive regard is positive. It makes your child feel good, and feeling good crowds out fear and freezing. So your child will take chances and explore his world more, which in turn will produce more mastery. So sheer positivity indirectly enhances mastery via enhanced exploration. On the other hand, unconditional positive regard is unconditional. Your child learns that good things come from his parents regardless of what he does. The lesson he will learn from that is passivity, and he will have trouble learning that his actions work when they actually do. So unconditionality directly undercuts mastery.

Resolving the dilemma depends, in my mind, on the kind of positive regard. Love, affection, warmth, and ebullience should all be delivered unconditionally. The more of these, the more positive the atmosphere, and the more secure your child will be. The more secure he is, the more he will explore and find mastery. But praise is an altogether different matter. *Praise your child contingent on a success, not just to make him feel better.* Wait until he fits the little peg man into the car before applauding. Also, *grade* your praise to fit the accomplishment. Do not overpraise and treat the peg man achievement as if it were an amazing accomplishment. Save your expressions of highest praise for more major accomplishments, like saying his sister's name for the first time and catching the wobbling football. To praise your child regardless of how well he does, to fail to grade your praise, is to render your child helpless. Such noncontingent praise also soon undermines his trust in you. That is why Ian's dad handled the spaceship building so poorly in chapter 2. If the task is very hard and your child fails grossly, try to break the task into smaller, more achievable steps, or unobtrusively shift to a different activity. But do not gloss over the failure and do not praise it.[5]

Punishment is less problematic. Skinner was simply wrong. Punishment, making an undesirable event contingent on an unwanted action, is highly effective in eliminating unwanted behavior. It is perhaps the most effective tool in the repertoire of behavior modification, and literally hundreds of experiments now demonstrate this.[6] But in practice, the child often can't tell what he is being punished for, and the aversiveness leaks over to the person who does the punishing and to the entire situation. When this happens, the child becomes generally fearful and constricted and he may avoid the punishing parent in addition to refraining from the punished response.

The reason children often find it hard to understand why they are being punished can be explained in terms of laboratory experiments with rats about "safety signals." In these experiments, an aversive event, like an electric shock, is signaled by a loud tone right before it happens. The tone reliably signals danger and the rat shows signs of fear as it learns that the tone is dangerous. Even more important, when the tone is not on, shock never occurs. The absence of the tone reliably signals safety and the rat relaxes whenever the tone is not on. Danger signals are important because they mean that a safety signal — the absence of the danger signal — exists.

The hypothesis is that when danger signals are not used and the rat is shocked on an unpredictable basis, the rat will be afraid all the time. When there is no reliable danger signal, there can be no reliable safety signal. Many experiments bear this out. When animals are in a situation in which shocks occur unheralded by any signal, they huddle in fear all the time. When the very same shocks occur but are preceded by a one-minute tone, the animals huddle in fear during the tone but all the rest of time go about their business without fear.[7]

Punishment fails frequently because the safety signals are often unclear to the child. When you punish a child, you must make sure that the danger signal — and therefore the safety signal — is completely clear. Make sure the child knows exactly what action he is being punished for. Do not indict the child or his character; indict only the specific action. It is not the child (personal, permanent, pervasive) who is bad, it is the action that is bad (impersonal, changeable, specific).

> Nikki, at almost three, is throwing snowballs point-blank at Lara and Lara is wincing. Lara's reaction eggs Nikki on. "Stop throwing snowballs at Lara, Nikki," Mandy shouts. "You're hurting her." Another snowball hits Lara. "If you throw one more snowball at Lara, Nikki, I'm taking you inside," says Mandy. The next snowball hits Lara. Mandy immediately takes Nikki, wailing in protest, inside. "I told you I would take you inside if you didn't stop throwing snowballs. You didn't stop, so this is what happens," Mandy gently reminds Nikki. Nikki sobs loudly, "Won't do 'gain, won't throw 'gain. No snowball. No."

Notice two things about the safety signals here. The punishment — being sent inside — "fits" the crime. It is a natural connection and therefore easy even for a two-year-old to see. In addition, Mandy gives a larger rationale for punishment — "you're hurting [Lara]." This provides the rudiments for Nikki's learning the overriding safety signal — not hurting others is safe, as opposed to not throwing snowballs.

Providing clear safety signals for your child is important. Bad events happen every day, and when you know a bad event is bound to happen — Mommy's leaving for the morning or a cavity needs to be filled — you should provide your child clear warning in advance. You must not tiptoe around it and let it take your child by surprise. When your three-year-old has to get a shot, tell her shortly before you go to the doctor's office that she will get a needle that hurts for a few minutes. A couple of minutes before the shot, tell her again that the doctor is about to give her a shot and it will hurt for a bit, but then she will feel fine again. If your child is warned clearly when something bad is about to happen, she will learn that *absent the warning, she is safe,* and bad events are unlikely. She will learn that going to the doctor's is *generally* safe. She will also learn to trust you. Providing danger signals is not fun for parents, because your child will be afraid and difficult in response. Many parents avoid doing so to avoid the short-term hassle. But the long-term cost is much worse.

When Amanda was about a year old, we began using babysitters for her when we would go out at night. When the babysitter arrived, we would introduce them to each other and wait until Amanda became absorbed in play. Then we literally tiptoed around the problem and sneaked out. We were first-time parents and wanted to avoid all the protesting and weeping we knew would occur. It didn't work. Not only did we lose our babysitter, but we noticed that Amanda's personality was changing from placid to fretful. I was doing experiments on safety signals at just this time and saw that we were violating the basic principle by not warning Amanda that we were about to leave. Next time, we held a big ceremony when we were about to leave, with hugs, singing "So long, farewell, auf Wiedersehen . . . ," going out to the car together with the babysitter, saying we'd be back in three hours, and waving bye-bye. Amanda understood enough of this to wail in protest, but we went anyway, and stuck to the ritual on subsequent evenings. Amanda soon resumed the calm personality she has had ever since.

An atmosphere of warmth and ebullience, clear safety signals, unconditional love but conditional praise, and lots of good events all add positivity to the life of your child. It is amazingly easy, however, for a child to be surrounded with good things and yet still have a gloomy mental life. What really matters, in the end, is how much positivity there is inside her little head. How many good thoughts and how many bad thoughts occur each day? An iconoclastic series of studies has appeared on this topic. Greg Garamoni and Robert Schwartz, two University of Pittsburgh psychologists, decided simply to count the number of good thoughts and bad thoughts that different people have and to look at the ratio. Sophisticated investigators, they counted "thoughts" in many different ways: memories, reverie, causal explanations, and the like. Using twenty-seven different studies, they found that depressed people had an equal ratio: one bad thought to one good thought. Nondepressed people had roughly twice as many good thoughts as bad thoughts. This idea is literally simple-minded, but it is a powerful one. It is also supported by the results of therapy: depressed patients who improve move to the 2:1 ratio from their original 1:1 ratio. Those who do not get better stay at 1:1.[8]

Is there anything you can do to help your child have a 2:1 ratio of good thoughts to bad thoughts?

Bedtime Nuggets. Those minutes you have with your child right before she falls asleep can be the most precious of the day. In our household, we use this valuable time to do "nighttime nuggets," a review of the good things and bad things that happened that day. We use this game to shape a positive state-of-mind ratio that, we hope, Lara and Nikki will internalize as they grow up.

The lights are out and Mandy, Lara, and Nikki are cuddling.

Mandy: What did you like doing today, Lara-Love?
Lara: I liked playing and I liked going to the park with Leah and Andrea. I liked eating crackers in my little house. I liked going swimming and diving in the deep with Daddy. I liked going to lunch and holding my own plate.
Nikki: I liked eating the chocolate strawberry.
Lara: I liked being silly with Darryl with his garage. I liked taking my dress off and just wearing panties.
Nikki: Me too.
Lara: I liked reading the words. I liked seeing the people row in

the river and rollerblade on the sidewalk. I liked getting the movie with Daddy and paying.

Mandy: Anything else?

Lara: I liked playing peekaboo with Darryl at dinner. I liked playing mermaids with Nikki in the bath. I liked playing the "Incredible Machine" with Daddy. I liked watching Barney.

Nikki: Me too. I like Barney.

Mandy: Did anything bad happen today?

Lara: Darryl bit me on my back.

Mandy: Yes, that hurt.

Lara: A lot!

Mandy: Well, he's just a little baby. We'll have to start teaching him not to bite. Let's start in the morning. Okay?

Lara: Okay. I didn't like that Leah's bunny died, and I didn't like Nikki's story about how Ready [our dog] killed the bunny by eating it.

Mandy: No, that was pretty gross.

Lara: Awful.

Mandy: I didn't like Nikki's story, but she's too young to understand. She just made it up. It's sad the bunny died, but he was very old and sick. Maybe Leah's daddy will buy them a new one.

Lara: Maybe.

Mandy: Sounds like you had a pretty good day?

Lara: How many good things, Mummy?

Mandy [*guessing*]: Fifteen, I think.

Lara: How many bad things?

Mandy: Two?

Lara: Wow, fifteen good things in one day! What are we gonna do tomorrow?

Nikki, almost three, needs some prompting, but Lara, at five, usually has a cascade of good events ready to talk about. The last thoughts a child has before drifting into sleep are rich in visual imagery, and they become the material around which her dreams are woven. The tone of dreaming is tied up with depression. Depressed adults and children have dreams filled with losing and defeat and rejection, and interestingly, every drug that breaks up depression also blocks dreaming. Bedtime nuggets, we believe, provides a foundation of a positive mental life, to say nothing of creating "sweet dreams."⁹

EXPLANATORY STYLE

With mastery at the base of your child's development and positivity forming the next layer, optimistic explanatory style can sit comfortably at the apex. By the age of two, children start to verbalize causal explanations (Nikki, just two, crying, "Lara meaned me," and at the computer, whining for Daddy, "I can't do"). By age three it becomes clear your child is trying to figure out the causal skein of the world. Many of her statements are now of the "cuz" variety, and many of her questions ask "why?" Nikki told me the other day that "the Prince wanted to marry Belle and not Sleeping Beauty cuz Belle was wearing a blue dress." When I asked her why she had a frowny face, she replied, "Cuz I need something to eat." At some point, a style — a consistent bias for certain explanations — forms out of this welter of different causes, and the explanations typically become either pessimistic or optimistic. Researchers have yet to pin down when a *style* comes into existence, but I assume that the style is inborn and then coalesces in the preschool years.

A parent can help teach an optimistic style in these crucial years. Teaching the monitoring and disputing of automatic thoughts, as we can do with older children, cannot be done with preschoolers. Preschoolers are not "metacognitive": they do not have the ability to think about and talk about their own thinking. But preschoolers are tuned in to the explanatory style of others, if not themselves. They passively absorb their parents' style; as we saw in chapter 8, the way you and your spouse talk and argue with each other and the way you criticize your child will be learned. We also observe that children learn the style of book, movie, and cartoon characters: they learn to talk like Ariel or Babar or Jafar.

Mandy and I use this uncanny mimicking ability to teach the beginnings of an optimistic style to our children. When Nikki is thwarted, we externalize the situation onto Flopsy, her story-tale bunny rabbit, and we have Flopsy make the optimistic explanations.

A few months ago, Lara began to attend ballet classes. Nikki had a very hard time with this, because she wanted to dance also but was too young to attend. She didn't see it this way; all she saw was privation. Being "too young" is a temporary explanation, since children get older. So we told Nikki the following Flopsy story and it consoled her greatly.

> Flopsy woke up very early one morning. The sun was shining and she jumped out of bed to look outside. Suddenly she remembered what day it was — Thursday. Thursdays her big sister got to go to ballet class and Flopsy had to wait outside. Flopsy wanted to dance so badly. It looked like so much fun and all the other little bunnies looked so pretty.
>
> "It is recital today," said Mummy. "Let's see what we can find to wear." Flopsy and her big sister got to wear some very special tutus. Flopsy found a blue one — her favorite color.
>
> When they got to school, all the little bunnies were wearing their special dress-up costumes. Mummy and Flopsy sat down and watched while Flopsy's big sister jumped and fluttered by. It was too much for Flopsy to bear. Flopsy started to cry and cry and cry until finally she ran outside.
>
> Mummy came out and she picked up Flopsy and hugged her and kissed her tears away. "I know it's hard, Flopsy. You want to be a ballerina too, don't you?"
>
> Flopsy nodded. "Why can't I, Mummy?"
>
> "You're not old enough yet, Flopsy. You have to be four to go to ballet class and you are only two and a half," said Mummy. Flopsy started to cry again.
>
> "I know," said Mummy. "Let's buy you some blue ballet slippers and then you can practice with your big sister after class. If Miss Alice sees how big you got and how well you dance, maybe she will let you go to class in September when you are only three. That's not too long to wait, is it?"
>
> Flopsy thought this was a great idea. Miss Alice agreed, and Flopsy felt much better.

15

The Limits of Optimism

YOU PROBABLY THINK by now that I am a gushing advocate of optimism. I am not, for I know that optimism is a mixed blessing. Its benefits for your child are clear: It will help him fight depression when the inevitable setbacks and tragedies of life befall him. It will help him achieve more — on the playing field, in school, and later at work — than others expect of him. And optimism carries better physical health with it — a perkier immune system, fewer infectious illnesses, fewer visits to the doctor, lower cardiac risk, and perhaps even a longer life. These benefits are considerable, but they are not unmitigated. For there is one thing that pessimists may do better than optimists.

They may see reality more clearly.

This is a disturbing finding that simply refuses to go away and is hotly debated. It began with an innocent experiment in the late 1970s done by Lauren Alloy and Lyn Abramson, who were then iconoclastic graduate students of mine. They gave students differing degrees of control over the lighting of a light. Some had perfect control over the light: it went on every time they pressed a button and it never went on if they didn't press. Other students, however, had no control at all: the light went on regardless of whether or not they pressed the button; they were helpless.

The students were then asked to judge how much control they had, as accurately as they could. The students with depressive symptoms were very accurate. When they had control, they assessed it accurately, and when they didn't have any control, they said so. The students without symptoms of depression astonished us. They were accurate when they had control, but when they were helpless they still judged that they had a great deal of control.

The people with symptoms of depression knew the truth. The nondepressed people had benign illusions that they were not helpless when they actually were. These findings disturbed me then and disturb me now. When I began as a therapist twenty-five years ago, I thought I was to become the agent of both happiness and reality. But reality and happiness seem to be in conflict.

Supporting evidence for depressive realism cascaded in:[1] Depressed people are accurate judges of how much skill they have, whereas nondepressed people think they are much more skillful than others judge them to be (80 percent of American men think they are in the top half of social skills). Nondepressed people remember more good events than actually happened and they forget more of the bad events. Depressed people are accurate about both. Nondepressed people are lopsided in their beliefs about success and failure: if rewards occur, they claim the credit, the rewards will last, and they're good at everything; but if it was a failure, you did it to them, it's going away quickly, and it was just this one little thing. Depressed people are evenhanded about success and failure.

While these findings are dramatic, there is a critical distinction that must be made. The studies that shed light on depressive realism do not, for the most part, compare people who are severely depressed to people who aren't. Rather, these studies compare students who have some depressive symptoms to students who have very few. These studies do *not* tell us that people who are in the throes of a severe depression, the level of depression that would benefit from therapy and the level of depression that this book is aimed at preventing, are more accurate than nondepressed people. In fact, the reason the realism findings are so hotly contested is that most therapists will tell you that severely depressed people are typically inaccurate. Severely depressed people blame themselves too much for problems; they believe they have no control when, in fact, they have some control; they remember only the harsh criticisms instead of the compliments. Indeed, therapists who work with suicidal patients try to reduce the risk of suicide by challenging the overly pessimistic belief that things will never get better, that life will always remain as horrible as it now seems. And hopelessness can usually be effectively challenged, because things, generally, will get better.

The debate surrounding depressive realism goes on. It may be that low levels of depression strip away our self-serving bias and force us to see things more clearly. But once depression becomes severe, people fall prey to the opposite error: self-serving bias gives way to self-harming bias. And one thing is clear: there is a much greater cost from the inaccuracy of severe depression than there is from the self-serving bias that affects us all when we are not depressed.

Accurate Optimism. In light of these findings, let me tell you why I believe the skills in this book are crucial, why I believe every child should master the techniques I describe. It should be clear to you by now what I mean when I use the term *optimism*. Let me remind you what optimism is not. Optimism is not chanting happy thoughts to yourself. Vacuous slogans of the sort "I am a special person," "People like me," and "My life will get better and better" may make you feel warm and fuzzy for a moment, but they will not help you to achieve your goals. Optimism is not blaming others when things go wrong. Dodging responsibility for problems will serve only to exacerbate them. Optimism is not the denial or avoidance of sadness or anger. Negative emotions are part of the richness of life and they are usually healthy responses that encourage us to understand or change the things that upset us.

When you teach your child optimism, you are teaching him to know himself, to be curious about his theory of himself and of the world. You are teaching him to take an active stance in his world and to shape his own life, rather than be a passive recipient of what happens his way. Whereas in the past, he may have accepted his most dire beliefs and interpretations as unquestionable fact, now he is able to reflect thoughtfully on these beliefs and evaluate their accuracy. He is equipped to persevere in the face of adversity and to struggle to overcome his problems.

Fully mindful of the tension between optimism and realism, I have come down strongly for teaching accuracy at every point in this book. There is one overriding reason: optimism that is not accurate is empty and falls apart. Life defeats it. Disputing and decatastrophizing work only when they can be checked against reality.

Unlike the Pollyannaish purveyors of "you are special" self-esteem, I aim to teach children to take a realistic view of themselves. Accurate optimism can be taught, even in the face of the tendency optimism has to drift toward self-serving illusions. The causes of bad events are always legion: Your child struck out to end the game and her team lost. Many factors contributed to the loss: among others, their relief pitcher had a blazing fastball, the umpire made a bad call at strike two, it started to rain at the end, and your child swung too late, striking out. Your child focuses on only one cause and then catastrophizes, "I swung too late. I'm no good." Accuracy warrants her to see the other causes as well, and to see that "I'm no good" does not follow from the facts. Teaching optimism here coincides, as it almost always does, with teaching accuracy.

Should we worry that the optimistic child will fail to appreciate real problems when they occur? I do not want to teach children to wear blinders to poverty and crime, hatred and envy, greed and suffering. I do not want a generation of children who will look at a polluted river coughing up dying fish and automatically think, "Nature will heal itself; I needn't worry." I do not want a generation of young people who will drive through the inner city and, sheltered in their upholstered cubicles, fail to take seriously the misery and hopelessness all around them, thinking, "Things will surely get better."

Accurate optimism does not fall into these traps. "Nature will heal itself" gets checked against reality: "Sometimes that's so. For example, when the United States tested nuclear weapons in the Pacific on Bikini Atoll, life was flourishing again in just a few years. But that's not so when the radiation has a half-life of one hundred years. Nor when an entire species is extinguished. Here human intervention is needed and I can play a role." Accurate optimism surely arms one against the exaggeration, alarmism, and nihilism that have replaced reasoned dialogue in our political life. "Our nation's economy will never recover. . . ." "There can be no peace in the Middle East."

"There are children starving all over the United States." "Minorities can never share in prosperity." — all get checked against reality: "The U.S. economy has grown for the last three years, and without inflation." "Jordan recently signed a peace treaty with Israel, and Syria may sign one too." "There is malnutrition in the United States but very little starvation." "The rate of employment for black and Hispanic college graduates is just as high as for whites." Accurate optimism is not a recipe for inaction in the face of suffering and injustice. "Things will surely get better" is checked against reality. The accurate optimist thinks, "When there is opportunity to be grasped and there is hope, then things get better. When there is no hope, things do not. What can I do to help the cause of providing opportunity and hope?"

Optimism, then, is not a cure-all. It will not substitute for good parenting. It will not substitute for a child's developing strong moral values. It will not substitute for ambition and a sense of justice. Optimism is just a tool, but a powerful tool. In the presence of strong values and of ambition, it is the tool that makes both individual accomplishment and social justice possible.

Afterword
A Progress Report on Optimism

MARTIN E. P. SELIGMAN

THE FIRST EDITION of *The Optimistic Child* (1995) and of its intellectual parent, *Learned Optimism* (1990), spawned a movement, now called "positive psychology." The year after we published *The Optimistic Child*, I was elected president of the American Psychological Association. Presidents are supposed to have themes, and I thought mine would be the prevention of mental illness, the endeavor into which these two books fit squarely. So I called together the dozen leading experts on prevention to discuss the possibility of a substantial presidential initiative on prevention.

I confess that I have the attention span of a ten-year-old, but this daylong meeting was excruciatingly boring. Each of the experts suggested that we take the therapies that work in adults and just do them earlier with kids at risk. Worthwhile, but boooooooooring! And with no intellectual backbone.

I was stuck, and it was my five-year-old daughter, Nikki, who, about a month later, got me unstuck (Seligman, 2002). Here's what happened:

I was weeding in our garden with her, and with a few words she turned my view of psychology and of myself upside down. Another confession: even though I have written a book and many articles about children, I'm actually not very good with them. I am goal-oriented and time-urgent, and when I'm weeding, I'm weeding. Nikki, however, was throwing weeds into the air and dancing and singing. I yelled at her. With a puzzled frown, she walked away. A few seconds later she was back, and said, "Daddy, I want to talk to you."

"Yes, Nikki?"

"Daddy, do you remember before my fifth birthday? From when I was three until when I was five, I was a whiner. I whined every day. On my fifth birthday, I decided I wasn't going to whine anymore. That was the hardest thing I've ever done. And if I can stop whining, you can stop being such a grouch."

This was for me an epiphany, nothing less. I realized something about Nikki, something about raising kids, not a little about myself, and a great deal about my profession. First, I realized that raising Nikki was not about correcting her shortcomings. She did that herself. Rather, I realized that raising Nikki was about this precocious strength she had displayed, naming it—I call it "seeing into the soul" or, in jargon, "social intelligence"—nurturing it, and helping her to mold her life around it. Such a strength, fully grown, will act as a buffer against her weaknesses and against the storms of life that will inevitably come her way. Raising children, I realized, is more than just fixing what is wrong with them. It is about identifying and amplifying their strengths and virtues, and helping them find the niche where they can live these positive traits to the fullest.

As for my own life, Nikki hit the nail right on the head. I was a grouch. I had spent fifty years enduring mostly wet weather in the soul, and the past ten years as a walking nimbus cloud in a household radiant with sunshine. Any good fortune I had was probably not due to being grumpy, but in spite of it. In that moment, I resolved to change.

The final part of this epiphany was to place my work on optimism in a larger context. What was optimism a piece of?

Raising Nikki was not remedial, but constructive. It was about identifying her strengths and then helping her construct the best niche in the world for her constellation of signature strengths. Isn't this the larger picture of what I was striving for in teaching kids optimism? Teaching children optimism is more, I realized, than just correcting pessimism, more than going from minus 5 toward zero. It is the creation of a positive strength, a sunny but solid future-mindedness that can be deployed throughout life—not only to fight depression and to come back from failure, but to be the foundation of success and vitality. It's going from plus 2 toward plus 10.

In the specific area of the optimistic child programs detailed in this book, there have been eleven full-blown replications (outside the University of Pennsylvania) of the depression-preventing power of teaching optimism to children. Eight replicated the results, and three found no effects. The three that did not find depression prevention all gave minimal training to teachers of the program. In the social sciences, eight out of eleven is, in my experience, pretty good.

In addition, at the University of Pennsylvania several new developments have taken place:

- We know something more about how long the depression prevention effects last. With no boosters, the optimistic child program prevents depression for two years. By the third year, the prevention effects fade (Gillham and Reivich, 1999).

- In our first prevention programs, we used clinically trained psychologists as the teachers. We then developed a two-week training program for middle school teachers. In the first week, the teachers learn how to apply learned optimism in their own lives. In the second week, the teachers learn how to teach optimism to middle school students. We replicated our depression prevention with teachers and found that they were just as adept as clinical psychologists. You can request the manual for teachers at info@pennproject.org.

- We developed a full-blown training program for parents that parallels the teacher-training program. Parents first learn how to apply learned optimism to their own lives. Then they learn in step-by-step fashion how to teach their children optimism. You can request the manual for parents at info@pennproject.org.

- David Yu, one of my recent Ph.D.s, took the optimistic child program to Beijing. He taught the program to middle school teachers and found that it reliably prevented depression, just as it had in the United States (Yu and Seligman, 2002).

- Esteban Cardemil, another recent Penn Ph.D., used the program in Philadelphia's inner city. He found that it prevented depression in Hispanic children but not in African-American children. Oddly, the issue among African-American children was that the untreated control group, as well as the prevention group, got markedly less depressed in the year following the intervention (Cardemil, Reivich, and Seligman, 2002).

Once we were satisfied that our optimistic child programs were replicable, we began to act on my realization that teaching optimism to children was only one aspect of positive psychology. Could we teach other character strengths to children, and what effects would these increased strengths have on their adolescent and later lives? Funded by a substantial grant from the U.S. Department of Education, our first effort to find the answers is now in its fourth year at Strathaven High School, outside Philadelphia.

Everyone in the ninth grade takes Language Arts. (It used to be called English.) The students read such masterpieces as *Lord of the Flies, Romeo and Juliet, The Scarlet Letter, Death of a Salesman, Night,* and *The Odyssey.* (You may have noticed that this is an unbroken diet of tragedy.) At Strathaven over the past four years, students are randomly assigned either to the usual Language Arts or to Language Arts with Positive Psychology.

The four sections of Language Arts with Positive Psychology receive a yearlong course that supplements literature with an examination of the Pleasant Life, the Engaged Life, and the Meaningful Life. More important, every week students are assigned a positive-psychology exercise in the real world. So when they read *Lord of the Flies,* for example, they have an eighty-minute session on the subject of kindness, and then they are assigned to do five kind acts and to write a reflection on what happened. Here are some other exercises the students are asked to do:

- Savor a pleasant sensory experience (The Pleasant Life).
- Identify their signature strengths and use their greatest strength in a new way (The Engaged Life).
- Make a gratitude visit (The Pleasant Life).
- Create a family tree of strengths (The Meaningful Life).
- Let go of grudges (The Meaningful Life).
- Positive service: Use a signature strength to serve something you believe is bigger than you are (The Meaningful Life).

In addition to these exercises, they analyze characters from literature, not just from the usual "hubris" and "weakness" characterizations that accompany the tragic view of life, but from the perspective of strengths: Achilles' courage, for example, is discussed, along with his pride.

How does this course affect the students? For the moment I can only say that both teachers and students love literature taught this way. We will publish the results of this study in 2008. The manual for this course can be requested from info@positivepsych.org.

What does the future hold for the teaching of optimism and positive psychology to children?

In July 2007, at the Positive Psychology Center of the University of Pennsylvania, we will train about one hundred middle school teachers from England to present the optimistic child program to their ten thousand students. This is an initiative of Richard Layard, a professor at the London School of Economics. Lord Layard was an adviser on unemployment for former prime minister Tony Blair. But he has transcended the "dismal" science and poses the challenge that government really exists to increase the happiness of the governed, not the gross domestic product. He seeks to end the epidemic of depression among young people in the United Kingdom by introducing learned optimism into the curriculum of the schools. We eagerly await the results.

The year 2008 will see our most challenging mission yet. The Geelong Grammar School, south of Melbourne, Australia, has decided to infuse its entire curriculum, from kindergarten through twelfth grade, with optimism and positive psychology. This great institution fifty years ago invented "Timbertop"—in which the entire ninth grade goes to a camp in the Victoria Mountains for the year, with no iPods or television, where they have to cut their own firewood, and each student ends the year by running in a marathon—and revolutionized education. Positive psychology will be their next Timbertop.

To accomplish this, the whole traveling circus of the world's leading researchers and practitioners of positive psychology will descend on Geelong. We will instruct the teachers on how to present the optimistic child program and the positive psychology program for language arts. More important, we will work with all the teachers to develop new curricula so that the positive psychology approach can be applied to the entire school.

Can history be taught that emphasizes human progress? Can mathematics be taught that emphasizes the beauty of proof and the idea that math is the most impeccable form of truth? Can biology be taught around the idea that human evolution has not only resulted in war and weaponry but also cooperation, sacrifice, love, and the building of cathedrals?

It is my vision and my hope that this work will be the beginning of the end of the worldwide epidemic of depression.

Notes
Acknowledgments
Index

Notes

Chapter 1: The Promissory Note

1. Fuller accounts and a complete bibliography of the helplessness experiments in animals and humans are found in M. Seligman (1993), *Helplessness: On depression, development, and death* (San Francisco: Freeman); and in S. F. Maier and M. Seligman (1976), Learned helplessness: Theory and evidence, *Journal of Experimental Psychology: General, 105,* 3–46. See also M. Seligman (1990), *Learned optimism* (New York: Knopf), chapter 2.

An account of a several-day debate between proponents of the behaviorist and of the cognitive views on learned helplessness was published in *Behaviour Research and Therapy* (1980), *18,* 459–512.

The special issue of the 1978 *Journal of Abnormal Psychology, 87,* began the large literature on helplessness as a model of depression. Since that time, there have been literally hundreds of journal articles and scores of doctoral dissertations written about explanatory style, learned helplessness, and depression. This massive literature has been controversial, but consensus has emerged that pessimistic explanatory style and depression are robustly related, as the theory predicts. See P. Sweeney, K. Anderson, and S. Bailey (1986), Attributional style in depression: A meta-analytic review, *Journal of Personality and Social Psychology, 50,* 974–991; C. Robins (1988), Attributions and depression: Why is the literature so inconsistent? *Journal of Personality and Social Psychology, 54,* 880–889; and H. Tenen and S. Herzberger (1986), Attributional Style Questionnaire, in J. Keyser and R. C. Sweetland (eds.), *Test Critiques, 4,* 20–30.

For reviews of the work on cancer and other illnesses, see my *Learned optimism,* chapter 10. For the most recent study of pessimism as a risk factor for a second heart attack, see J. Patillo, G. Buchanan, C. Thoresen, and M. Seligman (1995), Pessimism and cardiac death, *submitted.* For learned helplessness as a model of posttraumatic stress disorder, see B. van der Kolk and J. Saporta (1991), The biological response to psychic trauma: Mechanisms and treatment of intrusion and numbing, *Anxiety Research, 4,* 199–212.

The most complete coverage of the entire helplessness field and its various applications to humans is found in C. Peterson, S. Maier, and M. Seligman (1993), *Learned helplessness* (New York: Oxford).

2. For reviews of the extensive immunization against helplessness literature, see Seligman, *Helplessness,* and Peterson, Maier, and Seligman, *Learned
helplessness.*

3. I know of no perfect solution to the problem of pronoun gender. Here
is what I will do: When the sentence is equally applicable to males and females,
I will use either *he* or *she* unsystematically. When the sentence's referents are
predominantly female (as is true — intriguingly — for depression), I will use
she; when the referents are mostly male (as in substance abuse), *he.*

Chapter 2: From the First Step to the First Date

1. P. Lewinsohn, P. Rohde, J. Seeley, and S. Fischer (1993), Age-cohort
changes in the lifetime occurrence of depression and other mental disorders,
Journal of Abnormal Psychology, 102, 110–120; C. Garrison, C. Addy, K.
Jackson, et al. (1992), Major depressive disorder and dysthymia in young
adolescents, *American Journal of Epidemiology, 135,* 792–802.

Chapter 3: Building the Team

1. L. Jaycox and R. Repetti (1993), Conflict in families and the psychological adjustment of preadolescent children, *Journal of Family Psychology,
7,* 344–355.

Chapter 4: The Self-Esteem Movement

1. See especially the important work of Lilian Katz, an incisive critic of
the self-esteem movement. The examples come from her article All about me
(1993), *American Federation of Teachers,* summer, 18–23. The quote "the
basis for *everything we do* is self-esteem" comes from Sandy MacDonald
(1986), in Political priority #1: Teaching kids to like themselves, *New Options,* April 28, p. 27.

2. William James (1890), *Principles of psychology* (New York: Henry
Holt).

3. I summarize the four converging trends in the introduction to the
second edition of *Helplessness* as follows: (1) In 1959 Noam Chomsky
wrote his devastating critique of B. F. Skinner's seminal book *Verbal Behavior.* Chomsky argued that language specifically, and human action generally,
was not the result of strengthening past verbal habits by reinforcement. The
essence of language, he said, is that it is generative: sentences never spoken or
heard before (such as "There's a purple gila monster sitting on your lap.")
could nevertheless be understood immediately. (2) Jean Piaget, the great
Swiss investigator of how children develop, had persuaded most of the world
— the Americans last — that the developing mind of the individual child
could be studied scientifically. (3) By 1967 the field of cognitive psychology,
led by Ulric Neisser and George Miller, had begun to capture the imagina-

tion of the young experimental psychologists fleeing the dogmas of behaviorism. Cognitive psychologists argued that the workings of the human mind could be measured and their consequences studied by using the information-processing activities of computers as a model. (4) Behavioral psychologists found that animal and human behavior was inadequately explained by the concepts of drives and needs and began to invoke the cognitions — the thoughts — of the individual to explain complex behavior. Our work on helplessness embodied this trend.

4. S. Coopersmith (1967), *The antecedents of self-esteem* (San Francisco: Freeman). A parallel and important study of high school students was done by Morris Rosenberg ([1965], *Society and the adolescent self-image* [Princeton: Princeton University Press]), and additional intellectual provenance can be found in the work of Alfred Adler, G. H. Mead, Karen Horney, Eric Fromm, and Carl Rogers.

5. N. Branden (1992), *The power of self-esteem* (Deerfield Beach, Fla.: Health Communications).

6. *Toward a state of esteem* (1990) (Sacramento: California Department of Education).

7. Mistaking cause for consequence, and then shaping policy around this mistake, is not new to education. Remember the "Stay in School" campaign of the 1980s? Educators noticed that adolescents who dropped out of high school often went on to unemployment, welfare, and crime. Many assumed that dropping out caused such unfortunate results and that, therefore, if these kids could be persuaded to finish high school, they would do better in the job market and be more likely to stay out of jail. Ads on radio, TV, and even buses urged kids to "stay in school." Hundreds of dropout-prevention programs costing millions of dollars were instituted. Many potential dropout kids stayed in school. No evidence accrued, however, that these kids, who now got diplomas, went on to more employment, less welfare, or less crime.

Why? One possibility, rarely mentioned, is that dropping out of high school is often a symptom of other, more serious problems. These underlying problems, and not dropping out, cause unemployment, welfare dependence, and crime. Staying in school does not help much, because dropping out isn't a cause of the problems, just a consequence. The campaign did have other consequences, however: It probably made the high school environment worse for the rest of the students and for the teachers by keeping such kids there, rather than placing them in other programs that would address their problems. It probably also lowered standards globally so that these kids could get diplomas. And it probably enormously frustrated the kids who would have dropped out had they not been pressured into beating their heads against the classroom brick wall by well-meaning policymakers.

This is another remarkably gaseous literature. Dropout programs are reviewed and evaluated for their effectiveness at keeping children in school, but no clear effects on better employment, less crime, or less welfare are found. Representative studies: G. Natriello, A. Pallas, E. McDill, and J. McPartland (1988), An examination of the assumption and evidence for alternative dropout prevention programs in high school, in *Center for Social Organization of Schools report*, report 365 (Baltimore: Johns Hopkins University); J. Catterall and D. Stern (1986), The effects of alternative school programs on high school completion and labor market outcomes, *Educational Evaluation and Policy Analysis, 8*, 77–86; D. Muha and C. Cole (1990–91), Dropout prevention and group counseling: A review of the literature, *High School Journal, 74*, 76–80; and C. Pearson and M. Banerji (1993), Effects of a ninth grade dropout prevention program on student academic achievement, school attendance, and dropout rate, *Journal of Experimental Education, 61*, 247–256.

8. This is an example of the "prospective, longitudinal" method, the most widely accepted way of separating cause from correlation in a nonlaboratory setting. When coupled with the powerful statistical techniques known as "causal modeling," this method rivals the laboratory experiment as a way to discover underlying causality. Its main advantage over the laboratory experiment is that it has none of the artificiality of the laboratory. The only advantage the laboratory provides over the prospective, longitudinal method is the random assignment of subjects to groups.

9. The single best collection of scholarly research and writing on self-esteem is found in R. Baumeister (1993), *Self-esteem: The puzzle of low self-regard* (New York: Plenum). Remarkable is the contrast between the plethora of findings about things that cause self-esteem to become high or low and the absence of things that high and low self-esteem cause. Oddly, the researchers don't seem very disturbed by this.

10. Scientists have a derogatory phrase for endeavors like the attempt to bolster self-esteem directly: "manipulating epiphenomena" they call them. An epiphenomenon is a mere reflection of reality that has no impact on reality. The reading on the speedometer of your car is an epiphenomenon: it tells you how fast the car is going, but fiddling with the speedometer does not change the speed of the car.

In my emphasis on instilling "doing-well" skills that produce good commerce with the world and in my skepticism about "feeling-good" campaigns, you might wonder if I believe that feeling good is an epiphenomenon. You might even mistake me for a behaviorist. A behaviorist I am not, and here is the nub of my issue with the behaviorists: The behaviorist contends that all of mental life is an epiphenomenon — it doesn't matter a whit, since mental life is wholly a comment on the world that does not change the world. Thinking that it's a nice day, that turnips are cheap, that the war in Bosnia is a tragedy, or that triangles have three sides has no effect on the world. Indeed, behaviorism ignores mental life because it contends that mental life has no "causal efficacy." It should be clear from my emphasis on teaching the cognitive skills of optimism that I believe that some aspects of mental life have great efficacy. Self-esteem, however, is not one of them.

Chapter 5: The Epidemic of Depression

1. In The age of melancholy? (1979), *Psychology Today,* April, pp. 37–42, Gerald Klerman presents some of the alarming statistics on the prevalence of depression and coins the term. The first two of the four major studies that documented the epidemic of depression are L. Robins, J. Helzer, M. Weissman, H. Orvaschel, E. Gruenberg, J. Burke, and D. Regier (1984), Lifetime prevalence of specific psychiatric disorders in three sites, *Archives of General Psychiatry, 41,* 949–958; and G. Klerman, P. Lavori, J. Rice, T. Reich, J. Endicott, N. Andreasen, M. Keller, and R. Hirschfeld (1985), Birth cohort trends in rates of major depressive disorder among relatives of patients with affective disorder, *Archives of General Psychiatry, 42,* 689–693. The finding that depression now starts younger arose from the elegant mathematization of these data from this last-cited study by T. Reich, P. Van Eerdewegh, J. Rice, J. Mullaney, G. Klerman, and J. Endicott (1987), The family transmission of primary depressive disorder, *Journal of Psychiatric Research, 21,* 613–624. The third study, actually verifying the ongoing increase and greening of depression, is Lewinsohn, Rohde, Seeley, and Fischer, Age-cohort changes (see ch. 2, n. 1). The fourth study is Garrison, Addy, Jackson, et al., Major depressive disorder (see ch. 2, n. 1).

2. Lewinsohn, Rohde, Seeley, and Fischer, Age-cohort changes; Garrison, Addy, Jackson, et al., Major depressive disorder.

3. My student Sheena Sethi and I recently found that religious involvement, religious hope, and religious fundamentalism were all associated with greater optimism; see S. Sethi and M. Seligman (1993), Optimism and fundamentalism, *Psychological Science, 4,* 256–259.

4. The study of flow is the most exciting development in the psychology of positive affect in recent years. The notion of flow moves us beyond the increasingly vacuous categories of happiness, well-being, joy, and self-esteem. Any student of the good life, and how to get it, should read M. Csikszentmihalyi (pronounced "cheeks sent me high") (1990), *Flow: The psychology of optimal experience* (New York: Harper and Row).

Chapter 6: The Fundamentals of Optimism

1. The Jackson speech is quoted in Alice Felt Tyler's important book (1944) *Freedom's ferment* (Minneapolis: University of Minnesota Press). Tyler portrays the first half of the nineteenth century as centrally driven by the idea of the perfectability of humankind.

2. For documentation of the effects of pessimism on depression, see chapter 5 of my *Learned optimism;* for the effects on achievement, see chapter 6; and for the effects on health, see chapter 10. For a fifty-two-year longitudinal study of the stability of pessimism, see M. Burns and M. Seligman (1989), Explanatory style across the lifespan: Evidence for stability over 52 years, *Journal of Personality and Social Psychology, 56,* 118–124. The notes in *Learned optimism* give the references to many of the other original journal articles.

While poor achievement, depression, and ill health can all cause pessimism, it is important that many of the studies document that pessimism itself goes on to cause depression, poor achievement, and ill health. The studies use experimental designs, the longitudinal designs discussed in chapter 4 (which self-esteem studies do not), and the sophisticated statistical methods of causal modeling.

Chapter 7: Measuring Optimism

1. The Children's Attributional Style Questionnaire (CASQ) is the most widely used measure of explanatory style in children between the ages of eight and twelve (M. Seligman, N. J. Kaslow, L. B. Alloy, C. Peterson, R. Tanenbaum, and L. Y. Abramson [1984], Attributional style and depressive symptoms among children, *Journal of Abnormal Psychology, 93,* 235–238).

2. This table is derived from a five-year project involving 508 children (aged eight to twelve) who took the CASQ every six months (see S. Nolen-Hoeksema, J. Girgus, and M. Seligman [1992], Predictors and consequences of depression in children, *Journal of Abnormal Psychology, 101,* 405–422).

3. Nolen-Hoeksema, Girgus, and Seligman, Predictors and consequences.

4. The rating scale for your child's depression is my slightly modified version of the CES-DC (Center for Epidemiological Studies — Depression Child) test. This questionnaire was devised by M. Weissman, H. Orvaschel, and N. Padian and published in their article (1980), Children's symptom and social functioning: Self-report scales, *Journal of Nervous and Mental Disease, 168,* 736–740.

5. P. Rosenthal and S. Rosenthal (1984), Suicidal behavior by preschool children, *American Journal of Psychiatry, 141,* 520–525.

Chapter 8: Where Optimism Comes From

1. Some people still have the preconception that IQ is not at all genetic. They are wrong. If someone tells you so, he is either scientifically illiterate or ideologically blinded. The IQ data from identical twins and adoptive children (comparison of adopted children to their biological parents versus their adoptive parents) are massive and compelling: at least half of the variance

in IQ is genetic — 75 percent is genetic in the classic Bouchard study (T. Bouchard, D. Lykken, M. McGue, N. Segal, and A. Tellegen [1990], Sources of human psychological differences: The Minnesota study of twins reared apart, *Science, 250,* 223–228). What "intelligence" means, however, and what it predicts about achievement in life, is murkier.

The television-viewing study is R. Plomin, R. Corley, J. DeFries, and D. Fulker (1990), Individual differences in television viewing in early child-hood: Nature as well as nurture, *Psychological Science, 1,* 371–377. The religiosity study is N. Waller, B. Kojetin, T. Bouchard, D. Lykken, and A. Tellegen (1990), Genetic and environmental influences on religious interests, attitudes, and values, *Psychological Science, 1,* 138–142. The divorce study is M. McGue and D. Lykken (1992), Genetic influence on risk of divorce, *Psychological Science, 3,* 368–373. The other personality factors are from an analysis of the California Personality Inventory by T. Bouchard and M. McGue (1990), Genetic and rearing environmental influences on adult personality: An analysis of adopted twins reared apart, *Journal of Personality, 58,* 263–292.

2. P. Schulman, D. Keith, and M. Seligman (1993), Is optimism heritable? A study of twins, *Behaviour Research and Therapy, 6,* 569–574.

3. N. Pedersen, G. McClearn, R. Plomin, J. Nesselroade, J. Berg, and U. DeFaire (1991), The Swedish adoption/twin study of aging: An update, *Acta Geneticae Medicae et Gemellologiae, 40,* 7–20; and R. Plomin, M. Scheier, C. Bergeman, N. Pedersen, J. Nesselroade, and G. McClearn (1992), Optimism, pessimism and mental health: A twin/adoption analysis, *Personality and Individual Differences, 13,* 921–930. Because the Plomin study uses a different optimism measure, a different culture, and a different methodology from the Twinsburg study and still comes up with robust heritability, I am even more convinced that optimism has a heritable component.

4. Bouchard, Lykken, McGue, Segal, and Tellegen, Sources of human psychological differences, apart from being a classic experiment, is also articulate on this point. These alternative paths are examples of "gene-environment covariation." It is the environment that is primarily causal here, not the genes — and intervening to break the gene-environment covariation would demonstrate this.

Much of the future of environmental treatments for biologically loaded problems may involve discovering ways to break the gene-environment covariation. I will go as far as to predict that a field of psychology called "Breaking Gene-Environment Covariation" will come into being by the start of the next millennium.

5. Seligman, Kaslow, Alloy, Peterson, Tanenbaum, and Abramson, Attributional style. Although mothers' correlation to their children of either sex was robust, no correlation was found with fathers' optimism or pessi-

mism to either their children or their wives. But in the sample, the primary caretaker was almost always the mother, so our best guess is that a child learns and models the primary caretaker's explanatory style.

6. Carol Dweck is the leading researcher on sex differences in explanatory style and on learned helplessness in the classroom. See C. S. Dweck and B. Licht (1980), Learned helplessness and intellectual achievement, in J. Garber and M. Seligman (Eds.), *Human helplessness: Theory and applications* (New York: Academic Press, 197–222).

7. J. Barber, P. Badgio, S. Auerbach-Barber, P. Crits-Cristoph, M. Seligman, S. Nolen-Hoeksema, P. Schulman, and H. Zullow (1995), Gender differences in explanatory style: Achievement versus affiliation situations, Unpublished manuscript, University of Pennsylvania.

8. K. Arnold (1987), Values and vocations: The career aspirations of academically gifted females in the first five years after high school, Paper presented at the American Educational Research Association annual meeting, Washington, D.C., April 24.

9. The story of Hoving's adolescent transformation is told in John McPhee's book (1968) *A roomful of Hovings and other profiles* (New York: Farrar, Straus, and Giroux).

10. G. Brown and T. Harris (1978), *Social origins of depression* (London: Tavistock). A voluminous research literature repeats the finding that death of one's mother heightens the adult risk for depression. But the heightened risk, surprisingly, is not large, nor is there any replicable heightened risk for death of one's father.

11. V. Wolfe, C. Gentile, and D. Wolfe (1989), The impact of sexual abuse on children: A PTSD formulation, *Behavior Therapy, 20,* 215–228; and G. Stern (1990), The effect of childhood sexual abuse on adult attributional style, *Dissertation Abstracts International, 51,* 1007.

12. Seligman, *Learned optimism,* see pages 145–149; D. Pledge (1992), Marital separation/divorce: A review of individual responses to a major life stressor, *Journal of Divorce and Remarriage, 17,* 151–181; and L. Siegel and N. Griffin (1984), Correlates of depressive symptoms in adolescents, *Journal of Youth and Adolescence, 13,* 475–487.

13. W. Sloat (1987), About Men: Snakeskin, *New York Times Magazine,* January 25, p. 60.

Chapter 10: Changing Your Child's Automatic Pessimism

1. Chapter 8 of my book (1994) *What you can change and what you can't* (New York: Knopf) reviews the large literature on drug therapy and psychotherapy for depression.

The basic reference is the NIMH collaborative study I. Elkin, M. Shea, J.

Watkins, S. Imber, et al. (1989), National Institute of Mental Health Treatment of Depression Collaborative Research Program: General effectiveness of treatments, *Archives of General Psychiatry, 46,* 971–982. The reader should be warned that this is still a guild "hot potato" and even now the data are disputed and are in the process of re-analysis, with the drug lobby and the psychotherapy lobby each claiming it really did better than the other. My view is that it is roughly a tie among medication, interpersonal therapy, and cognitive therapy for *immediate* relief of symptoms, whereas once the drug is discontinued, cognitive therapy does much better at preventing recurrence: S. Hollon, R. DeRubeis, and M. Evans (1990), Combined cognitive therapy and pharmacotherapy in the treatment of depression, in D. Manning and A. Frances (Eds.), *Combination drug and psychotherapy in depression* (Washington, D.C.: American Psychiatric Press).

The more recent findings are about recurrence: M. Shea, I. Elkin, S. Imber, et al. (1992), Course of depressive symptoms over follow-up, *Archives of General Psychiatry, 49,* 782–787; and M. D. Evans, S. D. Hollon, R. J. DeRubeis, J. M. Piasecki, M. J. Garvey, W. M. Grove, and V. B. Tuason (1992), Differential relapse following cognitive therapy, pharmacotherapy, and combined cognitive-pharmacotherapy for depression, *Archives of General Psychiatry, 49,* 802–808. Both of these major studies find that cognitive therapy fares better than drug treatment (which is tapered off during follow-up) on recurrence of depression. But there is still considerable recurrence even in the cognitive therapy groups, with drugs showing about 50 percent recurrence over two years and cognitive therapy about 30 percent. In one well-publicized study, eleven patients who responded well to imipramine (a tricyclic) took the drug continually for five years and only one became depressed. Of nine patients given a placebo, five became depressed (D. Kupfer, E. Frank, J. Perel, et al. [1992], Five-year outcome for maintenance therapies for recurrent depression, *Archives of General Psychiatry, 49,* 769–773). This finding suggests that if antidepressant drugs work for you and curtail depression, to prevent recurrence, stay on them even when you're feeling fine.

2. Albert Ellis, (1962), *Reason and emotion in psychotherapy* (New York: Lyle Stuart). This book is still, along with Aaron T. Beck's 1967 classic *Depression* (New York: Hoeber), the most illuminating general reference I know of on the psychology of depression. An excellent guide to treatment is A. T. Beck, A. J. Rush, B. F. Shaw, and G. Emery (1979), *Cognitive therapy of depression: A treatment manual* (New York: Guilford).

The exercises in this chapter and in the next two originate in the seminal work of Aaron Beck and Albert Ellis. They formulated the first versions of our techniques in order to alleviate depression among those already afflicted. In 1987 Metropolitan Life asked me to adapt the techniques for a *normal* population and in a *preventive mode,* so that it could use them with its sales force — a very nondepressed group. I called on the considerable talents of Steve Hollon, professor at Vanderbilt, and Art Freeman, then professor at the New Jersey College of Medicine and Dentistry and one of the world's leading teachers of cognitive therapy, to help change the basic cognitive therapy techniques in these two ways. Dan Oran of Foresight, Inc., and Dick Calogero of Metropolitan Life administered the workshop project, and Karen Reivich was principal editor of the manuals.

Karen Reivich, Jane Gillham, and Lisa Jaycox then adapted these techniques for normal children and tested them extensively as described in chapter 9. See the Acknowledgments for an explanation of who did what. In these three chapters (10–12), I draw heavily on the thinking and hard work of all these people.

Chapter 11: Changing Your Child's Explanatory Style

1. We have found that the dimension of pervasiveness, which we routinely teach adults, is not easily taught to children. So both in the Penn Prevention Program and in this chapter we teach only permanence and personalization.

Chapter 13: Boosting Your Child's Social Skills

1. For more on the cyclic relationship between aggressive behavior, rejection by peers, and depression, see W. F. Panak and J. Garber (1992), Role of aggression, rejection, and attributions in the prediction of depression in children, *Development and Psychopathology, 4,* 145–165.

2. There is a large body of research on the similarity of cognitive mediators in depression and aggression. Kenneth Dodge is the leader of this field and has written comprehensive discussions focused on the hostile attributional bias seen in many aggressive boys: K. Dodge (1986), A social information processing model of social competence in children, in M. Perlmutter (Ed.), *Cognitive perspectives on children's social and behavioral development* (Hillsdale, N.J.: Erlbaum); K. A. Dodge and C. L. Frame (1982), Social cognitive biases and deficits in aggressive boys, *Child Development, 53,* 620–635; K. Dodge, G. Pettit, C. McClaskey, and M. Brown (1986), Social competence in children, *Monographs of the Society for Research in Child Development, 51;* B. A. Richard and K. A. Dodge (1982), Social maladjustment and problem-solving in school-aged children, *Journal of Consulting and Clinical Psychology, 50* (2), 226–233.

Dodge has more recently extended this work with colleagues Judy Garber and others to look at hostile and attributional biases in depressed children: N. L. Quiggle, J. Garber, W. F. Panak, and K. A. Dodge (1992), Social information processing in aggressive and depressed children, *Child Development, 63,* 1305–1320.

3. Pioneers in the study of problem solving are Spivack and Shure, who studied means-end thinking as it relates to psychological and social adjustment. For instance, see G. Spivack, J. Platt, and M. Shure (1976), *The problem solving approach to adjustment* (San Francisco: Jossey-Bass). In addition, Meichenbaum studied self-instruction as a means of slowing down impulsive behavior. See D. H. Meichenbaum and J. Goodman (1971), Training impulsive children to talk to themselves, *Journal of Abnormal Psychology, 77,* 115–126. From these basic concepts, many problem-solving programs have been developed which are similar to the five-step approach described here. For instance, in clinical populations: B. W. Camp, G. E. Blom, F. Hebert and W. J. van Doorinck (1977), Think Aloud: A program for developing self-control in young aggressive boys, *Journal of Abnormal Child Psychology, 5,* 157–169; A. E. Kazdin, T. C. Siegel, and D. Bass (1992), Cognitive problem-solving skills training and parent management training in the treatment of antisocial behavior in children, *Journal of Consulting and Clinical Psychology, 60,* 733–747; J. E. Lochman and J. F. Curry (1986), Effects of social problem-solving training and self-instruction training with aggressive boys, *Journal of Consulting and Clinical Psychology, 15,* 159–164; J. E. Lochman, P. R. Burch, J. F. Curry, and L. B. Lampron (1984), Treatment and generalization effects of cognitive-behavioral and goal-setting interventions with aggressive boys, *Journal of Consulting and Clinical Psychology, 52,* 915–916; and P. Yu, G. E. Harris, B. L. Solovitz, and J. L. Franklin (1986), A social problem-solving intervention for children at high risk for later psychopathology, *Journal of Child Clinical Psychology, 15,* 30–40.

Several other programs have been used with normal school children in a preventive format: M. J. Elias, M. Gara, M. Ubriaco, P. A. Rothbaum, J. F. Clabby, and T. Schuyler (1986), Impact of a preventive social problem solving intervention on children's coping with middle-school stressors, *American Journal of Community Psychology, 14,* 259–275; E. L. Gesten, M. H. Rains, B. D. Rapkin, R. P. Weissberg, R. Flores de Apodaca, E. L. Cowen, and R. Bowen (1982), Training children in social problem-solving competencies: A first and second look, *American Journal of Community Psychology, 10,* 95–115; and P. Weissberg, E. L. Gesten, B. D. Rapkin, E. L. Cowen, E. Davidson, R. Flores de Apodaca, and B. J. McKim (1981), Evaluation of a social problem-solving training program for suburban and inner-city third grade children, *Journal of Consulting and Clinical Psychology, 49,* 251–261.

4. These assertiveness techniques are modified from Sharon Bower's model of assertiveness for adults: S. A. Bower and G. H. Bower (1976),

Asserting yourself: A practical guide for positive change (Reading, Mass.: Addison-Wesley).

5. For useful reviews of the effects of parental conflict on child adjustment, see R. E. Emery (1982), Interparental conflict and the children of discord and divorce, *Psychology Bulletin, 92,* 310–330; and J. H. Grych and F. D. Fincham (1990), Marital conflict and children's adjustment: A cognitive-contextual framework, *Psychology Bulletin, 108,* 267–290.

6. E. Mark Cummings has studied the ways in which children react to naturalistic conflict between adults and the importance of resolving conflict: E. M. Cummings, D. Vogel, J. S. Cummings, and M. El-Sheikh (1989), Children's responses to different forms of expression of anger between adults, *Child Development, 60,* 1392–1404; E. M. Cummings, K. S. Simpson, and A. Wilson (1993), Children's responses to interadult anger as a function of information about resolution, *Developmental Psychology, 29,* 978–985; and E. M. Cummings, M. Ballard, M. El-Sheikh, and M. Lake (1991), Resolution and children's responses to interadult anger, *Developmental Psychology, 27,* 462–470.

Chapter 14: The Pyramid of Optimism: Babies, Toddlers, and Preschoolers

1. J. Watson (1967), Memory and "contingency analysis" in infant learning, *Merrill-Palmer Quarterly, 13,* 55–76. See also my *Helplessness,* chapter 7. Watson's classic experiments have been repeated in a number of forms with infants, using toys, strangers, and mothers' vocalizations. The consistent result is that noncontingency causes infants to fuss and become passive while mastery causes smiling and involvement. See M. Lewis, M. Sullivan, and J. Brooks-Gunn (1985), Emotional behaviour during the learning of a contingency in early infancy, *British Journal of Developmental Psychology, 3,* 307–316; M. Gunnar, K. Leighton, and R. Peleaux (1984), Effects of temporal predictability on the reactions of one-year-olds to potentially frightening toys, *Developmental Psychology, 20,* 449–458; and M. Levitt (1980), Contingent feedback, familiarization, and infant affect: How a stranger becomes a friend, *Developmental Psychology, 16,* 425–432.

For two representative studies of the importance of mastery for predicting later competence and for positive affect, see D. Messer, M. McCarthy, S. McQuiston, et al. (1986), Relation between mastery behavior in infancy and competence in early childhood, *Developmental Psychology, 22,* 366–372; and L. Mayes and E. Zigler (1992), An observational study of the affective concomitants of mastery in infants, *Child Psychology and Psychiatry, 4,* 659–667.

2. Angela Wilkes (1989), *My first cook book* (New York: Knopf), provides an excellent starting point.

3. C. Rogers (1957), The necessary and sufficient conditions of therapeutic personality change, *Journal of Consulting Psychology, 21,* 95–103. For representative articles advocating the same approach with children generally, see C. Ellinwood (1989), The young child in person-centered family therapy, *Person-Centered Review, 4,* 256–262; and S. Magura (1982), Clients view outcomes of child protective services, *Social Casework, 63,* 522–531.

4. The literature on appetitive learned helplessness is discussed in Peterson, Maier, and Seligman, *Learned helplessness,* and in Seligman, *Helplessness.* Both present extensive bibliographies of this research.

5. Deborah Stipek (1993), *Motivation to learn: From theory to practice* (Boston: Allyn and Bacon), has a useful list of guidelines for effective praise on page 55.

6. See the volume edited by B. Campbell and R. Church (1969), *Punishment and aversive behavior* (New York: Appleton-Century-Crofts), for massive evidence on the effectiveness of punishment.

7. My doctoral dissertation was the first of many studies to demonstrate this (M. Seligman [1968], Chronic fear produced by unpredictable shock, *Journal of Comparative and Physiological Psychology, 66,* 402–411). See chapter 6, "Unpredictability and Anxiety," of Seligman, *Helplessness,* for a review.

8. R. Schwartz and G. Garamoni (1989), Cognitive balance and psychopathology: Evaluation of an information processing model of positive and negative states of mind, *Clinical Psychology Review, 9,* 271–294; and G. Garamoni, C. Reynolds, M. Thase, and E. Frank (1992), Shifts in affective balance during cognitive therapy of major depression, *Journal of Consulting and Clinical Psychology, 60,* 260–266.

9. I believe that a high frequency of intensely negative dreams is more than just a mere correlation with depression. Depriving depressed people of dreaming either with drugs or by interrupting REM sleep is an effective antidepressant treatment. Just as coming across many bad events during the day causes depression, so too may experiencing bad events at night. See G. Vogel (1975), A review of REM sleep deprivation, *Archives of General Psychiatry, 32,* 96–97.

Chapter 15: The Limits of Optimism

1. Already a classic, L. B. Alloy and L. Y. Abramson (1979), Judgment of contingency in depressed and nondepressed students: Sadder but wiser, *Journal of Experimental Psychology: General, 108,* 441–485, was the first study to demonstrate depressive realism. P. Lewinsohn, W. Mischel, W. Chaplin, and R. Barton (1980), Social competence and depression: The role of illu-

sory self-perceptions, *Journal of Abnormal Psychology, 89,* 203–212, demonstrated depressive realism in the judgment of social skill. Depressive realism seems to hold for memory as well, but the evidence conflicts. See, for example, R. DeMonbreun and E. Craighead (1977), Distortion of perception and recall of positive and neutral feedback in depression, *Cognitive Therapy and Research, 1,* 311–329. Lopsidedness in nondepressed people is reviewed by C. Peterson and M. Seligman (1984), Causal explanations as a risk factor for depression: Theory and evidence, *Psychological Review, 91,* 347–374. See my *Learned optimism,* chapter 6, for a review of the evidence on this fascinating and robust illusion of control. The most recent piece showing realism as a risk factor for depression is L. Alloy and C. Clements (1992), Illusion of control: Invulnerability to negative affect and depressive symptoms after laboratory and natural stressors, *Journal of Abnormal Psychology, 101,* 234–245.

To top it off, realism doesn't just *co-exist* with depression, it appears to be a risk factor for depression, just as smoking is a risk factor for lung cancer. Nondepressed people who are realists go on to become depressed at a higher rate than nondepressed people who have these illusions of control.

But the reality of all these findings is hotly debated to this very day, and this is the reason I have used the words *may* and *seem* to describe the claims. There have been a fair number of failures to reproduce these findings, and when they are divided by the kind of task evaluated, depressed people seem more accurate in judging control but less accurate in recalling self-evaluative information (see R. Ackermann and R. DeRubeis [1991], Is depressive realism real? *Clinical Psychology Review, 11,* 365–384).

Afterword: A Progress Report on Optimism

Cardemil, E. V., K. J. Reivich, and M.E.P. Seligman (2002), The prevention of depressive symptoms in low-income minority middle-school students. *Prevention & Treatment, 5,* Article 8. Available at: http://journals.apa.org/prevention/volume5/pre0050008a.html.

Cohen, S., W. J. Doyle, R. B. Turner, C. M. Alper, and D. P. Skoner (2003), Sociability and susceptibility to the common cold. *Psychological Science, 14,* 389–395.

Csikszentmihalyi, M. (1999), If we are so rich, why aren't we happy? *American Psychologist, 54,* 821–827.

Danner, D., D. Snowdon, and W. Friesen (2001), Positive emotions in early life and longevity: Findings from the nun study. *Journal of Personality and Social Psychology, 80,* 804–813.

Diener, E., and M.E.P. Seligman (2004), Beyond Money: Toward an economy of well-being. *Psychological Science in the Public Interest, 5,* 1–31.

Fredrickson, B. (2001), The role of positive emotions in positive psychology. *American Psychologist, 56,* 218–226.

Gillham, J. E. and K. J. Reivich (1999), Prevention of depressive symptoms in school children: A research update. *Psychological Science, 10,* 461–462.

Giltay, E., M. Kamphuis, S. Kalmijn, et al. (2006), Dispositional optimism and the risk of cardiovascular death. *Archives of Internal Medicine, 166,* 431–436.

Maruta, T., R. Colligan, M. Malinchoc, and K. Offord (2000), Optimists vs. Pessimists: Survival rate among medical patients over a thirty-year period. *Mayo Clinic Proceedings, 75,* 140–143.

Peterson, C. (2006), *A primer of positive psychology* (New York: Oxford).

Peterson, C. and M.E.P. Seligman (2004), *Character strengths and virtues: A handbook and classification* (Washington, D.C.: APA Press and Oxford University Press).

Seligman, M.E.P. (1990), *Learned Optimism* (New York: Knopf).

Seligman, M.E.P. (2002), *Authentic happiness: Using the new positive psychology to realize your potential for lasting fulfillment* (New York: Free Press / Simon and Schuster).

Yu, D. L., and M.E.P. Seligman (2002), Preventing depressive symptoms in Chinese children. *Prevention & Treatment, 5,* Article 9. Available at: http://journals.apa.org/prevention/volume5/pre0050009a.html.

Acknowledgments

The Penn Prevention Program, and therefore this book, would not have been possible without the help of numerous people. First, I would like to thank my collaborators and coauthors, Karen Reivich, Lisa Jaycox, and Jane Gillham. This book reflects their hard work and their strong commitment to preventing depression in children. Karen, Lisa, and Jane have worked full time over the past five years to develop, implement, and evaluate the Penn Prevention Program. Karen and Jane created the cognitive component of the program, while Lisa developed the social problem-solving component. All three have been responsible for rethinking, revising, and expanding the program numerous times over these years. Karen adapted the program for use with inner-city children, and Jane created a parallel program to teach parents how to foster the development of optimism in their children. Karen, Lisa, and Jane have taught many of the intervention groups we have run for children.

Second, I owe much gratitude to the children and parents who participated in our research. They shared their lives with us, and we have learned a great deal from following these families over the years. Without their loyalty and commitment, this work would have been impossible.

I wish to acknowledge the foresight and dedication of those school administrators, teachers, and parents who were willing to expend extra energy and resources working with the program. Our first project was conducted in the Abington School District; the principal, Dr. Louis Hebert, along with Dr. Amy Sichel, helped us launch the Penn Prevention Program. Dr. Hebert passed away in August 1993. We remember especially his vision and integrity.

In the Wissahickon School District, Superintendent Bruce Kowalski and Dr. Mary Hornyak provided ongoing assistance on several projects. They enabled us to study the emotional development of children as they moved from elementary school through middle school and into high school. This allowed us to compare the effects of our Abington program with normal development. Jane Gillham later implemented the Penn Prevention Program in the Wissahickon School District, and the intervention program for parents was first tested there. These projects could not have succeeded without wholehearted support from the principals, assistant principals, and guidance counselors in the district. I am especially grateful to Neil Evans, Gary Bundy, Claudia Lyles, Dr. Lorraine Atkeison, Dale Stauffer, Austin Snyder, and Judy Guiliano. I would also like to thank Joanne West for her assistance in organizing follow-up assessments of the children.

In 1992 we launched our inner-city program and tested it at the Dr. John P. Turner Middle School in West Philadelphia. This project would not have taken place without the help of Dr. Ira Harkavy, Cory Bowman, and the Center for Community Partnerships at the University of Pennsylvania. Charles D'Alfonso, principal of the Dr. John P. Turner Middle School, and Cory Bowman were always able to find creative solutions to the many logistical challenges.

We are currently testing this program in the Upper Darby School District. A number of people made this phase of the project possible. Andrew Shatté, one of our star doctoral students at the University of Pennsylvania, came from Australia to do research on depression and joined our research team. Andrew has a dual specialty. His research focuses on understanding what makes therapies of depression work. Together with Karen Reivich, he developed a forty-hour program to train teachers to be program providers. He taught groups of teachers and helped oversee this large project. The Upper Darby project simply would not have happened had he not joined the research team. Barbara Shafer, Martha Menz, and Joseph Galli first approached us after reading *Learned Optimism*. They were eager to bring our work into their school district. Karen Reivich and Andrew Shatté taught school teachers from Beverly Hills Middle School and Drexel Hill Middle School to implement the prevention programs. These teachers (some of whom taught Karen when she was a middle school student at Beverly Hills) — Cathy Crawford, Holly Farnese, Gay Marshall, Faith Mattison, Barbara Mendell, and Brenda Vogel — are the first in the nation to run this program in the schools. These pioneers devoted more hours than any of us had predicted. Their dedication, support, and good cheer are making the program a success. I would also like to thank Mel Brodsky, Ed Speer, and Carolyn Felker, who gave us unflagging support in their schools. Finally, the guidance counselors, social workers, and school psychologists, particularly Dr. Carol Roberts, Pat Ritter, and Dave O'Connell, helped ensure that the program ran as smoothly as possible.

I would like to thank my colleagues who helped us sort through theoretical and methodological issues. In particular, I am very grateful to Drs. Jonathan Baron, Tyrone Cannon, Robert DeRubeis, and John Sabini, all of the University of Pennsylvania, and Steve Hollon and Judy Garber of Vanderbilt University, who provided insights and guidance throughout the many phases of this research. Gregory Buchanan, Emily Buss, Esteban Cardemil, Paul Grant, Melissa Hunt, Eileen Lynch, Andrew Shatté, Deborah Stearns, and Audrey Tyrka, all graduate students at the University of Pennsylvania, were helpful in reading drafts of articles, discussing design issues, and collecting follow-up data.

We were fortunate to have a team of dedicated and enthusiastic undergraduates at the University of Pennsylvania between 1989 and the present who were instrumental in every phase of this research in the Abington, Wissahickon, Philadelphia, and Upper Darby school districts. Our four artists, Susan Young, Kevin Colton, Lisa Jacobs, and Marios Koufarios, created cartoons to convey even the most complicated scenarios. Their artwork made the children's notebooks and homework much more appealing. Thomas Schiro proposed the book's version of the artwork. A large number of assistants helped us create the games and endless scenarios that make this program engaging: Petrina Alexander, Judy Atkin, Tara Bandman, Rishona Beck, Monica Bishop, Deborah Brown, Deirdre Byrnes, Barry Carty, Deborah Clark, Kevin Colton, Rick Dagrosa, Darion D'Anjou, Allison Fink, Jed Fishback, Michael Friedman, Valerie Golomb, Heidi Grenke, Karen

Grimm, Scott Harris, Amy Joseph-Mosely, Youval Katz, Denel Keister, Kirk Kicklighter, Jayne Klein, Caroline Koffler, Marios Koufarios, Robyn Lesser, Vaughn Mankey, Janet Miller, Kaplan Mobray, Juliet Nawara, Stephanie Newman, Jimmy Platt, Danielle Rabiner, Daniel Richter, Iris Rosenberg, Andrew Rozmiarek, Kim Saperstein, Raqiba Sealy, Helene Stein, Jessica Steitler, Cristine Santos Thompson, Caroline Tisot, Lisa Warren, Stacey Wruble, Susan Young, and Josh Zoia.

Peter Schulman, my research coordinator, and my secretaries, Elise McMahon and Carol McSorley, were helpful in ways too numerous to mention. I would also like to express special thanks to my former secretary, Terry Silver, who worked in my office when this project first began and who volunteered to help because of her experience teaching children Spanish. Terry assisted us in creating some of the games, role-plays, and "characters" we used to convey the ideas of optimism. She helped transform dry theoretical concepts into an exciting experience for children.

I would also like to thank a number of people who led groups in various school disctricts. Dr. Kimberly Wright Cassidy led groups in the Wissahickon and Upper Darby school districts. Kim, along with Dr. Leslie Rescorla, encouraged us to train Bryn Mawr College doctoral students to lead groups in Upper Darby. Ann Marie Borneman, Katherine Dahlsgaard, Rebecca Stetson, and Lynn Zubernis each implemented groups in Upper Darby. Their insight, energy, and devotion made them a joy to work with. Kirk Kicklighter worked with Karen Reivich in the Philadephia School District and was indispensable. Susan Moore led some of the children's groups, and Janet Miller, Juliet Nawara, and Jayne Klein co-led parent groups in the Wissahickon School District. Their help was greatly appreciated. Many of the undergraduate assistants listed above also came with us to the schools and helped lead the programs. Their professionalism, energy, and love for the children made the program the success that it was.

The people at Houghton Mifflin—my diligent editor, Gail Winston, as well as John Sterling, Lori Glazer, Tina Pohlman, and the insightful copy editor of the manuscript, Christopher Keane—have been a pleasure to work with and a constant source of optimism. My unflagging agent, Richard Pine, shaped the book, read every word of every draft, held my hand through the difficult times, and shouted with joy when things worked. The National Institute of Mental Health has supported my research (MH-19604) for the last twenty-five years, and many of the ideas and procedures in this book were drawn from my NIMH projects. Dr. Peter Muehrer and Dr. Jack Maser of NIMH have been true friends and supporters.

Finally, I thank my wife and the five Seligman children. My wife, Mandy McCarthy Seligman, urged me, against my inertia of feeling wholly "written out," to do this book, the last in a trilogy. She read every chapter as it was drafted and, with the gentlest of red pens, commented candidly. Chapter 14 on babies and toddlers is more her creation than mine. Mandy is a ray of sunshine on the gloomiest day, and her love and optimism pervade these pages. Amanda Seligman, my oldest, commented wisely on a draft of the manuscript, taking time out from her dissertation in social history at Northwestern University. David Seligman, now finishing his senior thesis on fairness at Swarthmore College, amazed me by deciding to become a psychologist in the middle of this project. My three youngest, Lara, Nikki, and Darryl, have been the inspiration for this book. Lara learned to read and do arithmetic as the book was being written, Nikki revealed the most astonishing social skills, and Darryl was born when the project began and is now shouting "Dump the Dodo" in the background as I write the very last words. It is to these children, each a world (skillfully curled), that I dedicate this book.

Martin Seligman
Wynnewood, Pennsylvania
April 3, 1995

Index

ABC (adversity, beliefs, consequences) model, 139–44
  diary for, 146–48
  disputing and, 195–97
  introducing, 152–57
  practice with, 144–49
  and real-life situations, 161, 175–76, 185–86
  teaching to child, 149–61
  use of terminology, 154
ABCDE (adversity, beliefs, consequences, disputation, energization) model, 195, 211–25
  completing practice sheet with child, 224–25
  real-life, 215–16
Abington, Pennsylvania, Penn Prevention Program in, 115–30. *See also* Penn Prevention Program
Abramson, Lyn Y., 295, 314n1, 315n5, 321n1
Accuracy
  of beliefs, 167–69
  disputations and, 208–11
  of optimism, 297–99
Accusers, disputers and, 194
Achievement, movement away from, 40–41
Ackermann, R., 322n1
Action
  optimism and, 12

path of, in problem solving, 256–60
  self-esteem movement and, 27
Adaptive behavior, 2. *See also* Learned helplessness
Addy, C., 310n1, 313n2
Adler, Alfred, 311n4
Adults. *See also* Parents
  disputation practice for, 200–3
  period of birth and depression in, 38
  rapid-fire disputing for, 204–8
Adversity, 137–39
Age-cohort changes, depression and, 310n1, 313n2
Ages, of onset of depression, 38–39
Aggressive behavior, 235, 318n1, 2, 319n3
Alloy, Lauren B., 295, 314n1, 315n5, 321–22n1
Alternatives, generating, 198
Always, permanence and, 52–54
Anderson, K., 309n1
Andreasen, N., 313n1
Anger
  depression and, 234–35
  personalization and, 58
  value of, 43
Animal experimentation, 2–3
  punishment and, 288–89
Anxiety
  as depression symptom, 89